THE PARENT'S GUIDE TO SOLVING SCHOOL PROBLEMS

First published by Wellness Institute/Self-Help Books, LLC, 2002
Published by arrangement with the author by
        Selfhelp Success Books, L.L.C., 2009

First printing, 2002
First Selfhelp Success printing, 2009

ISBN 9781935235026

Selfhelp Success, Selfhelp Success Books, and
are imprints of Selfhelp Success Books, L.L.C.

Printed in the United States of America
Published by Selfhelp Success Books, L.L.C.
900 Burmaster Street, Gretna, Louisiana 70053

GRETNA 2009

TABLE OF CONTENTS

ACKNOWLEDGEMENTS

While there are many sources of learning experiences, I am very grateful to the numerous children and parents with whom I have come into contact with during my professional career. They have provided many learning experiences reflected in much of the information used in this book. The interaction I have had with teachers, pediatricians and other mental health professionals has also increased my knowledge base.

While the majority of the information in the book is based on my philosophy, experience, and how I conduct my practice, I did use some experts to help me in some of the areas where I felt my knowledge base was weak. Dr. Annell McGee, a speech and language pathologist, basically wrote the chapter on Trouble Following Directions Auditory Processing Problems. The International Dyslexia Association has numerous books, pamphlets, fact sheets, etc., available to the public which they allow to be reproduced. Almost all of the information in the chapters on reading and spelling problems, as well as the chapter on Forty Ways to Help Your Learning Disabled Child, was taken from information provided be this organization. Some of the information in the chapter on writing problems was also obtained from them. Barbara Bruno, M.ED., an educational diagnostician, and Denise Nagim, M.A., C.C.C., a speech and language pathologist provided me with some information that I used in some of the chapters on learning problems.

Most of the information in the chapter on the Individuals with Disabilities Education Act was obtained from handouts, information for parents, etc., used by the Jefferson Parish Public School System's Department of Special Education.

Carla, my wife, Colleen Coogan, Jeanne Dufour, Alan Fontenelle, Gladys George and Kim Gervin handled the typing and computer applications. Tabitha Murphy-Godwin, M.A., a psychologist, helped me review some of the information in the book. Alan Fontenelle and Kim Girvin did most of the corrections and modifications, as well as scanning the book onto the computer so the above could be done.

To my children, Jason and Alan,
for teaching me the most about children
and to my grandchildren,
Trent and Marissa,
who are sure to provide me
with new learning experiences.

PART I

INTRODUCTION

Attending school and doing school related activities (e.g. homework, projects) consumes 50 to 60% of the time most children are awake. For some, it may be 70 to 80% of the time. If a child is experiencing problems in school, the majority of his life involves negative attention, frustration, failure, emphasis on unacceptable behavior, conflict and/or not meeting the expectations of others. For most people, activities that are difficult or produce negative attention are things that we avoid, lack of motivation to become involved with and generally show a lack of interest in performing. School, for some children, becomes a negative experience in the early school years.

The first goal of this book is to give parents a better understanding of the causes of school related problems, as well as to present some methods and techniques to effectively deal with these difficulties. The information presented in the book should make your child's school experience more positive.

Another goal is to provide information that will improve family life by developing an ease in living with, relating to and raising children on a daily basis. Although this book is concerned with specific learning and behavioral problems, I've primarily focused on normal everyday problems most parents encounter regarding school. I have included the problems and concerns that I see most frequently in my practice. By increasing your skills and providing alternate techniques to deal with your children, problems will decrease. The home environment will improve. The hassles you encounter working with your children should decrease.

Another goal is to provide methods that allow you to interact and deal with your children without conflicts, hollering, screaming, getting upset of buying antacids. Consequently home life will be happier.

The fourth goal, probably most important to me, is to present information so you can easily understand it. This book is written for parents, not professionals. I've avoided using technical terms, jargon and psychological phrases.

Some mental health professionals, when communicating with parents, use special terminology or unusual words parents may not understand. As a result, parents leave a conference more confused then when they came in. They may not have any additional information to use in helping their child.

This book is written in everyday language. It will make sense and can be easily understood. I use several examples to explain an idea; hopefully one of them will be similar to what you are experiencing.

The majority of children that I see in my practice have difficulty in school, either academically or behaviorally or both. Because of this I have written another book entitled *"How To Be A Good Parent By Effectively Dealing with Your Child's Behavior Problems."* This book addresses a wide spectrum of behavior problems exhibited in children from their early toddler years up to and including adolescence. The book contains some materials found in this book, as well as other valuable information to assist the parent in dealing with these problems.

PART II
TYPES OF SCHOOL CONCERNS

Problems that occur in school are often related to academic performance, behavior or a combination of the two. Communication between the parent and teacher or administration is an absolute necessity to deal with problems effectively, such as trouble completing work, passing tests, getting along with other children, paying attention in class, following classroom procedure.

The first step in eliminating the problem is to establish an open line of communication between you and the appropriate school personnel—counselor, teacher, principal. This helps you stay informed about the problem so you can deal with it before it gets out of hand.

I frequently hear parents say, *"Why did the teacher wait till Christmas to tell me he wasn't turning in his homework? They didn't tell me he was in danger of failing until the end of the year. If he has been a behavior problem since September, why didn't I know about it sooner? If we had known about this problem when it started, we could have done something about it. Now it's out of hand."* Or parents wait one to two months into the school year or until the first P.T.A. meeting or parent-teacher conference to make contact with the school.

You May Have To Make First Contact

Waiting for the first meeting or for the teacher to contact you is a bad practice, especially if you have a child with a history of difficulty in school or if you suspect some type of problem. You have 1 child in Mrs. Smith's class, but Mrs. Smith has 30 to 175 other students. Her time for dealing with 1 student is limited. Teachers don't always get a positive reaction when they call parents. Parents may be uncooperative, disinterested, blame the school or teacher for the problems or defend the child and not listen to details of the problem. Parent contact often is a negative experience or a waste of time for the teacher, so it may be avoided.

When a teacher encounters a cooperative, concerned parent, he usually makes every effort to open the lines of communication. Even so, it is usually better if you initiate the call or visit rather than waiting for the teacher to call.

Don't assume no news is good news. I often suggest a parent

put an "X" on a calendar every two or three weeks to remind them to talk with the teacher.

Academic Problems

Many parents explain a child's academic troubles by saying, *"He's lazy. He's not interested in school. He does not want to work."* But there are many other reasons children have difficulty with schoolwork. Some problems may be related to behavior; before one can say a child has a true academic problem, the behavior must be controlled.

Almost all children who have learning difficulties eventually develop behavior problems. A child may have only academic trouble, but after a few months or years of not being able to grasp the material, he won't be able to keep up. He finds himself in a situation where he doesn't understand what's going on in the class. Very little makes sense.

Children who have trouble learning, experience a great deal of failure, frustration and negative attention. They are eventually identified as having behavior problems. A discussion of methods for dealing with school-related behavior appears later in this section.

Deal With Problems Early

Establish good communication between you and the teacher to become aware of and deal with school problems early, before they get out of hand. This is extremely important in effectively correcting academic difficulties. The sooner the problem can be identified, diagnosed and appropriate recommendations made, the easier it is to treat. And it's unlikely that future problems will develop. Many times I see children in fifth or sixth grade who have had academic problems since kindergarten or first grade but for some reason nothing has been done earlier.

Seek Professional Help

If a child has problems with his schoolwork, seek professional help and get an evaluation as soon as possible. Most school systems have evaluation teams that test and diagnose children who experience learning difficulties. The evaluator should also make recommendations about what can be done to minimize the child's difficulties.

Evaluations can also be obtained from mental-health centers, state agencies or private psychologists. When selecting a person or team to evaluate your child, be sure they are licensed, certified or have the appropriate credentials. You can also ask the child's pediatrician, teacher or school to recommend someone.

Evaluations are extremely helpful in assisting children with learning problems. There are many reasons children have trouble with schoolwork. They may have learning problems due to perceptual-motor deficiencies, to auditory or visual processing problems or to poor memory. They may have a poor learning foundation, an achievement level below their grade placement (in fifth grade but reading at a third-grade level) or be slow learners. Appropriate testing will help pinpoint the area of difficulty.

Always have a child evaluated before he repeats a grade. Some children may benefit from repeating a grade, but for others, other interventions may be necessary to correct their learning problems.

Behavioral Problems

When a child shows behavioral and academic problems, first attend to the behavior before trying to make an accurate assessment of the learning problem. If a child is doing poorly but is not completing his work and not paying attention in class, try to eliminate the interfering behavior.

Try Positive Attention

Children attend school about half of the time they're awake. If you add homework, class projects and school-related activities, it involves 50 to 80% of a child's life. When a child has trouble in school, a large portion of his life involves negative attention. It's very important for you to provide positive attention to children who have school difficulties. These children should receive more positive attention at home than the child who is not experiencing difficulty at school. This is needed to offset the excessive negativeattention.

Look Beyond School Behavior

The greatest mistake most parents make is they only zero in on school behavior. The major problem for Joey is he doesn't follow classroom procedure. You set up a program to deal with this school behavior, but it doesn't work. Why? Because behavior seen at school is only part of a larger behavioral pattern. Taking a broader look at Joey, we see this behavior is typical in many other situations.

A child's behavior is part of his total environment. To produce change in one area (school), other areas must also be dealt with. If you isolate only ten percent of the behavior and try to change it, there's a strong probability your attempts will fail.

Examine Child's Total Environment

When I work on a child's school behavior problems, I get the parents to identify situations in the child's total environment where this behavior is also seen. When first trying to produce change, we focus on the behavior at home and in the neighborhood rather than at school. If not listening in school is his major difficulty, we try to get him listening at home before we deal with his academic behavior. If irresponsibility is the source of trouble, we first try to build and establish responsible action at home.

There are several reasons for taking this approach. First, you have more control of the child's behavior at home than at school. You are much closer to the source of the problem. And you deal with a greater variety of situations where the behavior is seen.

Second, in trying to promote change in this fashion, you can deal with a larger portion of the total behavior pattern. The child's irresponsible behavior in school may represent only ten percent of the total pattern. By dealing with the behavior at home and in the neighborhood, you may influence 90% of the pattern.

Finally, patterns of behavior develop elsewhere and get transferred to school. If a child has learned to manipulate you to satisfy his needs, there's a strong probability this behavior will be seen at school. The child may do what he pleases, refuse to work when he doesn't feel like it and ignore classroom procedure. Bad behavior developed at home is transferred to school. Get the reverse process to occur.

Produce Changes At Home

By producing change at home, the new or good behavior can be extended to school. Often we see the child's behavior improve at school without directly working on it. By getting him to listen better or show more responsibility at home, the child's school behavior may improve at the same time. When trying to change any behavior, work with it in the context of its total environment. When it starts to change, you may see improvement in areas you have not directly tried to change.

Once a behavior shows significant improvement at home, about two weeks later the changes often extends to school. However, sometimes this process doesn't occur easily, and further steps must be taken to help the behavior be seen in school. When you start working directly with the school behavior, increase communication between you and the school.

If you establish some control or change at home but a corresponding improvement at school has not occurred, several techniques can be used. Behavioral charts or some communication procedure may be helpful. Keep the system simple.Several procedures are described in the chapter on Monitoring School Behavior & Performance.

Before discussing specific school problems, I will discuss some general behavior management techniques that parents can use on a daily basis with their children. A general understanding of these fundamentals will be necessary to help deal with some of the specific concerns discussed later in the book. As mentioned above, to change a school behavior or problem, frequently other behaviors must be changed. For example, a child is failing three subjects in 5th grade because he is not turning in homework and projects. He is not bringing the proper books home to study, he is not prepared for class, etc. What happens in most cases is that the parents start punishing him for not doing homework, make him bring home all his books, etc. In other words, they try to change the problems at school. However, if you look at the situation in a broader sense, in 90 out of 100 children the child is not irresponsible only with school, he is irresponsible in most aspects of his life (e.g. his room looks like a disaster area, he never cleans up after he eats, he seldom hangs the towel up after he takes a bath, he leaves his bike in front of the house).

Although hanging a towel up after you take a bath and doing math homework is like night and day in terms of what is important, it is the same behavior—that is, not doing what you are supposed to do—irresponsibility. Therefore, in order to make a child more responsible in school you have to make him more responsible overall! If you cannot get him to go to bed when you tell him, clean his room and do other responsible things around the house, you are not going to be able to teach him responsibility toward schoolwork.

Another example would be the six year old who is refusing to separate from his mother and go to school. He gets extremely upset and fearful when he has to be independent of his mother. In most of these cases if you only focus on the refusal to attend school, the interventions will usually be ineffective. Looking at the broader picture, these children are often too dependent on or with the parent too much. They often sleep with the parent, and the mother does things for the child that he could be doing himself (e.g. dress him, bathe him, clean his room). Therefore in order to make it easier to change the refusal to go to school, we have to make this child more independent overall.

While this book focuses on school-related problems, very often other behaviors have to be changed in order to make it easier to deal with the school concern. This is the reason I am first presenting some general techniques of behavior management.

PART III

METHODS AND TECHNIQUES

Chapter 1

Deciding Which Behavior To Change

Parents bring their children to my office for a variety of reasons.

"He won't listen"

"I have to fight him to do homework"

"The teacher says he's immature and should repeat the grade"

"He doesn't behave in school"

"My child is failing 5th grade"

"He has problems with the children in school"

"She seems angry and has an attitude problem"

The first thing I do is ask the parent, "What do you mean he doesn't behave in school? Give me some examples. "What behaviors is he showing to make the teacher think he is immature?" "Give me an example of what you mean when you say he doesn't listen."

I ask the parents to describe or specify the exact behavior, not to look at it in general terms. As an example, what the teacher might mean when she says the child is immature is that he does not pay attention, complete his work, or pay attention like other children his age.

Behavior Must Be Specified

Behavior to be changed must first be specified by stating it in detail. I may not be able to make a child mature, but I can help you to get him to complete his seat work, stay in his desk and pay attention.

Most of us find it difficult to be specific in our descriptions because we look at children and behavior in general terms. The first thing we have to do is specify the behavior. "My child is very angry."

OK, what is he doing? "He's sticking a pencil in his sister's ear. That's what makes me think he's angry." What is anger? What is immaturity? Is he 13 years old and still has to be dressed for school? The first step in changing any behavior is being specific in describing it.

ABCs Of Change

Once the behavior has been specified, we can move to the next step and analyze the behavior. Let's look at a child who has temper tantrums, whines or pouts frequently.

Parent: "My child has temper tantrums every time we sit down to do homework."

Psychologist: "Can you describe or define for me what you mean by a temper tantrum?"

Parent: "He throws himself on the floor or curls up in a chair and whines, screams, hollers, rolls around and sometimes gets violent."

Psychologist: "What usually comes before the temper tantrum? Can you give me an example of what makes him have a temper tantrum?"

Parent: "After he finishes his snack, I say it's time to start homework." He says 'No, I want to watch TV first and then do homework'. I say 'No.' you can't" and then it starts. He begins the whining, complaining, telling me I'm mean and finally the full-blown temper tantrum. He rolls on the floor, screams, hollers, and won't stop cyring."

Psychologist: "What happens next?"

Parent: "Well, he gets me so irritated and upset I finally start hollering. He's hollering. I'm hollering and after a while I yell 'Go watch your stupid TV program, I don't care if you fail 2nd grade. You're going to put me in a mental hospital."

In this situation, what I have asked the parent to do is to analyze the behavior. We look at the temper tantrum (behavior) and look at what comes before the behavior (antecedents) and what comes after the behavior (consequences). In any behavior, there are three parts-Antecedents, Behavior and Consequences. These are the ABCs!

A	B	C
Child Is Told	Temper Tantrum	He Watches TV
Let's do homework		

With this information, we have taken the first step in producing a change. We have analyzed the behavior. We have looked at the specific behavior and what comes before and after the action.

In analyzing a behavior, it's also important to see how often it occurs. How many times an hour, day or week does it occur? 10 times a day? Once a week? 3 times an hour? There are reasons for this analysis. I have had many parents tell me, "Once I started looking closely at the behavior and kept a record of how frequently it occurred, I realized it wasn't as bad as I thought it was."

Another reason for analysis is a child doesn't wake up one morning behaving a specific way. His behavior gradually develops over a period of weeks, months or years. To modify behavior, a similar process is necessary. Results are based on a gradual improvement that will occur.

Usually we look at a actions in general terms and cannot see the small changes. Parents may come to me and say, "My child is giving me trouble doing homework." We then decide on a treatment plan and ask the parents to try my suggestions.

After 2 weeks, the parents return. If they looked at the overall behavior, they may say, "He's giving me trouble with homework." But they didn't look at the child's action closely and actually note how frequently the problems occurred. Otherwise, they might have observed that before the treatment plan was started, the child was giving them problems doing homework four out of four days. After the two weeks period, they were only having trouble on two out of four days. This is a 50% improvement!

Behavior changes gradually. Look for small improvements.

CHAPTER 2

Why Children Do The Things They Do

In analyzing behavior as described in Chapter 2, we look at an important factor in behavior change—consequences. The reason most of us do what we do is because of the consequences of our behavior. The reason we go to work instead of staying home is because the consequences are different. We get paid if we work and do not if we stay home. The same is true for children. They behave in certain ways because of the consequences of their actions.

The child described in the previous chapter who was having temper tantrums—why is he misbehaving? The consequence of this behavior is he gets what he wants—he watches TV. His behavior is maintained because it has a purpose. Let's look at another behavior sequence.

Parent: *"My child always has to have the last word."*
Psychologist: *"What do you mean?"*
Parent: *"He's sassy. He talks back and always has a smart answer."*
Psychologist: *"Can you give me an example?"*
Parent: *"I tell him something he doesn't like. 'Go take your bath. Go pick up your toys. Come inside.' He says, 'Wait a minute' or something similar in a sarcastic, harsh voice. If someone saw or heard him do this, they would think he has no respect for me."*
Psychologist: *"Then what happens?"*
Parent: *"I usually say, 'You have ten more minutes' or I remind*

him several more times. He says 'Stop nagging.' 'Get off my back.' or some other smart answer. After a few more remarks, I'm very angry and we're in a shouting match. Eventually we're in an argument, and I have to drag him to do what he should have done 30 minutes ago."

The consequence of this behavior is the child is getting his parent upset. Perhaps that's the reason he continues the behavior.

When I ask most children, *"Why are you sassy?"* they usually give me a routine answer—a shrug of the shoulders or *"I don't know."*

Or they give me some equally revealing response, such as, *"My father won't buy me a motorcycle."*

"I have to wear black shoes to school."

"My brother's stupid."

Many children honestly do not know why they behave in certain ways. They are usually responding to the environment, events and people in their lives.

One question does not lead to the basis of that response. At our center we usually do some psychological testing and interviewing to determine the reasons for and consequences of a child's behavior.

Let's imagine I have a magic wand with which I can tap the child on the head and have him tell me some of the reasons for his behavior. The following are a few examples of what I might learn about a child's actual behavior motivation.

Example 1

The child has to be told many times to do his homework or the parent must get upset before the son will listen.

Psychologist:" *Jason, why does your mother have to tell you 37 times then get upset and holler before you will do your homework.*

Jason: *"Well, it takes 37 times because the first 30 times she doesn't really mean it. She's says, 'Jason, do your homework' in a normal voice. She's really talking to hear herself talk, and I let it go in one ear and out the other."*

Psychologist: *"Then what happens?"*

Jason: *"About the 31st time, her voice starts getting louder. Around 32 and 33, she starts hollering and saying in an angry voice, 'I really mean it.' Somewhere around the 34th or 35th time, her face starts turning red. She starts pounding on the table."*

Psychologist: *"What do you do then?"*

Jason: *"Well, the next thing is the hair on the back of her neck stands up. This usually happens around the 36th or 37th time. When I see this, I know she means business. I'm going to get it if I don't do what she says so I run like crazy and start my homework."*

Psychologist: *"It sounds like you wait around for the right signal or cue that tells you a consequence is coming or something is really going to happen. When you see it, you do what your mother wants."*

Jason: *That's right."*

Example 2

The child won't get dressed for school. He continually fools around; every morning's preparation for school is a battle.

Psychologist: *"Joe, why does your mother have a lot of trouble with you before you go to school?"*

Joe: *"I don't like getting dressed, and I'd rather look at TV. If I fool around long enough, I can look at TV, and after a while my mother will come in and dress me."*

Example 3

Psychologist: *"Your mother tells me that you are always forgetting your lunch money at home. Why can't you remember to bring it to school? What happens?"*

Jeff: *"I have never missed eating lunch."*
Psychologist: *"What do you mean?"*
Jeff: *"Every time I leave my lunch money home, my mother brings
        it to school."*

I could go on with many more examples, but the point should
already be clear that children often behave as they do because of
the consequences of their behavior.

Any time two people get together, parents and children
included, we teach each other different things about behavior and
its consequences. Whenever people relate to one another, they
teach each other certain behavior. This is called social learning
theory. When we interact with our children, we are teaching them
behavior, and they are teaching us to respond to them in certain
ways. We often teach our children how to be helpless, dependent,
immature, to have temper tantrums, to be sassy and not listen. At
the same time, they teach us to holler, nag, scream, get upset,
criticize or worry. Social learning, or behavioral interaction, is a
two-way street.

If we can teach our children to misbehave, we can also teach
them good, acceptable behavior. Unfortunately, most of us go
about it the wrong way. We try to change the child directly. How
many times have you looked at your children's behavior as their
problem and said, "I buy you things, clean your clothes, feed you
and you're bad? Why don't you behave?" In other words, "Why
don't you change your behavior, and I'll be happy and pleased
with you?" It's a very difficult thing to change other people's
behavior directly without an intermediate change in your
relationship with them. It is much easier if you change the way
you relate to your children. In doing this, you encourage them to
change their behavior and the way they relate to you.

Suppose I work with someone who continually criticizes what
I do. I arrive at work before he does and start on some paperwork.
He comes in and says, *"Why are you doing that? That's a waste
of time. What you are doing is worthless."* He goes on and on.
Each morning we almost come to blows. We yell at each other
and have heated arguments. Each day is a hassle. This disruption

has continued for two years, and I keep telling this man, *"Please leave me alone. Be nice. Quit calling me names."* But I have responded to him in this fashion for two years, and he has not changed. My techniques have not worked.

All of a sudden I say to myself, *"Maybe I'm beating my head against a brick wall trying to change him. It would be much easier if I change the way I respond to him."* The next day he comes in and starts his verbal assault, but I stay calm. He criticizes me, but I keep doing my work. He rants and raves for three hours, but I don't respond. The next day he comes in and does the same thing, but I keep doing my work. He hollers for about 45 minutes. The next day the criticism lasts for 15 minutes. The following day it lasts about three minutes. After about a week of this, he comes in and says, *"Good morning. Do you want a cup of coffee?"* Now I have him doing exactly what I want him to do. I accomplished this by changing my responses.

Much of the behavior—good or bad—seen in children, especially under age ten, can be viewed as a response to the environment. Without a change in the environment, it's difficult to change a child's behavior. However, if the surroundings are modified, it's easy to achieve behavioral change in children, A child's most significant environment is his home, so a change in the way you respond to your child often produces a significant behavior change in him or her.

The information following focuses on ways you can change you own behavior. By responding to your children differently, you can change their behavior. Just as important as analyzing and looking at your children's behavior is the need to look closely at what you are doing and how you respond to your children.

If you can change how you respond to your children, you'll change their behavior. To change your child's behavior, you must look at the total environment. You are a significant part of the picture.

CHAPTER 3

Being A Consistent Parent

Since the early 1970s, many parents have participated in our parent-training workshops. At the first meeting, all parents are asked to list at least three kinds of behavior they would like to change in their children. The behaviors parents list most frequently include:

"Hardheaded, stubborn, not doing what I ask,"

"I have to really get upset before he'll do what I tell him" or some other phrase that identifies the child's problem as not listening.

One of the primary reasons for Listening problems is inconsistency in the parents' approach to a child's behavior. They do not mean what they say or do not follow through with what they say. Although this inconsistency seems like a small omission, it's often one of the main reasons why techniques tried by parents do not work.

Consistency can be viewed as the foundation of effective child management. Like the foundation of a house, if it is solid there is a good probability the structure it supports will be fine. However, if the foundation is shaky, problems are certain to arise. By being consistent, parents increase the probability that the techniques they use will work. On the other hand, an inconsistent approach to child management almost assures failure.

We don't listen to adults who say one thing and do something else. We can't expect our children to listen to us if we behave the same way. Suppose you have a friend named John who tells you, *"I caught 100 pounds of shrimp today and, I'll bring you 25 pounds tonight."* You go home and don't bother to cook. You wait, but John never brings the shrimp.

The next week you talk to him and mention your car is broken, but you have to go to the store to get something. He says, *"I can take you. I'll be over around 3 pm to pick you up."* You get dressed, but he never shows up. The next week John agrees to help you move some furniture but again fails to do what he says.

This interaction occurs for many weeks. Three months later, he calls you and says, *"I have 2 tickets to a new movie. I know you want to see it, so get dressed and call a friend. I'll drop the tickets off at your house at 6 pm."* What will you do? Will you hurry home, get dressed and call a friend? Probably not, because John usually says one thing and does something else.

How would you respond to John? You wouldn't listen to him. You'd think he was talking to hear himself talk. More important, he can't control you or get you to do what he wants. He tells you to go home, call a friend, get dressed and wait for him to come. However, you go about your daily business as usual because you've leaned John is inconsistent. He says one thing and does something else.

If you are inconsistent in your approach to your child, he feels the same way about you and will respond to you the same way you would respond to John. There are many ways you can be inconsistent and teach children to be confused, to ignore directions and to manipulate.

Making Statements You Don't Mean

You are driving across town and your 2 children are in the back seat. They're picking on one another, and you keep asking them to be still. However, they continue, and their behavior intensifies. Soon they're arguing and you're telling them to be quiet. Then they start to fight, and you're at the end of your rope.

You say something wonderful like, *"If you don't stop, I'm going to stop at the next bridge and throw both of you off it."* Naturally, they don't stop.

Your child is doing poorly in school. To make him study harder you say, *"You know, if you don't do better in this school, we'll have to put you in a home or boarding school."*

I could give other examples, but the point is we often say things we have no intention of carrying out. We know this and, more important, the child also knows it. Your threats don't stop the behavior, and your child keeps doing whatever you're trying to prevent.

Overstatements

You are sitting down with your son trying to get him to do his homework. He's counting the dots on the ceiling, daydreaming and beating the pencil on the table. Fifteen minutes worth of homework has exhausted 2 hours; all your attempts to get it finished have failed. You are frustrated and finally tell him, "*Go to your room; you're punished for the night.*" He starts crying but goes to his room and pouts.

In a few minutes, he sticks his head out of the door and says, "*I'm sorry. I love you. I'll be good; I'll never do it again.*" You start feeling sorry for him or feeling guilty for what you've done, and 2 minutes later you let him out of his room.

Overstatements like those above are major sources of inconsistency in families. We get angry and make statements we could never follow through. Or we say or do something then start feeling guilty and try to undo it. In both instances, the child interprets your behavior as implying, "*Don't believe or listen to what I say because I don't mean anything I'm saying.*"

Turning "No" to "Yes" and "Yes" to "No"

Another way to be inconsistent is to say one thing and do something else. It's about 30 minutes before supper, and your 6-year-old son comes up to you and says, "*Can I take my new truck to school. I want to play with it at recess and I can show it to my friends.*"

You respond, "*No, I don't think that is a good idea. Your teacher also said not to bring toys from home to school.*"

However, he doesn't accept this and keep badgering you. "*Why can't I take the truck? My sister took her doll to school last week. Why can she take her stuff to school and I can't? That's not fair. You love her more than you love me.*"

While all of this is going on, you tell him to calm down, quit complaining and stop whining. After a few minutes you tense, upset and your stomach is in knots so you let him take the truck to school to preserve your sanity. In doing this, you reversed your original *"No"* and changed it to a *"Yes."*

Or how many times have you said something like, *"I'll take you to the show this Saturday if you are good in school this week."* He is good, but when Saturday comes, you say, *"I'm a little too busy this weekend, so we'll go to the show next week."*

The examples are endless, but in this form of inconsistency, a *No* is changed to a *Yes* or a positive statement becomes negative. This teaches your children not to listen to you when you respond in this way. You also show them how to manipulate you. You say, *"If I tell you something you don't like, do this or this* (have a temper tantrum, whine, pout, get me upset*), and I'll change my mind."* You are showing them how to be con artists. Children are very good at manipulating adults on their own and don't need additional help. Avoid this type of interaction.

See If What You Requested Has Been Done

You can also produce inconsistency by telling your child to do something then not checking to see it has been done.

You tell your child *"If you write all of the assignments down in your notebook every day so I can see if you are doing your homework you can go out and play that day. If you do not write all of it down you will not be able to go outside and play with your friends."*

The child comes home all week with assignments written in his notebook. Each day you say, *"Is this everything you have to do?"* He says *"yes"* and goes outside to play. On Friday you get a note from his teacher that he missed five assignments this week.

This form of inconsistency is not important for some children, but for others you have to follow-up. For some kids, I would not buy a car from them until I drove it. You must see if the child has done what he or she has been asked or what he is supposed to do. Some children will try to get away with as much as possible if you let them. This is especially true of homework. This form of inconsistency tends to interfere with the development of responsibility and also teaches children to be manipulative and sneaky.

Consistency From Both Parents

Consistency comes from both parents and from the mother and father as a unit. Each parent must mean what he or she says when dealing with the child, but each must also support and back up the other.

A child misbehaves in school and comes home with a great deal of homework as punishment from his teacher. He does not start it right away but plays and wastes his time. His mother has told him to do his homework. *"I've told you ten times to finish that work. If you aren't finished by the time you're supposed to go to baseball practice, you're not going."*

However, these threats produce no action. Some time later, the child starts getting ready for baseball practice. His mother sees him putting his shoes on and getting his glove. She tells him, *"Didn't I tell you you couldn't go if you didn't finish your work?"*

The child says, *"I'm going; you can't stop me."* The mother replies with some further threats, then the child starts hollering. They begin arguing heatedly, and soon they are in a power struggle.

"You're not going."

"Yes, I am."

The father, who is sitting in another room, hears the arguing and comes into the boy's room. He asks, *"What's going on?"*

The mother tells him what has happened, and the boy gives his side of the story.

Then the father says, *"The team is depending on him, and he needs to go to practice. Now son, you go to practice and do your schoolwork when you come home."*

The boy goes out to play, leaving his parents arguing.

Parents can produce inconsistency by undermining each other and not presenting a unified approach to the child. There are several results to this inconsistency. First, the child is learning to play one parent against the other and to manipulate them to get his way. When one parent disciplines a child and the other countermands it, the first parent's authority is reduced. Consequently, the child views this parent as the one who holds final authority and will not listen to the other.

By presenting this type of approach, parents tend to differentiate themselves as the bad guy, or the mean one, and the good guy, or the one who steps in and rescues the child from the evil being done to him. This type of inconsistency also produces arguing and fighting between parents. When this happens, some children identify themselves as the cause of the conflict between their parents. This isn't a good situation in which to place a child because the child may then view himself as the root of all the problems and conflicts between his parents.

It's extremely important for parents to be consistent as a unit. If you disagree with your partner or another person who has a significant part in disciplining your child, it's best to support him in front of your child. Later, when your child is not around, discuss the difference of opinion and, more important, resolve it.

Suppose your husband takes your son's bike away for a month because he got a detention in school. Although you feel this is too severe, you should support him in front of the child. Later discuss the problem, and decide how you will handle it the next time it occurs. Maybe the next time it happens the child won't be allowed to ride his bike for 2 days. When the behavior occurs again, a rule and consequence have been established so you and your husband are in agreement and can present a unified front.

Different Parent Responses To The Same Behavior

Depending on how you feel or your mood, people often treat the same behavior in very different ways.

One day a child comes home with a poor test paper and we sit down with him and go over the test to show him what he did wrong. Tomorrow when he brings home a similar test we holler, scream and get upset. The third time this happens we punish him for a week. The next time he comes home with a low grade on a test we give him a lecture on the value of education.

When you respond to your children inconsistently, you

establish a situation similar to that in the following example. Let's say that today when I see you, I smile and shake your hand. Tomorrow when I see you, I smile and punch you in the nose. The next time I see you, I smile and take your car away. Another day I smile and give you money. This goes on for several weeks. How are you going to respond to me when you see me? How are you going to feel?

First of all, you can't predict my behavior. Although I am nice to you at times, you never know what to expect. When you see me, you'll probably tighten up, be confused and feel uncertain, tense and insecure. You'll probably try to place some physical distance between us and won't be able to become emotionally close to me or form a friendship. Children who experience inconsistency from their parents feel the same way. This inconsistent, unpredictable, unstructured interaction is difficult for them to handle.

It's best to set up a specific consequence for each behavior, whenever possible. For example, it may be a standard rule at your house that whenever anyone comes home with a poor test and he did not study for it, he will not be able to sleep out or have a friend sleep over that weekend. Or the days the child does not bring his math book home and cannot do his homework, you will make up math problems and the child will have twice as many to do as he would have had for his homework.

Setting up rules and consequences reduces inconsistency and makes the environment more structured and predictable. This decreases the probability that the problems mentioned above will appear.

Consistency In The Environment

Consistency as discussed above relates to how adults interact with children. Interpersonal consistency is very important in child management. Consistency, structure or routine in the environment can also reduce behavioral difficulties.

A child with a set bedtime gives you less trouble when it's time to go to bed than a child who is allowed to retire at different times every night. Homework is less of a chore if it's done at the same time each day. Other chores, such as bathing, feeding the pets and taking out the garbage, require less reminding and nagging from parents if a routine is established. You don't have to make your home a military operation, but structure it as much as you reasonably can. Establish some routines to make the environment more predictable for the child.

Consistency may seem like a minor concept but it can eliminate about 50% of "not listening" in children. It's a major principle in child management and parent training. Consistency serves as a foundation on which other techniques and methods are built.

Following are two good rules to keep in mind when interacting with your child: Don't say anything you can't or don't want to do. Do everything you say you're going to do. You must follow through for any intervention to work.

CHAPTER 4

Setting Rules For Behavior

Another major problem common to many child-rearing situations is setting rules or behavioral expectations. Parents usually have thousands of rules and regulations around the house.

- Don't get into any trouble today at school.
- Listen to your teacher.
- Don't be mean to your classmates.
- Let's start homework.
- Bring all your books home from school.
- All your homework must be done before your favorite TV program comes on.

Random Discipline

Parents frequently do an excellent job of setting expectations but spoil their good work when the child breaks the rules or doesn't live up to behavioral expectations. This is where the mistake is made. If the child gets in trouble at school, the parent then decides what is going to happen—he gets hollered at, his bike taken away for a week, a lecture, etc.

You state the expectation beautifully but wait till the rule is broken. Only then do you decide what the consequence will be. You should try to avoid this.

When you discipline or try to enforce rules and expectations in this way, several things happen that make effective child management difficult.

Random Discipline Doesn't Make Child Feel Responsible

A child doesn't feel responsible for what happens to him when he's not in control of the consequences of his behavior. He doesn't develop responsibility or feel he influences what occurs to him. Many children have told me something similar to, *"If I'd known they were going to take TV away for a week, I would have never misbehaved."* Children do not develop responsibility and feel others determine what happens to them. They blame others for what has happened to them.

"The teacher didn't tell us we should study that; that's why I failed the test."

"Daddy hollered at me; that's why I broke my toy."

"My sister kept bothering me; that's why I punched her in the nose."

Random Discipline Creates Anger

If you discipline randomly or wait till your child breaks a rule then decide the consequences, your child is likely to get angry with you. He feels you are responsible for the bad things that happen to him. When rules are enforced in random fashion, a child is justified in being angry at his or her parents and feels as if he or she is not in control of the consequences of the behavior.

To understand how your child feels under these circumstances, take an example pertaining to the adult world of work and paychecks. Let's say you go to work and your boss tells you exactly what he expects of you. *"Come to work every day. Take an hour for lunch. Work from 8 am to 5 pm."* He spells out the rules and expectations very clearly.

After you've been working for him for a few weeks, you miss a day of work and receive a paycheck that is $5 less than usual. The next week, you miss a day and your check is $10 short. Another week, you stay home a day and your boss deducts $35 from your check. The next week, the check is $75 short, the next $130, the next $135.

After a couple of months of this, you go to the boss and ask, *"What's going on? I miss work, and you take different amounts of money out of my check."*

The boss responds, *"That's what I think you deserve. I needed you on the day I took out $130, but I didn't need you when I just deducted $5."*

How would you feel if you were the employee? You would be angry and think he was mean and unfair. You would also feel he was responsible for what happens to you. You would tend to blame him for your behavior.

Continuing with this example, a friend comes up to you and says, *"Why didn't you buy that TV you said you were going to buy?"*

You'd probably reply, *"My boss took a lot of money from my check, and now I can't buy it."* You would make your boss responsible.

This situation occurs many times every day in most families and is a primary reason why some forms of discipline don't work. A child has a difficult time developing a sense of responsibility if disciplined in this manner. He may develop anger and resentment toward you, be confused and have a difficult time knowing where he stands. In addition, he may have trouble becoming emotionally close to you.

Random Discipline Makes You Feel Guilty

If you discipline randomly, you may feel guilty for what you have done and try to undo it. This results in an inconsistent approach to the child. For example, you and your children are watching a cartoon special on TV, and the kids are fighting and teasing each other. You tell them repeatedly to stop, calm down and behave, but they continue. You finally reach your breaking point and yell at them, *"I've told you 10 times to stop, but you will not listen. Now go to your rooms. You can't watch TV!"*

They put their heads down and walk to their rooms. You pick up the newspaper and start reading it. Then you start thinking-you may feel mean, guilty or upset for what you've done. *"Maybe I was a little too hard on them. This cartoon special only comes on a few times a year, and I've made them miss it."*

After some thinking, you feel like a bad guy, so you go to

their rooms and ask them if they can be good. In a few minutes, they're back watching TV, and you've eliminated your guilt feelings. However, nothing constructive has been accomplished.

Rules And Consequences Must Be Clearly Defined

In setting rules, state your expectations and state the consequences before a rule is broken. Both the rule and the consequences of the child's behavior must be clearly spelled out.

Let's take the previous example pertaining to work and paychecks to see how clear definition is provided. When you come to work the boss states the rules or expectations. *"Come to work every day. You have an hour for lunch. You work from 8 am to 5 pm."* But he takes his specifications a step further and states the consequences of failing to meet expectations.

"Each day you come to work and are here a full day, you will be paid $100. If you do not show up, you will not receive the $100."

Now you know each day you miss work your weekly check will be $100 short. At the end of 2 months, you look at your check stubs and note there has been a $100 deduction for each day you missed. By having the expectations and consequences spelled out, you can't make your boss responsible for the deductions. There's only one person to blame—yourself. You are responsible for what has happened to you.

If your friend comes up to you and asks, *"Why didn't you buy that TV you said you were going to buy?"* you should respond, *"Because I decided not to go to work, I didn't get a full paycheck. I don't have enough money to buy the TV."* In setting up the rules and consequences, your boss has made you accountable and responsible for your own behavior.

To set effective rules, tell your children, *"Here is what I want you to do. This* (consequence A) *will happen if you do it that way, and this* (consequence B) *will happen if you do it that way."* By defining the consequences of behavior, your child can decide for himself what's going to happen to him.

Completing Class Work
"Your teacher is telling me you're not finishing your seat work. I'm going to talk to her everyday when I pick you up. On the days that you have completed all your work we will be able to stop at the store on the way home from school and get some candy. If you do not complete your classroom, we will not."

Bringing Home Books
"The day you bring home all your books from school you can look at TV. The days you don't, no TV."

Getting Ready For School
"The mornings that you are dressed and ready to go to school at 7:30am, we will have time to stop and get a donut on the way to school. If you're not dressed at that time we will not be able to get a donut."

Getting Along With Classmates
"Your teacher told me that you have been fighting and arguing with your classmates at recess, lunch and P.E. I'm going to check with her on Friday and if there weren't any problems, your friend can come over and sleep Friday night."

Doing Homework
"You mentioned to Dad you want to go to the basketball game Friday night. That's fine, but you know we've been having a great deal of trouble getting you to do your homework. I'll tell you what we will do. If you come home three out of four days this week and do your homework without a fight, you can go to the game. But if you give us trouble about the homework more than once this week, you can't go to the game."

In the examples given, the parent is in control. The adult specifies the expectations and consequences, but the child decides what will happen. A map is drawn; all you have to do is sit back and wait for your child to tell you what to do. You don't have to remind him 50 times, nag or cajole. By his behavior, your child will tell you if he wants to watch TV, stop and get candy, go to the basketball game or have a friend sleep over. All you have to do is be consistent and follow through with the consequence the child chooses.

I believe it's extremely important to teach your children they are responsible for their own behavior. Good and bad things happen because of their decisions. Many adults never learn this. They fail to accept the responsibility for the consequences of their behavior.

If a child feels he or she is responsible for the consequences of his or her behavior, then the child will feel a situation can be changed. If things are bad, he can make them better. If he's happy with what's happening, he can maintain it. If he feels a parent is responsible, he is like a puppet on a string who has to wait until others decide to make him feel good.

Expectations And Consequences Must Be Specific

One morning while I was getting ready to go to work, my wife was trying to get our oldest son up to go to school. He wouldn't budge and continued lying in bed. I passed his room and said, *"You'd better be out of the bed by the time I'm finished shaving."*

When I finished, I went to check on him and, sure enough, he had done exactly what I told him. He had taken his pillow and blanket off his bed and was now lying on the floor! Children often do exactly what you tell them. When you state rules or behavioral expectations, be as specific as possible! *"I want you to get out of bed, put your clothes on and be sitting at the table ready for breakfast in 15 minutes."*

You may also encounter problems with a child's behavior if expectations or consequences are stated in general or cloudy terms. The statements " *I want you to behave in school today"* or *"The grades have to get better"* are too vague. What does behave or better mean? They mean different things for different people. For and eight year old, behaving in school might mean hitting other kids ten times instead of twenty. His parent defines behaving as not getting into any fights. For the twelve-year-old getting better grades might mean raising his grade point average from 70 to 72, whereas the parent perceives better as 80.

When the child and parent get together to compare notes, they come up with different interpretations of the same expectation. The parent feels the child has misbehaved, but the child feels he has behaved as required and he has been unfairly disciplined.

The same misunderstanding results when you state consequences in general terms. *"If you don't do homework, you're going to get it"* or *"If you get a detention, you'll be punished."* What does this mean to a child? Probably not much.

In stating expectations, rules and consequences, be specific and spell out exactly what you mean. You can't assume the child knows. Both of you must have the same idea of what is expected and what the consequences of failure will be. There should not be a mystery or guessing game for the child. If there is, the child is apt to be confused and resent being disciplined.

How To Set Up Clear Expectations And Consequences

Expectations and consequences must be spelled out ahead of time to be effective. A map is drawn for the child, and he decides what path to take. There are three general ways to accomplish this.

Natural Consequences

Some behavior carries with it natural consequences, and these are often sufficient to produce change. If I beat my head on the floor, the natural consequence is that my head will hurt.

That result may be enough by itself to prevent me from continuing the behavior. If the only thing a child obtains by having a temper tantrum is a sore throat, upset stomach or hurt head, that behavior will quickly decrease. Natural consequences can be used to manage some problem behavior, and often this is a good place to start.

However, the natural consequences have to be important to the child to effectively work. For example, for some children, we could tell them *"If you're not dressed for school when the bus arrives, you will not go to school today."*

For some kids this would kill them. Other kids wouldn't get

dressed until they were 18 years old and didn't have to go to school. A few other examples follow.

You have 2 children one gets ready every morning for school and the other does not. You may tell them *"The people who are dressed for school—when it's time to go I will take them to school. Whoever is not dressed I'll take whenever they are dressed and they will be tardy and have to deal with the principal."*

A child is constantly losing pencils, pens, notebook, coats or whatever. They could be told *"I will supply you with three pencils a week. If you need more, I'll buy them for you, but you'll pay me back."*

"If you lose you jacket and I have to buy you another one, you will owe me for the jacket."

In most situations we don't have the children pay actual money. We give a list of chores with assigned value. For example, folding clothes is worth .50 cents, washing the car $5.00, emptying the dishwasher .50 cents. We then tell the child, *"The jacket, pencils or whatever cost $25. Since you lost it, and I didn't, you have to pay for it. Here's a list of chores and what they are worth. Every time you do a chore come tell me so I can check it off and give you credit for it. I will not give you money for anything until you pay me back my money. If you work real hard you can finish this in a few days. If you fool around and don't pay me back till you are 17 years old I'll have a lot of extra money to spend on your sister."*

Another example would be *"I passed 5th grade a long time ago. I don't need this and I'm not fighting you with the homework. If you don't want to do it, don't do it. But you'll have to go to school tomorrow and deal with Ms. Buteria and suffer the consequences."*

The natural consequences of not doing homework at some schools are you get a detention, have to go see the principal, etc. Another natural consequence of not doing homework is you get bad grades and may fail. Now this will work for the child who cares about good grades and passing. Some kids don't and this natural consequence will not work.

Children often get sick to avoid unpleasant situations such as school, tests or other obligations. Later, when the child gets home or when other children are home to play, he recovers very rapidly. Natural consequences can be used to alter this problem behavior.

"If you're sick, you have to go to the doctor." Most kids love that! Or the house rule could be that when a child is sick he must remain in his room, in bed, without play or TV time.

The consequences of being well far outweigh the natural consequences of being sick. The child will probably not be tempted to feign sickness.

Parents who have trouble with children failing to put their dirty school uniforms in the proper place may state, *"I only wash clothes that go in that dirty-clothes basket. Those articles that are left in other places will not be washed."* In this situation, the natural consequence of the child leaving his school uniforms in his room is he won't have a clean one to wear or he'll have to wash them himself. Again, it is important to note that the natural consequences have to be important to the child. For the twelve year old who is starting to notice girls and wants to "fit in" socially, this is an important consequence. For the twelve year old who would wear the same pair of drawers for a month if you didn't tell him to change them, it is not!

In these types of situations, you must respond in a matter-of-fact manner and not get upset. Consistency and following through with what is said are also extremely important.

Grandma's Rule

This is a principle many parents use frequently. It can be stated very simply. *"First you do what I want you to do, then you can do what you want to do."*

Our grandmothers or parents often said, *"Eat your meat and potatoes, then you can have your dessert."* This method of setting consequences can be used on the spur of the moment. However, it must usually include some type of activity that is of interest to the child. You're having difficulty getting your child ready for school, and you know he enjoys watching TV before school. Using grandma's rule, you would say, *"The TV is not turned on until you're dressed and ready for school."*

A few other situations illustrate the principle.

"If the teacher tells me you've finished all your class work when I pick you up, we can stop and feed the ducks on the way home from school."

"You can't talk on the phone until the homework is completed."

"The days you bring home all your books, you can watch TV."

In these examples, the parent sets expectations and consequences and gives the child a decision to make. As a parent, all you do is carry out the consequence the child decides on.

Arbitrarily Setting Consequences

When natural consequences or grandma's rule can't be used, you can always identify consequences that are important to the child and set rules or behavioral expectations according to these.

A sassy child might hate being confined in his room. You could tell him, *"I don't like you talking back to me and being sassy. Each time this happens, you have to go to your room for 13 minutes."*

Another child who's doing poorly in school because he fails to do his homework may love to stay up past his usual bedtime. To improve this child's behavior, you might tell him, *"For every homework assignment you bring home and complete, you can stay up three minutes past your bedtime."*

This child gives you a great deal of trouble getting dressed for school. Use what he loves to change his behaviors by telling him *"On the mornings you are dressed and ready for school without a hassle, we'll play a game that night. On the morning you are not, we won't play any games."*

A child who loves to have sleepovers could be told, *"If you do not get a detention this week your friend can sleep over."*

In these situations, you have identified a consequence that is important to the child and then set the behavioral expectations. It isn't a natural consequence or something that follows an activity but something devised and individualized according to a child's particular interests.

It could be a positive consequence—something the child enjoys and that does not happen everyday at your house. Or, it could be a negative consequence that the child would like to avoid or a loss of privileges.

CHAPTER 5

Changing Behavior

Consequences are the most important aspects of modifying a child's behavior. The previous chapter discussed the most effective way to use them. Parents can use three major consequences to discipline their children.

Reward Or Positive Consequences

If you see a behavior you like, reward it. Follow the behavior with positive attention—something that is important or enjoyable to the child.

Punishment Or Negative Consequences

If you see a behavior you don't like, punish it. Follow the behavior with negative attention—something the child views as unenjoyable or withdrawing something positive.

Ignoring Or No Consequences

If you see a behavior you don't like, ignore it. Maybe the attention you give it is the reason it exists. Don't follow the behavior with negative or positive attention.

Rewarding, punishing and ignoring behavior are the three major consequences you can use to discipline your children. These tools are essential to changing behavior as discussed in detail in the following chapters.

CHAPTER 6

Reward

There are three major consequences—rewarding, punishing and ignoring—that you can use to discipline or manage child behavior. But most parents usually rely on punishment. By punishment, I mean negative attention, emphasis on bad behavior, anything from hollering at a child to spanking him. Many times a week, I hear, "*I've tried everything on this child, but nothing works!*"

The first question I ask is, "*What have you tried?*" The usual answers I get are varied.

"*I've taken him off the baseball team.*"

"*We put her in her room.*"

"*My husband took TV away.*"

"*We wouldn't let him play outside.*"

"*My wife made him write lines.*"

"*I wouldn't let her go out Saturday night.*"

"*We spanked him.*"

What most parents tell me is they've used every form of punishment they could dream up.

Many problems occur when punishment is used as the main method to control or discipline children. This is discussed in detail in Chapter 7.

Most parents pay more attention to misbehavior than to appropriate behavior. If everything is going well, they don't say anything. But when something goes wrong, they're quick to punish the child. A few examples follow.

On Friday, the young child brings home twenty-five papers

from school that he did that week. Twenty-four are great, have stars on them, rocket ships or smiley faces. One is bad. We spend 8 seconds going over the good ones and an hour and a half on the bad one.

You tell a child to bring home all his books from school. What happens when he forgets a book? You give him attention by yelling or punishing him or give him a lecture. What happens if he brings home all his books? Nothing.

A child with poor penmanship is writing his ten spelling words five times apiece. We tell him, *"Take your time and do it neat so I can read it."* He takes his time and forty-five of the words look great. Ten don't. We tend to emphasize the 10% bad work and minimize or overlook the 90% that looks great.

Parents usually stress only bad behavior. Try changing your approach, and you may find your child's behavior changes!

The Positive Approach

Most counselors and child psychologists stress a positive approach to discipline. They stress shifting the emphasis from what the child does wrong to what he is doing right. In doing this, you pay more attention to good behavior and less to inappropriate actions or misbehavior. This positive approach is primarily achieved by using the consequence of reward.

Parents tell me, *"I've tried everything,"* and go through their list of punishments.

I then usually ask, *"Have you tried rewarding him for doing good?"*

Parents think I'm speaking another language or I've mentioned something that has never crossed their minds. And many parents have the wrong idea of what I mean by "reward." They usually view it as a bribe, money or something similar.

Reward can be defined as something that will serve as an incentive; an emphasis on anything that is important to the child or anything that will increase the probability good behavior will recur. The primary purpose of reward is to get a child to want to do what is asked or expected. Reward often changes the child's motivation. It will change a behavior the child views as undesirable into something he wants to do.

Many parents ask me, *"What can I use for a reward?"* This is difficult to answer because reward must be individualized for each child. What is important to my son may not be important to yours. What may serve as a reward for one child may be a punishment for another.

When trying to identify possible rewards for children, throw out your values and observe closely what the child considers important.

Types Of Reward

Possible rewards might be found to occur among any of the following categories.

Activity Rewards

These could be activities that are important to the child staying up past his bedtime, having a friend sleep over, playing a game with you, staying out later on Saturday, going to sleep at grandmother's house, playing pitch and catch with you, extra time to ride his bike, extra TV time or going to a dance or football game.

Foolish Rewards

These usually involve an activity you might view as foolish or stupid but the child views as a reward—washing the car, cutting the grass, using the vacuum cleaner, taking a shower.

Material Rewards

These are usually concrete or material things the child values—an extra dime for school, a toy, candy, a snack at night, a bag of potato chips, football cards, an album, a basketball.

Things You'd Usually Buy

These rewards usually involve material things that parents would get the child anyway. A child comes home and says, *"I want a kite."* You would probably buy him one; however, take the opportunity to use the child's desire for the kite as a means to reward good behavior.

Another child might say, "*Joey has a pair of new tennis shoes. I wish I had some like his.*" You look at his shoes, see they're old and he needs a new pair. Instead of going out on Saturday to buy the shoes he needs, use the desire for a particular style of shoe as an incentive to change behavior.

Token Rewards

These rewards have little value in themselves. But they represent something important, or they can be traded for a desired object. Money serves as a powerful token reward for adults.

The kindergarten child who behaves or performs in school to get a star on his forehead or a happy-face stamp on his hand is actually working for a token reward. These represent approval, positive attention and acceptance. Points or stars on a chart often serve as tokens that can be traded in for some desired object or activity.

Social Rewards

This is the most powerful reward you have, and you have it with you all the time. It doesn't cost a penny. It's praise, recognition and positive attention for good behavior.

Many children will do a great deal to get social rewards. Often social rewards are sufficient to change and maintain behavior. These rewards might be verbal approval, laughter, a smile, a hug or a kiss. They might be recognition for helping you set the table, attention to an everyday behavior (picking up clothes, brushing teeth), telling your child how pleased or proud you are of him and various forms of praise.

Social reward, praise, positive attention, non-verbal approval of good behavior—these are very important and become a major part of the total approach to child behavior described in this book. Use social rewards with all the rewards described above. If your child earns an activity reward (staying up past his bedtime) for not being sassy, praise him for this behavior change.

Intrinsic Rewards

This is self-reward or behavior that is performed because it feels good. Patting yourself on the back for a job well done or engaging in a behavior because you enjoy it are types of intrinsic reward.

You have just finished reading a book. Your friend comes up to you and says, *"What did you get out of that book? Did it tell you how to fix your car, build a house or make meatballs and spaghetti?"*

You respond, *"I read it because I enjoyed it. It was fun to read."*

Another person likes to go fishing. He doesn't catch many fish but leaves in the morning with an ice chest full of beer and food. In the afternoon, he comes back home tired. The ice chest is empty, and he has spent $20. You ask him, *"Why do you go fishing? You never catch fish, and it costs money."*

This fellow might reply, *"It gives me a lot of pleasure to be on the water; I enjoy it."*

Throughout this book I stress a positive approach to child behavior using reward. Although I emphasize material, social and activity rewards, the purpose of the whole approach is eventually to get your child to function on intrinsic rewards. He does things (making his bed, listening, not being sassy, doing his homework) because he enjoys them or because they make him feel good. The process of how this can be accomplished is discussed in detail in the following section.

The Purpose Of Reward

When I start talking about reward at a workshop, school meeting or in my office, several questions are usually asked by parents who do not agree with this notion. They ask two questions: *"Isn't that bribery? Are you telling me to bribe my child to be good?"*

The answer to both of these questions is No. A bribe is paying someone to do something that is illegal or giving a person a reward for an inappropriate behavior. If you get a traffic ticket and pay somebody to fix it, that's a bribe.

I go to work every day. I don't feel my wages are a bribe. You would probably think it was foolish if someone said, *"Your boss bribes you to go to work."* You and I go to work because of consequences. The positive consequences (rewards) of going to work are greater than staying home. So we show up at work every day.

We do many of the things we do because of positive consequences though we seldom view them this way. If you are in control and set behavioral expectations and consequences, you are doing the same thing an employer does to get his employee to come to work. By using rewards, you can set up situations so a child will want to behave in an appropriate fashion. Positive consequences of being good far outweigh the negative consequences of being bad.

Reward Child For Something He's Supposed To Do?

Another question parents commonly ask me is, *"Are you telling me to pay or reward my child for something he's supposed to do?"*

Children learn what is right and wrong and what they're supposed to do. When your child is born, he doesn't know, *"I'm supposed to do my homework. I shouldn't talk back to my parents. I'm supposed to pick up my clothes and keep my room clean. I should go to bed when I'm told,"* or the many other demands you will make on him. If your child isn't doing what you want him to do, you must assume he hasn't learned it. Using positive consequences (rewards) is a very effective way to teach your child what he should and should not do.

Will He Misbehave To Get Rewarded?

"Won't my child learn to misbehave to get rewarded?" Parents who ask this question are actually saying, *"My child will become a con artist and will learn to manipulate me by bad conduct to get paid for being good."* This won't happen if you are in control and set expectations and consequences. Manipulation primarily occurs when you are inconsistent, as discussed in Chapter 4.

This behavior will also develop if your child is allowed to

manipulate a situation to his advantage. You tell your child 20 times, *"Go pick up your toys,"* but he doesn't respond. Then you say, *"If you pick up your toys, I'll give you a dollar."* Or the child misbehaves then asks you what you'll give him if he's good.

You must be very consistent and in control to prevent manipulative behavior from developing. Follow through with what you said when you set the rules and consequences. Although you are in control, your child actually determines what will happen to him.

Rewards For The Rest Of The Child's Life?

"Am I going to have to reward my child the rest of his life for being good?"

The answer to this question is both "yes" and "no." Hopefully, you'll continue using social reward (praise) for good behavior throughout your child's life. Use praise in family interactions. But phase out material and activity rewards as soon as possible. The goal of this system is to get the child functioning on intrinsic reward. The child engages in behavior because it feels good and he wants to do it.

Suppose a child views getting dressed for school as an undesirable behavior. You have difficulty every morning getting him up and ready. Some common approaches to the problem include hollering at the child, dressing him, criticism, punishment and emphasis on failure to do what is expected.

A positive approach first identifies an incentive or reward for good behavior. Let's say the child loves potato chips. (You can use anything that's important to him.) Tell him, *"When I wake you up for school, I'm going to set the timer on the stove for 15 minutes. If you're dressed when the bell rings, we'll stop on the way to school and get a bag of potato chips. If you aren't dressed, we don't get the chips."*

The aim of reward in this example is not to continue giving the child a bag of potato chips for getting dressed in the morning until he is a junior in college. The purpose is to change what the child considers undesirable action (getting dressed for school) into behavior the child wants to do. While he is getting dressed for school, praise his getting dressed on time. Give his new behavior a lot of attention. During the first and second week, the child can't wait to get to the store to get the potato chips. By the third or fourth week, the chips will become less important. He may not ask to get them in the morning even though he is still getting dressed for school.

The purpose of the reward or incentive (potato chips) is to make him want to do something he previously thought was undesirable. Once you can get him to do it, you are halfway to changing the behavior. When he is doing what you want, all you have to do is associate verbal approval and praise with the new behavior,

Most children will do a great deal to get verbal approval. Often this is sufficient to change and maintain behavior. Eventually, the child will engage in the new behavior because it is more enjoyable and pleasurable (intrinsically rewarding) to get dressed on time than to fool around and get hollered at, punished and be late. Instead he'll want to get dressed for school!

Start with material or activity rewards to motivate the child to engage in the new behavior. Once the child changes his behavior, use social reward. Eventually the material reward can be phased out. Intrinsic rewards will take over.

The following is a silly example, but it stresses the ideas stated above. Let's say I ask you to go into your yard and count the blades of grass. I ask you to separate the different types of grass, the light-green ones from the dark-green ones. I tell you I'll be back the next day to get the results, and I'll give you $5.

What would you think? You'd probably think I was crazy for asking you to do that, and you wouldn't count the grass. The behavior I have requested is undesirable and something you don't want to do (like doing homework, picking up clothes, not being sassy or any other problem behavior you see in your child).

Let me rephrase my request. I ask you to go into your yard and count the blades of grass. I ask you to separate the different types of grass, the light-green ones from the dark-green ones. I tell you I'll be back the next day to get the results, and I'll give you $13,000.

In this case, you'd probably count the grass to get part of the $13,000. What have I done? By using a reward, I have increased your desire to engage in a behavior you thought I was crazy to ask you to do. I've changed an undesirable behavior into something you want to do. Now I have half of the ball game won. Let me stretch a point in this silly example to emphasize the process that occurs when reward is used effectively.

Let's assume I'm an important person to you, such as your mother or father, and I can get you to count grass every day. When you do what I ask you to do, I use social reward and say, "*You're doing a beautiful job. I'm proud of you and never knew you could do this so well. I never saw people count grass so fast.*" Eventually my praise will gain importance, and the material reward will decrease in importance. Soon you'll be counting grass to receive the social reward. In the next step, intrinsic reward would take over. You'd engage in the behavior because you enjoyed it and derived pleasure from it.

Although this is an extreme example, much of our adult behavior is based on intrinsic reward. People start working to eat and have money. Many who could retire continue working for the pleasure they derive. Some people get involved in coaching Little League baseball for pleasure (intrinsic reward) or engage in other behavior that requires great effort just for enjoyment.

Use material and social rewards as a means to an end. That end hopefully will be children who engage in appropriate or responsible behavior because they enjoy it or want to do it (intrinsic reward).

Reward—Things To Consider

Reward can be used to change behavior, but keep in mind the following points so reward works effectively.

Reward Must Be Individualized

A consequence that is rewarding for one child may not produce the same effect for another. When trying to identify a reward for a particular child, look closely at the child's needs, interests and habits. Throw out your values, what you feel is important and what has worked for another child. Some children will work their hearts out to earn ten cents, while others wouldn't move a finger for $10. If you use extra TV time as a reward for your daughter and it works well, don't automatically assume it will work for your son.

Some parents ask me, *"What can I use as a reward?"* This is a very difficult question because different children value different things. I tell them to observe their child closely to identify activities that are important.

Another statement I hear frequently is, "Nothing interests my child. I don't know what I can use as a reward." I haven't met a child for whom some reward could not be identified. For some children, a reward is easily found. For others, it's difficult, and a more-detailed investigation is necessary.

I usually tell parents, "Listen to your children very carefully. Observe their play. Ask them what is important to them or what they would like to work toward." All children can be motivated by incentives, but for some children incentives are more difficult to identify.

Always Use Social Reward

Regardless of the type of incentive (material, activity) used, always use social reward (praise). The main purpose of material or activity reward is to motivate the child to behave in a certain way. Eventually intrinsic reward should take over, but praise must be used for this to occur. Whether a child has earned time past his bedtime, a bag of potato chips, a toy or whatever, praise and positive attention should always accompany the behavior.

Don't Put The Cart Before The Horse

Parents often use reward but make the mistake of rewarding the child before the behavior.

"I'm going to buy you this bike, and I want you to be good at school."

Consider what can happen if you pay someone to paint your house before the job is complete. It's usually done half way or not completed to your satisfaction. The same thing happens when you give a child a reward then expect him to behave in a certain fashion.

To be effective, base reward on behavior and always give rewards after the expected action. If the reward comes before the desired behavior, you can't expect it to work.

Rewards Earned Must Be Received

When a reward is earned, be sure your child receives it!

Parent: I've used that reward system you told me to use. It worked fine for a few days, but now nothing's happening."

Psychologist: "Tell me about it. What did you use for reward? How did you set it up?"

Parent: "Well, we were going to work on his behavior in school. We used staying up past his bedtime as the reward. If he was good in school he would be able to delay his bedtime by 30 minutes. It worked fine for about five days, but now he's just as bad as before."

Psychologist: "What happened? Did he earn the reward?"

Parent: "He did fine for the first five days. Good behavior in school, and he earned the 30 minutes. But he gave us so much trouble about getting dressed for bed or teasing his sister, we didn't let him stay up."

Often children earn rewards for one behavior but lose them for doing something else. This is a sure way to destroy the effectiveness of a reward system. Rewards earned must be received. How would you feel if I told you, "Please clean this chair, and I'll give you $25. Then clean this one, and I'll give you another $25." You clean the first one, and I give you $25.

Then you say, "I don't feel like cleaning the other chair."

I tell you, "Give me back the $25 you earned because you wouldn't clean the second chair." You'd be angry and think I was unjust. If I took money away that you'd already earned, it would be difficult for me to motivate you toward the same behavior again.

The same thing happens if a child earns a reward but you don't bother to see he receives it. A child earns a breakfast at a restaurant for doing what he's supposed to do in school. But you never take him or keep delaying the reward. Earned rewards must be received as soon as possible. This brings me to another point.

Reward Should Occur Immediately After Desired Behavior

If a child does something this minute, ideally he should be rewarded right now-not next week or next month. The effectiveness of a reward is, in part, based on how closely it follows the behavior you're trying to control. How well a reward works is not based on quantity or cost but immediacy. Rewards should be given as soon as possible.

Let's take the example of a 9-year-old who has trouble hanging up his clothes after coming home from school. You know this child loves potato chips and motorcycles. One day you might say, 'Tm going to check your room at 3:30 pm. If your clothes are hung up or put away, we'll get a bag of potato chips." The next day you could tell him, "If your clothes are put away by 3:30 pm, we'll go to the dealer and get the motorcycle you've been wanting."

Let's say both rewards work and the child hangs up his clothes or puts them away. But one reward costs .75 cents, and the other costs $850. Even so, the motorcycle is not going to change the behavior permanently any more than the bag of potato chips. The immediacy of a reward is more important than the quantity or price. In regard to school performance or behavior, it's better to reward on a daily or weekly basis than to wait after each report card or grading period.

It's not always immediately possible to reward a child for his behavior, so social and token rewards should be used frequently. The chapter that discusses responsibility explains how to construct behavioral charts. Social and token rewards are employed to provide immediate reinforcement for desirable behavior.

Reward Improvement

Often a reward system doesn't work because parents expect too much change too rapidly, and they don't reward improvement

Many times parents come to me and say, "My child won't listen when it comes time to do school work."

We set up some type of reward system to change that behavior. Two weeks later the parents return and say, "He's still not listening." This may be a fact if we consider the overall behavior. But behavior change must be broken down into steps and evaluated for gradual improvement. A child might not be cooperating at homework every night before we started the reward. After two weeks, the not listening behavior has decreased to four times in two weeks. While the child may still not be cooperating every day, he has improved and is 50% better than he was two weeks ago.

In using reward, behavior or goals must be broken down into steps. Reward small goals (gradual improvement). You can't attempt to change behavior 100% or to change the child overnight.

Look at where the child is now and where you want to go. A child who isn't listening 30 times a day should be rewarded if he can decrease that rate to 20 times a day the first week. After that, the amount of improvement necessary to receive the reward can be increased each week. The second week's reward would be received for 13 times a day, the third week ten times a day and so on. Eventually the child would be rewarded for not listening only three or five times a week. Allow some room for error. Do not expect 100% improvement to receive the reward.

Reward Must Be Changed

The purpose of using reward is to change behavior. In most cases, interests and attitudes are also modified. A reward that may initially be important to a child might lose its effectiveness with time and use.

Suppose you enjoy steak dinners. I could probably motivate you by saying, "If you help me, Ill take you out to the restaurant of your choice for a steak dinner. However, if you've eaten steak every day for a week, I wouldn't be able to motivate you or change your behavior with the same reward. You'd probably be tired of steak, and the reward wouldn't be seen as important or desirable.

Children respond the same way and become either tired of or disinterested in the same reward. If a reward has worked beautifully in the beginning but is no longer effective, change it because it's probably been used too much or too long.

When you first try a reward, use it consistently for a period of time (usually a week or so) before trying another even though the reward appears ineffective. Often you identify a reward that is important to a child, but because it does not work the first, second or third time it is used, you try another one immediately. Rewards need to be varied but not too quickly.

Reward Should Be Attainable

When a reward system is first started, it shouldn't be too complex or too difficult. The goal should not require a great deal of change, and it should be set up to ensure success and attainment of the reward. You have to lock the child into the system. If you make it too difficult at first and the child isn't able to attain the behavioral goal and incentive, the whole system will probably fail.

Consider the child who gets up out of his desk twenty times a day. You set up a positive system to decrease the behavior. "Your teacher is going to put a check on your folder every time you get out of your desk. If you only have four checks when you bring it home today, you can stay up 30 minutes past your bedtime. When it is time to go to bed you and the child look at the folder and he has ten checks. The child doesn't receive the reward.

In this case, the total system is likely to fail because the expectations were set too high. The child improved his behavior by 50% and, in a sense, was punished for doing this. Soon the child will become disgusted with this system.

Expectations must be realistic so the child will receive the reward. A good rule to follow is to expect about 30% change at first. In the above example, the child should have received a reward if he eliminated 6 behaviors in a day and received 14 checks.

Another problem that occurs is reward systems are often too complex or difficult. Too much work or change is required for the child to receive the reward. For example, a child may have to:

1. Get out of bed when called in the morning.
2. Be good in school.
3. Put his clothes away when he comes home from school.

4.   Do his homework.
5.   Come in on time from playing.
6.   Not fight with his brother.
7.   Pick up his toys.
8.   Take his bath when told.

If he does all this, the reward is having a story read to him at bedtime. The child will probably think, "The heck with this it's not worth it," and the system fails.

When starting a reward system, the child must be able to achieve the reward easily to accept the system. This increases the probability that future reward will be effective and that change will occur.

CHAPTER 7

Punishment

Most parents are punishers. They pay more attention to their child's mistakes, failures and misbehaviors than to their successes, achievements and adaptive actions.

By "punishment," I mean any negative attention, from hollering to whipping a child. Report cards or grades are an example. A child brings home 5 A's, 4 B's, 2 C's and 1 F. The grade that usually gets the most emphasis is the failure. The parent asks, "What happened? Why did you get the F? You are going to have to try harder in that subject."

Parents generally pay more attention to mistakes and failures than to accomplishments and successes. By responding to your children this way, you set up a situation in which the only thing the child receives for being good is not being punished or criticized. This type of parental response also results in children who feel it is useless to do nice things because they are never good enough and no one pays attention to them.

Like adults, children avoid things that are negative. If sitting down to do homework is a negative situation (there is a lot of punishment or hollering), the child tries to avoid homework and you have trouble getting him to do it. For some personality types, punishment actually makes matters worse. It doesn't work.

I'm not saying you should not use punishment in disciplining children. But punishment should not be used as the main method of behavior management. Many times a parent tells me, "I've tried everything on this child, but nothing works. In fact, his behavior seems to be getting worse. "

The first question I ask is, "What have you tried?" Most of the time, the answers I get are fairly similar.

"I've spanked him."

"We sent her to her room."

"My husband took him off the baseball team."

"I wouldn't let her watch TV."

"We decided to take his bike away."

What parents generally are saying is they have tried all types of punishment.

About 95% of parents use punishment as their main form of discipline. When I ask, "Have you tried rewarding him or ignoring his behavior?" parents usually respond as though I am speaking another language. The most effective way to use punishment is to combine it with other consequences. Use rewarding and ignoring about 60 to 70% of the time. Use punishment only 30 to 40% of the time. Certain problems can occur if parents use punishment as the main method of control.

Problems With Punishment

Children Behave Because Of Fear

If I came up to you and said, "I can get your child to do whatever you'd like him to do in one of two ways. First, I can get him to do what you want him to do out of fear of what's going to happen. Or I can get him to do what you want him to out of satisfaction from learning new behaviors or because he feels he's accomplishing something." Which method would you prefer? Most people would pick the latter. But most parents use the fear method (punishment).

A problem with using punishment as the main method of control is most of the time you get the children to behave out of fear of what is going to happen to them.

Most forms of punishment are based on fear. "If you don't bring your grades up, you won't be able to play baseball this summer."

"The next time you are disrespectful to your teacher you will

lose your TV, computer and video game privileges for a month."
In these examples, the children behave out of fear of what will
happen to them rather than out of a sense of accomplishment.
Fear is not an emotion most parents would want to develop
excessively in their children. However, when punishment is used
as the main method of control, fear may develop.

Anger, Aggression And Rebellion May Develop

Using punishment as the main method of control often
produces anger and resentment toward parents. This is especially
true if the discipline is decided on and administered after the
misbehavior. Children who are disciplined this way often feel
unjustly treated and develop considerable hostility toward parents.
Sometimes these feelings are expressed directly ("I hate you."
"My father's mean.").

But more often this anger is expressed through a variety of
passive-aggressive behaviors, such as opposition, resistance,
stubbornness, defiance and rebellion. For instance, you say it's
black, and he says it's white, or she does just the opposite of what
you tell her. Anger may also be displaced to other situations and
cause fighting with or anger toward siblings, peers and other
authority figures.

Emotional Distance Is Created

Let's say you have a boss who controls you by fear (if you
aren't on time, you'll be fired). He pays more attention to your
failures and mistakes than to your successes and accomplishments.
Whenever he comes around, you know he's going to criticize
your work. You often feel he unjustly disciplines and reprimands
you.

How would you feel toward this person? Would you feel close
to him? Would he become your friend? Would you feel secure
and comfortable when he's around? You probably wouldn't want
anything to do with him. You certainly wouldn't want to socialize
with him or take him on a fishing trip with you.

When punishment is primarily used to discipline, children
often feel emotionally remote from their parents. You don't feel

close to people you fear or whom you feel give you more negative attention than positive recognition. In this situation, a significant amount of emotional distance is created between the child and parent. This may result in a lack of verbal interaction (only talking to the parent when necessary) or withdrawal (spending more time alone, minimizing contact with the family). A close emotional relationship will fail to develop.

Escape/Avoidance Behavior May Develop

We all tend to avoid situations that produce negative attention. What would you do if every time you made gravy it turned out badly and you received a great deal of criticism and negative attention? Would you run home every day to cook it? No, you would avoid it. Suppose every time you went by a friend's house, he told you everything you were doing wrong and spent three hours talking about your failures but devoted only ten minutes to your accomplishments. How often would you want to go by his house? Probably once every 6 years.

Children often show the same feelings and behavior when punishment is used as the main method of discipline. When fear and negative attention are primarily used in discipline, avoidance and escape behavior develops. If every time a child cuts the grass all his mistakes are pointed out, he'll learn to avoid grass cutting. If a child encounters only hollering, fighting or negative attention every time he sits down to do his homework, he won't want to do homework.

Lying, manipulating and running away from home are avoidance behaviors learned by children who experience these situations. You hear a lamp fall off the table and break. Your youngest child is in the back room, and this is where the lamp was broken. You go into the back room and say, "Did you break that lamp? What happened?"

The child knows if he admits to the behavior he'll get punished, receive lecture No. 26 or get a great deal of negative attention. So he says, "I was watching TV, and a band of gypsies came through the house and knocked over the lamp. I don't know where they went after that. That's how it was broken." When you see a child not telling the truth, trying to manipulate his parent or using the ultimate escape behavior, which is running away, look at the consequence being used. If punishment/negative attention is the main method of discipline, it may be the cause.

Punishment Doesn't Work With Some Personality Types

Reward must be individualized. Some types of reward work with some children but not with others. The same is true for punishment. For some personality types, punishment is sufficient to control behavior. But for others, punishment doesn't work at all, or it only works for short periods of time.

Let us take the example of two children, Alan and Jason, going to rob a bank. I picked robbing a bank because it serves as a good example, but any type of inappropriate behavior could have been used. Alan is getting ready to rob the bank and is thinking, "If I rob the bank, I might get caught and be sent to prison. I won't be able to watch TV, play with my friends or go outside."

On the other hand, Jason is thinking, "I'm going to rob that bank and get some money. Then I'll buy a motorcycle, candy and toys."

Here we have two children getting ready to engage in the same behavior, but the motivations are entirely different. For Alan, whether or not he robs the bank depends on what will happen to him-negative consequences. However, Jason's behavior is motivated only by pleasure and by what he will gain from the behavior. Alan, who is concerned about negative consequences, can be controlled by punishment. But the pleasure-oriented Jason cannot be controlled by punishment. Either the money has to be taken out of the bank so the behavior is not pleasurable anymore or not robbing the bank has to become more pleasurable than robbing the bank. It has been estimated that 30 to 40% of the children in the United States have Jason's personality type. They are more concerned with the pleasure they receive from their behavior than with the negative consequences or punishment they receive. It often appears they act before thinking and don't profit from past punishing experiences. Being caught or punished only temporarily affects their behavior.

These children also show the characteristics of a skilled manipulator or con artist. They often tell you what they think you want to hear but will turn around and do exactly what they please. It is estimated that 3 or four children out of ten will not respond to punishment when used as the major method of discipline. Using this type of consequence to prevent certain behavior is ineffective and proves very frustrating to the parents. Other consequences (rewarding and ignoring) must be used to discipline these children.

Some Develop Personality And Emotional Problems

All children are individuals, and their responses to punishment vary. Some children comply; others become angry and rebel. Others may withdraw, bottle up emotions and become nervous and feel guilty.

One of the primary types of punishment most parents use involves verbal negative attention—hollering, screaming, criticizing and name-calling. When used frequently, this type of punishment interferes with healthy personality development. It is usually a very ineffective method of discipline.

Hollering and screaming only create an emotional distance between parent and child and upset both. Criticism ("Your brother can do that better than you. You never can do anything right.") and name calling ("You're stupid.") only make the child feel badly about himself. Controlling children by guilt ("I cook, take care of you, wash your clothes. Why aren't you good in school? I bought you that bike and took you out to eat, but you still won't listen.") or fear ("If you don't straighten up, I'll put you in a home. If you and your sister don't stop fighting, I'm going to leave and let you all take care of yourselves.") only serves to develop unhealthy emotions and feelings in children.

This type of punishment is very ineffective and should not be used because personality and emotional problems are apt to develop.

Model Behavior Develops Until . . .

Many times I hear, "My child didn't give me any problems until recently. He was a model child. But now he won't listen and does just the opposite of what I tell him. Generally I have a hard time controlling him. When he was little, he did exactly what we told him and almost never objected to what we said. It's a different story now, and it seems like he won't listen to anything we say."

When punishment is the main method of discipline, children with certain personalities often develop model behavior when young. It seems these young children are too good. They always listen and never give their parents any trouble. However, between ten and 13 years of age, they reverse their former behavior. It seems as if the anger that has been developing in them for years suddenly emerges. It is primarily expressed through the passive-aggressive methods described above. This type of personality often fools parents who mainly use punishment because the child behaves so well when young. This model behavior is temporary.

Different Behaviors Receive Same Type Of Punishment

Parents often overuse a certain type of punishment, and it loses its effectiveness as a motivator. A child may have to go to his room for being sassy, hitting his brother, not picking up his toys or coming home late. Another child may receive a spanking for not being good at school, talking back to his mother, fighting, or not cleaning his room. Hollering is probably the most overused punishment because it's used for hundreds of different behavior patterns. When this happens, the punishment becomes a very ineffective form of discipline.

The following example shows how children feel and respond in this situation. Let's say you really like to go out and eat seafood. I tell you, "If you'll help me paint my house, I'll buy a seafood dinner tonight." You'll probably help me because the seafood is a good motivator. However, if you have eaten seafood every day for two weeks and I try to motivate you with the same consequence, I'll probably be unsuccessful.

The same thing happens when you use one form of punishment for many different behaviors. The negative consequence is no longer important to the child, and it loses its effectiveness as a motivator. Determine a specific punishment for specific misbehavior. A child could lose TV privileges for misconduct in school, but for nothing else. Going to bed early could be reserved for giving trouble with homework and so fort.

Punishment Only Temporarily Changes Behavior

Some people disagree on this point, but many experiments prove punishment does not result in a permanent or long-term change in a behavior pattern. The effects of punishment are only temporary. And after a period of time, the punished behavior reappears. This is the reason some children show good behavior or a period of control after punishment that lasts only for a few days or, with some children, only a couple of minutes. When punishment is used as the primary method of control, something like the following situation occurs.

I tell you I'm going to drop by your house in ten minutes to have a cup of coffee. You look around and see your house is a mess. You want it to look nice when I come over, so you quickly make the house presentable. Things are stuffed in the closet, thrown behind the sofa or put under chairs. Now the house looks OK, but have you really changed anything? No, you've just rearranged things. Eventually, you'll have to go back and put everything in its proper place. This is how punishment often works. It only changes behavior on the surface like sweeping dirt under the carpet.

When reward is used, the behavior may not be changed as quickly, but the improvement will be long-lasting. Reward has the same effect as putting a few things where they belong. Although the house won't look as clean immediately, eventually it would be permanently changed. You won't have to go back and put things away because the situation would have been permanently changed.

With punishment, you can only expect behavior to be modified for short periods of time. After awhile, it will reappear and have to be dealt with again. The best way to use punishment is to sandwich it between rewards. I discuss this in further detail in another section of this chapter.

Punishment And Negative Attention May Maintain Certain Behaviors

A phrase often overused in analyzing child behavior is, "He's doing that to get attention," While "getting attention" is frequently used inaccurately to explain certain behavior in children, this statement is sometimes accurate. Some children often misbehave to get negative attention because this is better than no attention at all. Positive attention is very scarce in some families, so children seek whatever type of attention they can provoke.

In other situations, children behave in certain ways to get a reaction from their parents. Whining, complaining, stubbornness and similar behavior is often used by children to get a parent nervous, upset or frustrated so the child can get his or her own way.

Your child asks, "Can I go outside and play?" You tell him no. Then the child starts complaining, whining and hitting his sister. After a few minutes of this disruption, you become agitated and nervous. You eventually say, "Go outside and play. I'll call you when it's time to eat."

Children often behave in certain ways to get attention as a method of expressing their anger and as a way to get back at you. You tell your child, "Go to your room. You're punished."

Now he's angry. He doesn't want to go to his room, and he resents what you've done. What can he do? He can't punch you in the nose so he starts mumbling under his breath. He says things like, "You're mean. You like my brother better than me. I hate you. I'd rather live at Ted's house."

What do you do? You start to get upset and yell, "What are you saying? Speak up. If I hear that again you'll stay in your room longer."

What's happened? You've given the behavior a great deal of attention. This is often sufficient to maintain the child's actions.

In the situation described above, another problem develops. You wind up punishing the child because of his reaction to the punishment. Then you punish him again because of his misbehavior. Now he has to stay in his room for four hours instead of 13 minutes. Maybe both of you have forgotten what he was sent to his room for in the first place! The punishment snowballs, and the reason for the initial discipline is lost.

Misbehaving or behaving to get attention is usually not consciously planned by the child. One method of dealing with this type of behavior is by ignoring it. This method of discipline is discussed in the chapter on Ignoring Specific Behavior.

Punishment May Not Offset Reward Or Pleasure From Misbehavior

A child is told "You will be grounded this weekend, if the teacher reports that you have failed to turn in homework this week."

The child does half of the homework and is grounded for the weekend. For some children this may be worth it. The amount of pleasure they got from not doing the homework may offset any punishment.

One problem with punishment is in some situations the behavior being punished has received a significant reward. If punishment is used as the main method of discipline, it probably won't work or will have to be used extensively to counter the effects of the reward and pleasure received from the misbehavior. This is one reason punishment works more effectively when sandwiched between rewards. In the above example, reward for appropriate behavior would produce better results than punishment for not listening.

Parents And Punishment

You Serve As Models For Your Children's Behavior

Children learn behavior by observing other people. This is called the modeling theory of learning and is the basis for not showing certain programs on TV during prime time or family viewing hours. Children exposed to certain behavior may imitate it and may incorporate it into their patterns of dealing with conflicts, solving problems and interacting with others.

Whether a child models or imitates a certain way of responding depends on two general factors. First, it depends on how similarly the model resembles the child. Secondly, it depends on how significant the child considers the model. As parents, you are the most significant people in your children's early lives. You serve as very powerful models from which behavior is learned. Your children learn many behavior patterns just by observing how you deal with certain situations, conflicts and problems.

Many times I hear a parent say, "My daughter acts just like her mother when she gets mad."

"I get nervous very easily, and so do my children,"

"My son's fears are similar to mine."

Then I hear, "He must have inherited that way of acting." While children are often born with behaviors, some are learned from models.

If a child sees his father throw things when he's angry or deal with conflicts by screaming and hollering, it's highly probable this child will adopt these patterns of responding when faced with similar situations. If a mother is afraid of storms, her child may learn this fear. Psychologists have found a large percentage of parents who physically abuse their children were abused themselves as children.

If you deal with conflicts by hollering, arguing and screaming at one another, your child may be learning to deal with his siblings or peers in a similar way. This brings us to an important point regarding physical punishment (spanking or threats involving control by aggression or force). If I encounter a child in my office whose primary problem involves fighting, hitting other children, losing his temper or trying to control others by physical means, I ask the parents, "How is he disciplined? If he doesn't want to do something, how can you get him to do it?"

The usual answers I get in nine out of ten situations include:

"I give him a spanking."

"I tell him if he doesn't behave or do what I want, I'll go get the belt."

"I threaten him with a beating."

The child who is controlled by physical means or threats of aggression learns if people do not do what he wants, he should be aggressive and threaten them with force.

So when another child cuts in front of him in line at school, he shoves or hits him. If a child takes his pencil and won't give it back, a fight will start. The child's primary method of problem-solving involves physical means, force and threats of aggression because he has modeled his behavior on the significant people in his life, his parents.

The mother of a three-year-old told me, "Every time I slap my child for doing something bad, he hits me back. Lately he's been hitting me whenever he doesn't get his way. He shouldn't hit his mother. What can I do to stop this?"

My answer was very simple. "Stop hitting him!"

If a child lives with hostility, he learns to fight. If he lives with criticism, he learns to condemn. If punishment is used as the main disciplinary tactic, your child may be learning and adopting these methods to control others-peers, authority figures, siblings and eventually his or her own children.

Punishment May Make You Feel Guilty And Unfair

Guilt often results if punishment is administered in a random fashion. The type of punishment is decided on after the child misbehaves and is not spelled out ahead of time.

A child comes home with a failing test paper on the day his favorite TV program comes on. His mother tells him because of this he can't watch his program and needs to go to his room. The mother sitting in the quiet of the back room starts thinking, "Maybe I was too hard on him," I probably over reacted. This is the first bad paper he's brought in a month. He's been talking about the TV program all week, and now I've made him miss it.

Guilt starts to develop, and the mother feels responsible for what has happened to the children. To undo the wrong she has done and to feel better, she says, "Come on out of your room. You can watch TV if you're good."

Administering and reacting to punishment in this way results in a very inconsistent approach to child management. Consistency is of major importance to behavior change and management. The approach described above is certain to result in ineffective discipline and continued misbehavior.

Types Of Punishment

Most parents tend to be punishers. That is, attention to misbehaviors, mistakes and failures are usually employed as primary disciplinary tactics. The types of punishment used by most parents can be grouped into six general areas. Some are effective, while others should be used sparingly or avoided altogether.

Response Cost

Response-cost is a very effective form of punishment. It is a system in which the child is fined and loses privileges or desired activities for misbehavior. "When you do something bad, it's going to cost you something." This is used frequently in our daily lives. If you get a speeding ticket, you have to pay a fine. When your income tax is late, you are assessed a penalty.

A good example of a response-cost system can be seen when allowance is based on daily chores. Let's say a child has to feed the pet each day and put out the garbage five times a week. For these chores, he gets an allowance of $3 each week. He has to perform 12 tasks each week to earn his full allowance (25¢ a task). A record on a calendar or a chart of his performance is kept. Each time he performs the required duty without being told, he earns 25¢ toward his weekly allowance. However, if the task is not performed by a certain time and the child has to be reminded, he loses 25¢. It is totally up to the child whether he earns nothing or his full allowance each week. This is similar to the situation most of us face each day.

We can go to work and be paid or stay home and receive nothing.

I have used loss of money as a punishment because a response-cost system can be described easily this way. However, the fine or loss could really be any privilege or activity. You may have a child who loves to watch TV or get on the computer and he is misbehaving (i.e. getting out of his desk) in school. You can set up a response-cost system to modifying the school behavior by using loss of TV or computer time as the fine for this behavior. A system could be set up so the teacher would inform you on a daily about the child's classroom behavior. See the chapter on communicating with the school to get more information on how to effectively communicate with your children's teacher.

The child is told, "Your teacher will let me know everyday how many times you get out of your desk without permission. Every time you get out of your desk you will lose 15 minutes of TV time. How much TV you watch each night is totally up to you and how well you can behave in school." Any type of activity, privilege or event that is important to the child can be used as the fine in a response-cost system of punishment. However, several points must be kept in mind when using this system.

Define Behavior

Clearly define the behavior that will be fined and exactly what failure will cost the child.

Use Positive Consequences And Rewards

This type of system works best when positive consequences and rewards are also used.

Don't Set Up A Debit System

Do not set up a system in which the child will owe you, or the loss will be unrealistic. If a child gets $3.00 a week allowance and the parent says, "For each book you fail to bring home for homework you will lose 50¢ of your allowance" the child may have a minus allowance at the end of the week and owe the parent $5.00.

Or a parent may tell a child, "Each time you get out of your seat in school without permission, you'll have to go to bed ten minutes early." If the child gets out of his seat enough, he may wind up going to bed when he comes home from school! This type of response-cost system is sure to fail.

Assess Fines

Fines must be consistently assessed whenever the misbehavior occurs.

Time Out

This is an effective form of punishment used frequently by parents. A child going to his room or standing in the corner are examples of time out. There are two general ways to use this procedure.

With the first method, a time-out area is designated (a room, a corner, the hall). The child is sent there for a particular misbehavior. Every time a child whines when doing homework, he is sent to the time-out area. This punishment can be used for temper tantrums, sassiness, fighting between siblings and other behaviors.

The second method involves removing a child from a pleasurable activity.

Two brothers are watching cartoons on Saturday morning. You know they love the cartoons, but they constantly argue and fight with one another. You might tell them, "If I hear any fighting, the TV will be turned off for five minutes." The activity from which the child is removed can be anything that is important to him (riding his bike, watching TV, playing with his friends).

Several things must be kept in mind to make the time-out technique successful. It must be very clear what the child must do to be punished. The misbehavior has to be defined and spelled out. You may say, "I don't want to hear or see any more fighting. By that I mean hitting each other, name calling or teasing." Hearing this, the child knows exactly what behavior will be followed by time out

Some type of warning should also be given.

"The next time I see you do that, you'll have to go to your room."

"I'm going to count to three, and if the fighting doesn't stop, the TV will be turned off."

The child should know how long he will be in time out or what he must do to get out of the time-out area. "Go to your room for five minutes. I'm going to set the timer on the stove, and when the bell rings, you can come out."

Or a child who is whining might be told, "Go to your room when you stop whining you can come out."

The time-out procedure must be used consistently and may have to be employed several times to control the behavior. If your children are watching cartoons and fighting, you may have to turn the TV off for five minutes 7 or 8 times during the morning.

Time out should be given in a very matter-of-fact way without displays of emotion. When bringing the child to time out or when he is in the time-out area, don't lecture, fuss, scold, get upset or excited, nag or apologize.

Not Receiving Reward

When a reward system is used and the child does not receive the positive consequence, it can be viewed as a type of punishment. Often when I am designing a technique using reward to change a behavior, parents ask me, "If he doesn't do what we want him to do, how do we punish him?"

My answer is, "You don't have to punish him. Not receiving the reward can serve as the consequence." "Your child teases and can't get along with his sister when sitting at the kitchen table doing homework. He loves to stay up past his bedtime and is told, "If you and your sister get along during homework time, you can stay up 30 minutes past your bedtime." When he doesn't comply, he doesn't necessarily have to be punished. Not receiving the reward can be considered as the punishment and is often an effective disciplinary tactic.

Some parents have a hard time accepting this and feel they need to punish the misbehavior in addition to withholding the reward. This is not always necessary. This is similar to the way most of us are disciplined regarding attendance at work. If you go to work, you are paid. If you stay home, you receive less on payday. We are not punished for missing work. We just do not receive the reward, and this is sufficient to keep most of us going to work on a regular basis.

Verbal Punishment

Hollering, criticizing, name-calling and lecturing, as well as telling the child things to make him feel guilty, embarrassed or fearful, fall into this category. This is a very ineffective form of punishment because some children totally ignore their parent's ranting and raving. The hollering goes in one ear and out the other.

Other children develop emotional difficulties or behavioral problems as a result of verbal punishment. Some children develop resentment and anger toward their parents when this is used, while others become emotionally distant.

Earlier in this chapter, I discussed problems that may occur when punishment is used as the main form of discipline. Most of the potential problems described can occur when verbal punishment is used frequently. I will not restate the behavioral and emotional difficulties that can occur, but negative verbal discipline must be avoided.

Physical Punishment

Spanking and hitting children fall into this category. I personally feel there are many other forms of discipline that can be used with children. Use physical punishment very, very sparingly. Parents serve as primary models for child behavior, and children who are physically punished often learn aggressive methods to control others. Other children withdraw, become angry, develop rebellious tendencies or show a variety of emotional and behavioral difficulties.

If and when physical punishment is used, use it infrequently and only for certain specific behavior. A child should not get a spanking for hitting his sister, getting a detention, coming home late, breaking a toy or 40 other different misbehavior types. Reserve spanking for certain behavior.

I also believe physical punishment is more effective when used with younger children (under four years). A small child may get a spanking for crossing the street unattended or for fooling with an electrical outlet. But it should not be used for hundreds of different behavior lapses ranging from wetting his pants to hitting his baby sister. Some parents should not use physical punishment because it does not fit their personalities. The spanking upsets them more than it does the child-they feel guilty, mean, unfair and brutal.

Control By Force Or Intimidation

This is similar to physical punishment, but the parent doesn't have to touch the child. "I'm going to get the belt if you don't hurry up and get dressed for school." The child runs and gets dressed. The control or the way we get the child to do what we want is by threats of force. This type of punishment should be avoided.

Another form is by intimidation or the fact you are bigger than the child. Because of this you can control him. This should also be avoided. People who use this type of discipline forget a child grows; he or she will soon be as big as you. When the child is in adolescence, you need more appropriate control than ever.

If this is the main method used on the child, you'll lose your control when you need it the most. In addition, these techniques teach the child to deal with other children by using force, intimidation and control by overpowering. Also the child's school will not use this type of discipline.

Punishment: Things To Consider

Punishment is a consequence that can be used to change behavior. However, keep several things in mind to make punishment work effectively and to minimize the occurrence of problems.

Use Other Consequences

Three major consequences can be used in disciplining children. Punishment is more effective when ignoring and especially rewarding are also used. When punishment is used as the main method of control, it is less effective than when it is used in conjunction with reward. Reward and ignoring should be used about 60 to 70% of the time, with punishment being used 30 to 40% of the time. Time-out and response-cost punishment are more effective if the child is earning rewards and privileges for other acceptable behavior.

Define Behavior And Consequences

Avoid ambiguous statements, such as "be good." State exactly what you mean by being good. "I want you to go to school today and don't get out of your seat without permission and complete all your seatwork."

Avoid random punishment. Don't decide the punishment after the behavior; spell out the negative consequence along with the rule before the behavior occurs. "We're going to the store. If you stay by me, you can go outside and play when we get home. If you run all over the store and don't listen to me, you'll have to stay inside when we get home."

Determine Length Of Punishment

Parents often say, "Go to your room" or "You can't ride your bike" or something similar.

The child asks, "For how long?"

The parent responds, "When I decide to let you out" or "When I think you deserve to ride your bike."

This is not a productive situation. When a child is punished, he should know for how long and what he has to do to get out of the punishment. "Go to your room for five minutes. You won't be able to ride your bike tomorrow."

"Go to your room. When you calm down, you can come out."

"You can start going out to play after school when you bring home all your books."

These statements clearly identify what the child must do to avoid punishment.

Clearly define the behavior to be punished, state the negative consequence ahead of time with the rule and tell the child how long he will be punished and/or what behaviors he must show to get out of the punishment.

Use Behavior To Set Rule

Try to avoid punishing a behavior the first time it appears, but use it to set a rule. You can't always do this, but the principle can be employed in most situations.

A fifth grader comes home with the first detention he has ever received. You feel like setting down some type of punishment. However, punishment in this situation is often ineffective because this was a new behavior whose consequences had not been spelled out ahead of time.

A better way to deal with this situation would be to use it to set the ground rules. "The next time you get a detention you will lose your phone privileges for a week."

Use Warnings Or Signals

In an earlier chapter, I used the example of a child who had to be told 37 times to do his homework. He was told over and over again. With each request the mother's voice got louder and louder. Eventually her face turned red, then she began hollering and screaming. Only then did the child start his homework. The child was responding to signals. He sat around and waited for the signal that came immediately before the negative consequences; then he responded. He knew hollering immediately preceded spanking or other punishment. When these signals appeared, he performed the desired behavior to avoid the negative consequence.

Most parents use signals or warnings, but often they involve actions like those above (hollering, getting the belt, getting upset). Using appropriate signals and warnings can make things run more smoothly and eliminate a significant amount of distress at home.

Events in the environment can be made to serve as signals.

"You have to be dressed and ready for school before your cartoon comes on." "The homework has to be completed by 7:00pm."

You can let events or clues in the environment warn the child rather than your voice.

Counting to three, giving three warnings, holding up 1 finger at a time, saying, "The next time that happens" or some other verbal statement said in a very matter-of-fact way can also serve as effective signals.

For example, every time the phone rings and the mother starts talking, her young child begins a series of interruptions. "Let me talk. Where's my ball? I'm thirsty." The conversation is interrupted a number of times, and the mother loses patience. The mother could use hand signals to deal with the behavior. The rules, behavioral expectations and consequences would be set up ahead of time and the child told, "When the phone rings, I don't want you to interrupt me. (Explain what this means to the child). Each time you interrupt me, I'm going to hold up a finger. If I get to three fingers, you'll have to go to your room for five minutes" or some similar punishment.

Reward can also be used. "If I don't get to three warnings, I'll read you a story" or some similar reward. Pennies, pencils or some other object could be placed on a table to serve as signals. The child is told "Each time I have to tell you to get back to your homework, I'm going to take a penny off the table. When we finish homework if there are no pennies left, you will not be able to play video games tonight."

You must be consistent when using this type of warning system and give the third or final warning when appropriate. You can't say, "I'm going to count to three. 1. 2 ...2. . 2," but 3 never comes. You can't tell the child, "The next time you do that, this is going to happen," but three months later you're still saying, "The next time . . ." and the consequence of the misbehavior never occurs.

Using signals to create a buffer period may also serve as a way to reduce some behavior problems.

Your child is outside playing baseball. It's almost his turn to bat when you stick your head out the door and say, "Come in; it's time to do homework." You'll probably get a great deal of resistance.

You can avoid this by giving the child a five-minute warning. A little while before it's time to come in, call him and say, "I'm going to call you in five minutes to come in. Start getting ready. The next time I call, you must come in."

Sometimes it isn't wise to demand a child do what you expect at that minute. Giving him a signal as a buffer period may reduce some of the resistance.

"I want those toys picked up by the time this program's over."

"We're going to do this three more times, then we'll stop."

Individualize Punishment
When deciding on a negative consequence, the interests, values and preferences of each child must be considered. What

may be punishment for one child may not be punishment for another child. For some children, going to their room is a major punishment; others couldn't care less. You may tell your child, "If you don't get dressed on time for school, you'll miss the bus and won't be able to go to school." Some children would consider this a negative consequence, while others would see it as a reward. What may work effectively on a child's sister may not work with him. In determining a punishment, consider what is important to the child. The individualization of consequences is discussed in detail in the chapter on Reward.

Punish Behavior, Not The Child

When you use punishment, comment on the behavior not on the child as an individual. If a child fails a test in school, it doesn't mean he's stupid (a statement concerning a child's self image). It means he did not adequately study for the test. If a child hits his brother, he isn't necessarily a mean person. However, this type of behavior can't be tolerated.

Stay Calm When Punishing

When punishment is administered, try to remain calm. Treat the behavior being dealt with in a matter-of-fact fashion. If a child loses a privilege (response-cost) or is put in a timeout area, avoid nagging, scolding and lecturing,

When using negative consequences, use specific punishments for specific behaviors and nothing else. Use loss of TV time only when certain behavior is seen (homework isn't done) and not for everything under the sun. Relate physical punishment or confinement only to specific actions.

By doing this, you can avoid the problems that occur when negative consequences are overused.

Punishment Should Occur Immediately

The importance or effectiveness of punishment is primarily determined by how closely it follows the behavior you're trying to control and not by its severity, length or harshness. The statement, "Make the punishment fit the crime" isn't always true.

Punishment should occur as soon as possible after the misbehavior.

Negative consequences that immediately follow undesirable behavior have the most impact and produce the most change. Avoid delaying punishment. Let's say that right after school a brother and sister get into a terrible fight. You come in and separate the children, saying, "Wait till Dad gets home. You'll both be punished." About three hours later, the children are playing together and having a good time. The father comes home and hears about the incident that occurred earlier. He goes in, gives the children a lecture and administers a punishment. What behavior is most affected by the punishment? That which occurred immediately before the negative consequence—playing together cooperatively.

A child's perception of time is different from yours. A 6-year-old may perceive 13 minutes as we perceive 2 hours. If the consequence is too far removed from the behavior, the child may not remember why he is being punished. Avoid delays in punishing when possible. This can't always be done but by using behavior charts. The chapter on Irresponsibility talks about using behavior charts. Punishment can be delivered immediately in many situations.

Administering Punishment

How much punishment should be given? This is a question I am frequently asked. Parents really mean different things.

"How much should I take away?"

"How severe or harsh should the punishment be?"

"Should I take him off the baseball team or merely not let him ride his bike?"

These are difficult questions to answer mainly because much depends on the individual child. But several points can be made regarding this concept.

One of the main factors that control or change behavior is not large or severe consequences that occur every now and then, but the small consequences that occur and follow a misbehavior each time it happens. Why do you avoid touching fire? Probably not because you think you'll die, get third degree burns or have to be hospitalized. The main reason you avoid it because every time you touch fire or something hot, it hurts. It's the little consequence that occurs each time you perform this action that prevents the behavior, not the severity or amount of the negative consequence.

Let's say your child isn't doing all his homework because he forgets some of his books at school. You have told him for three weeks to bring all his books home, but it isn't working. You finally reach the end of your rope and tell him, "Unless you bring all your books home, I'll have to take you off the football team." This is a pretty significant punishment because this child lives for football. However, the behavior doesn't change, and he is not allowed to play on the team.

Usually in cases of severe punishment, the child feels, "What's the use?" In this example, he probably wouldn't bring home any books at all after being punished this way.

A better way to handle this same situation is to identify something that is important to the child to be withheld each time books are left at school. Suppose you are using a response-cost system. This child loves to watch TV-die cost could be any other privilege that is important to him. He is told, "Every time you don't bring all your books home, you lose your TV privileges for that night. If you want to watch TV, all you have to do is bring your books home."

Each time he fails to do as told, this consequence follows. Using negative consequence in the latter fashion has a greater impact on eliminating undesirable behavior than the former extreme method.

How Long Should Punishment Last?

How long do you punish? This frequently asked question involves principles similar to those discussed above. It mainly involves response-cost and time-out types of punishment. The closer the punishment occurs to the inappropriate behavior, the greater the effect.

I'm sure you have experienced something like this. A child misbehaves on the way home from school and is sent to his room for an hour. He goes to his room, and for the first five or ten minutes lies on his bed and pouts, complains, cries or makes statements about how unfair and mean you are. After a short period of time, he gets a toy and starts playing with it, reads a book, counts the dots on the ceiling or occupies himself in some way. After a brief period of time, it appears the punishment doesn't bother him.

Or you take your child's bike away for 2 weeks for being disrespectful to his teacher. During the first day or so, the child is concerned about the punishment. She doesn't like what has happened and asks to ride her bike. After the brief period at the beginning of the punishment, it seems as if she could care less about not being able to ride her bike.

In both of these examples, the probable reason the child developed the I-don't-care attitude about the punishment was because it was too long. Negative consequences do not have to last a long time to work. The most effective part of any form of negative consequence occurs in the beginning.

Let's look at the example of sending a child to his room for I hour for being sassy. From the above chart, you can see the first ten minutes have a 90% effect on the sassiness, the second ten-minute period has an 8% effect and the third ten-minute period has a 2% effect. Punishment has no impact on behavior during the remaining 3 ten-minute blocks.

The latter part of the punishment is very ineffective. During that time the child occupies himself with other things or develops anger and resentment toward the parent for placing him in this situation.

Rather than sending your child to his room for an hour, it is more effective and behavioral change will occur more rapidly if he is sent to his room for 10 minutes six different times. If he's sassy, he goes to his room for 10 minutes then comes out. When this behavior occurs again, the same consequence occurs. The same principles apply in the example of taking a child's bike away for 2 weeks. Rather than taking the privilege away one time for 14 days, it is better to restrict the child one day 14 times.

All people have different psychological time clocks. They differ in how accurately they estimate time. The same is true for children; that's why it is difficult to answer the question, *"How long to punish?"* an individual child. A child's estimate of time is vastly different from yours. A 6-year-old may perceive the passage of 15 minutes as the same amount of time an adult perceives the passage of 2 hours. Punishing this child for 1 hour is equivalent to punishing an adult for 8 hours. As children get older, their perception of time gradually approximates that of an adult. For some small children, a 30-second time-out punishment is sufficient, while for older children 20 minutes may be necessary.

A good rule of thumb to keep in mind when trying to determine how long to punish your child is to watch him closely to see how he reacts. Observe how long it takes before he occupies himself with something else and appears unconcerned about the punishment. In sending a child to his room for an hour, we observed whining, complaining, crying or similar behavior during the first ten minutes. But there was hardly any reaction during the remaining 50 minutes.

This gives us some idea of how long to punish the next time— ten minutes. For the child who had his bike taken away for 2 weeks, we see punishment affected him the first day but apparently had little impact on his attitude after that. One day is more appropriate the next time this punishment is used. Punishment does not have to be severe, harsh or long to work. Its effectiveness is primarily determined by how closely it follows the behavior you are trying to change and how frequently it occurs.

CHAPTER 8

Ignoring

Ignoring Specific Behavior

Some behavior in children exists because of the reaction given to it by their parents. Some kids know whining, complaining, pouting, sassiness, temper outbursts or crying get a reaction from their parents. Or it gets them their way. Such behavior is often continued because of the consequences a child receives for his or her behavior.

All behavior exists for a reason. To eliminate some types of behavior, it is necessary to remove the consequence (parents hollering, getting upset, becoming nervous). It's necessary to ignore the behavior. Ignoring undesirable actions is a very powerful method of discipline, but it is not often used effectively by most parents.

What To Ignore

Ignoring changes or eliminates only certain behavior. For other kinds of behavior, it has no effect. The obvious question is, *"What should be ignored?"* To determine what behavior to ignore, analyze the action and ask, *"What is my child getting out of the behavior?"* If your answer includes the following, consider ignoring the behavior all together.

"He's getting me upset."
"He's making me holler.
"I get nervous."
"We get into a power struggle or screaming match."
"I cry or leave him alone."
"I give in to him."

"He gets his way."

Ignoring can be very effective in changing or eliminating behavior that primarily serves the purpose of getting a reaction from you or getting the child what he wants.

Let's say you ask your child to start his homework. While he's doing what you requested, he starts mumbling under his breath. You can't understand most of it, but every now and then you hear something like, *"I've been in school all day doing work and now I have to do more work" "This is stupid."*

Although your son is doing the homework like you asked, you start reacting to the mumbling. *"Speak up. What are you saying? You'd better cut that out. Stop mumbling."* Each time you speak, your voice gets louder. You may become more upset.

Your child probably continues mumbling because of your reaction to it. Ignore it. If the behavior is ignored and the child doesn't get a response from you, the behavior usually disappears because it serves no purpose.

Also ignore behavior that is manipulative and designed to get a child his way (whining, pouting, temper tantrums, a thousand questions).

Your child asks *"Can I play video games before I do my homework?"* You say, *"No, we are going to do homework first."* This brings a violent reaction from the child. He starts screaming, hollering and throwing himself on the floor. After a little while, you can't take it, so you tell him, *"All right go play the game. We'll do homework later."* Children can wear you down with continuous whining or pleading and finally get their way.

How To Ignore

Ignoring the behavior described above usually produces behavioral change, but this procedure has to be used consistently. There are two ways to provide no consequences to a specific behavior in a child.

Withdraw All Attention

Act as though the behavior doesn't exist or the child isn't there. Don't talk to the child. Don't give him any facial or gestural indications of disapproval. Don't mumble to yourself. Withdraw all attention. If you decide to ignore whining and the child exhibits this behavior while you're talking to someone, talk over the behavior. Turning up the TV, putting on the stereo headset, going outside to work in the garden, taking a walk or getting involved with some task are techniques you can use to help withdraw all attention from the misbehavior.

Withdraw Emotional Attention, But Deal With Behavior

With this type of ignoring, your verbal reprimands and emotional attention are eliminated. But some disciplinary action, usually time-out or response-cost punishment, is taken. The rule at your house may be, *"When someone has a temper tantrum, he goes to his room. When he calms down, he can come out."* When your daughter throws a temper tantrum, tell her to go to her room or take her there. Don't get upset. Don't tell her to stop. Don't threaten her with a spanking. Don't react to her misbehavior in any way other than that specified.

Sassiness may be dealt with by stalling, *"I won't talk to you when you are sassy."* (Explain exactly what you mean by sassy.) When the child starts being sassy, ignore it and say, *"When you can talk in a normal tone of voice, I'll respond to you."*

Your children may like to make various noises or gestures to aggravate you. When this happens, stay calm and carry out the consequence that was previously determined. If your child makes noises that bother you, try setting up a chart in the kitchen. Tell the child, *"Every time you make noises, I'm going to put an X on the chart. For every X you have, you lose five minutes of TV time tonight."* When the child makes the noise, very calmly remind the child he has received an X and record it. You give no emotional attention or consequence to the behavior.

Things To Consider
Be Consistent

Be consistent when this disciplinary consequence is chosen to deal with a certain behavior. If you choose to ignore pouting, do it every time the behavior occurs. You can't ignore it one time then attend to it the next. If the child gets what he wants from the behavior every now and then, it may be sufficient to sustain the behavior.

By being inconsistent, you may set up a situation for the child similar to that of a gambler. He may lose seven or ten times but wins once. One win is enough to keep him trying many more times.

Be Sure Behavior Is Ignored

You may think you're ignoring a behavior, but you don't totally eliminate all attention or consequences. When you ignore, be sure all verbal (lecturing, hollering, mumbling under your breath) and non-verbal communications (an angry expression on your face, slamming a door) are withdrawn from the child's undesirable behavior.

Behavior May Get Worse

Sometimes when attention or consequences that are usually given a behavior are withdrawn, the behavior gets worse or intensifies before it diminishes.

Consider a child who has temper tantrums to get his way. It usually takes a 5-minute tantrum to coerce his parents to give in to his desires. Now they have attended one of our workshops and have decided to stick to what they say and ignore the behavior.

The child comes in and asks his mother, *"Can we go rent a movie?"*

She says, *"No, you've already had two."*

The temper tantrum begins, and the child starts his five-minute routine.

At the end of this period the parent has not attended to his behavior and has not given in. What's going to happen when the child doesn't receive the consequence he usually gets? The behavior intensifies. His voice may get louder. Crying may occur more frequently, and the length of the temper tantrum may increase. It may last ten, 30 or 60 minutes or until the child realizes the behavior is not going to bring him the consequence he normally receives.

The child will eventually realize the behavior is not working and the only thing the temper tantrum gets him is an upset stomach, sore throat and a headache. It serves no purpose and should stop or decrease in frequency and intensity.

The same thing happens when this consequence is used to deal with whining, complaining, pouting, noise making and similar behavior. The behavior intensifies and increases in frequency until the child realizes the behavior isn't serving its purpose. Then it will start to disappear.

When the behavior gets worse, continue doing the same thing. Don't give in, and don't go back to your old methods of dealing with the undesirable behavior. The increase in the inappropriate behavior should last three to 5 days at the most. However, in most situations, the increase in the undesirable behavior lasts only one or two days.

If the above procedures are used correctly, the most severe temper tantrums and other similar behavior can be successfully dealt with in a few days.

Other consequences may have to be used

A good rule is to ignore first when trying to change behavior. This produces successful results when the aim of behavior is to get a reaction from you and get the child what he wants. In some cases, ignoring the behavior is not sufficient to change it. In these situations, positive or negative consequences must be employed when the ignored behavior does not improve.

Ignore reaction of others

When you are ignoring behavior and other people are around (at a store, company at your house), you may feel embarrassed or pressured into some action to counteract what you are trying to accomplish. Disregard the reactions of others and how you think they perceive you. Deal with your child's behavior—not other people's!

PART IV

MEMOS FROM YOUR CHILD

As I was going through my files, I discovered some papers reproduced from the Leaders' Manual for Children: the Challenge by Driekurs and Soltz (1967). One paper, "A Memorandum From Your Child," included some of the concepts and major points I am trying to convey in this book.

Below, I have reproduced some of Dreikurs' statements, modified others and included some of my own to stress some very important concepts in child management to keep in mind when dealing with your children.

1. Don't spoil me. I know quite well I shouldn't have all I ask for. I'm only testing you.
2. Don't be afraid to be firm with me. I prefer it. It makes me feel more secure.
3. Don't let me form bad habits. I have to rely on you to detect them in the early stages.
4. Don't correct me in front of other people if you can help it. I'll take more notice if you talk quietly with me in private.
5. Don't make me feel smaller than I am. I'll make up for it by behaving stupidly big.
6. Don't make me feel my mistakes are sins. I have to learn to make mistakes without feeling I'm no good.
7. Don't protect me from consequences. I need to learn from experience.
8. Don't be too upset when I say, *"I hate you."* I don't mean it, but I want you to feel sorry for what you've done to me.
9. Don't take too much notice of all of my small ailments. I may learn to enjoy poor health if it gets me a lot of attention.
10. Don't nag. If you do, I'll have to protect myself by appearing deaf.
11. Don't forget I can't explain myself as well as I would like. This is why I'm not always very accurate.
12. Don't make promises you may not be able to keep. I feel let down when promises are broken, and this discourages my trust in you.
13. Don't tax my honesty too much. I'm easily frightened into telling lies.

14. Don't be inconsistent. That completely confuses me, makes me not listen and teaches me to manipulate you.

15. Don't tell me my fears are silly. They are terribly real. You can do a lot to reassure me if you try to understand and accept my feelings.

16. Don't put me off when I ask honest questions. If you do, you'll find I stop asking and seek my information elsewhere.

17. Don't ever suggest you are perfect or infallible. It gives me too much to live up to, as well as too great a shock when I discover you are neither.

18. Don't think it's beneath your dignity to apologize to me. An honest apology makes me feel surprisingly warm toward you.

19. Don't forget I love experimenting. I can't do without it, so please put up with it.

20. Don't forget how quickly I am growing up. It must be very difficult to keep pace with me, but please try.

21. Don't use force with me. It teaches me to be aggressive and hostile and that power is all that counts.

22. Don't fall for my provocations when I say and do things just to upset you. I'll try for more such victories.

23. Don't do things for me I can do for myself. It makes me dependent, and I feel like a baby. I may continue to put you in my service.

24. Don't let my bad habits get me a lot of attention. It only encourages me to continue them.

25. Don't try to discuss my behavior in the heat of conflict. For some reason, my hearing isn't very good at this time. My cooperation is even worse. It's all right to take the action required, but let's not talk about it until later.

26. Don't try to preach to me. You'd be surprised how well I know what's right and wrong.

27. Don't demand explanations for my wrong behavior. I really don't know why I did it.

28. Don't answer silly or meaningless questions. I just want to keep you busy with me.

29.   Don't let my fears arouse your anxiety. Then I'll be more afraid. Show me courage.

30.   Don't pay more attention to my mistakes, failures and misbehaviors than to my successes, accomplishments and good behaviors. I need lots of understanding, encouragement and positive attention. I can't pat myself on the back; I rely on you to do it. Treat me the way you treat your friends, then I'll be your friend, too. I learn more from a model than a critic.

PART V

"SHOULD I BE CONCERNED
ABOUT THIS?
WHAT IS NORMAL?"

What should I be concerned about? What is normal behavior or achievement? Is a child being disrespectful to his teacher or assertive? How many times should a second grader get out of desk a day? How many failing papers should a child get a week before I should be concerned? He doesn't listen to his teacher and talks a lot in class. Is he "all boy" or is this a problem?

These questions are difficult to answer. *Normal* behavior doesn't interfere with a child's ability to cope with his environment or get along with others.

It's fairly easy to find a child-development book that tells you at what age a child should walk, talk or get his first teeth. Other books tell you what behavior to expect at certain ages (terrible twos). But what is a normal amount of fighting in school, detentions, incomplete seatwork or activity? When trying to decide what is normal or what to expect from a child, several factors must be taken into consideration.

Frequency

All children get out of their desk, blurt out answers without raising their hands or have temper outbursts at some time. To determine if the behavior should produce concern, observe how frequently it occurs. A child who has a temper outburst once a month isn't revealing excessive behavior. If it occurs four times a day, analyze it more closely. Consider how often it occurs. The more frequently the behavior is seen, the more it deviates from normal.

How Does Behavior Interfere With Child's Ability To Function?

Most children don't like to do homework or class work. But most do it. The child who isn't doing his schoolwork may fail or have to go to summer school. If a child's behavior restricts or prevents functioning like an average child, it may be considered *abnormal*.

How Does The Behavior Interfere With Others?

Most children talk in class or get out of their desk at some time or another. However, if this behavior disrupts the class or prevents others from learning, it may not be considered normal. If the behavior significantly interferes with other people's routines, behaviors and activities, it may deviate from the norm (not normal).

Take Peer Groups Into Consideration

I'm the last person to say you should keep up with the Jones's. In determining what to expect from your child, consider his peer group. Take into account the behavior and actions of his age-mates. You must compare your child with other children his age.

Your child comes home every Friday with 25% of his seatwork incomplete. To determine if this is something to be concerned with you would have to talk to the teacher and/or find out how the other children in the class are doing with completing their seatwork.

The child's peer group's behavior must be taken into consideration before deciding what is normal for your child. It may be necessary to become familiar with other children to determine what to expect from your child or how much his behavior differs from the average.

Individual Differences

Children have different personalities. One child may be sensitive, another talkative, a third shy. In determining whether behavior is normal, consider the child's peer group and the individual child. Also consider family differences and expectations. You may expect your child to say, "Yes ma'am" and "No sir," while I don't expect it from my children.

Listen To Others Who Know About Child Behavior

Teachers, coaches, dance instructors and others who work with children are usually familiar with age-appropriate and normal behavior. Although they may not be able to give reasons for certain behavior or recommendations for dealing with them, they can easily identify unusual actions that differ from those of the child's age group.

Listen to these people if they tell you that your child's behavior should be investigated. I see many children in fourth or fifth grade whose abnormal behavior was first reported to their parents by teachers in preschool, kindergarten, first and second grade and by other teachers.

If you still think your child's behavior differs from the average after reading this, contact your child's doctor or a mental-health professional who deals primarily with children. He or she will be able to give you information or direction to help answer your questions.

PART VI

SHOULD I HAVE MY CHILD EVALUATED?

A saying I use frequently is, "*If it's not broken, don't fix it.*" If a child is not having any behavioral, emotional or academic trouble, I would not have him evaluated. If your child is having trouble at school, at home, in the neighborhood, on the playground or with his friends and his behavior is not typical for his age group, you may want to consider an evaluation.

If your child's teacher, coach, dancing instructor or some other person involved with him tells you something is unusual, listen. See the section on What is Normal? to get more information to help you decide if your child's behavior deviates from the norm. An evaluation may be appropriate. This may involve your child talking to a mental-health professional or formal testing.

Some professionals believe if a child experiences academic or behavioral problems, he should be evaluated or tested. Psychological and educational testing is usually more upsetting to you than to your child. Evaluations are designed to provide more information regarding a child's behavior, ability and performance. The more information you have regarding any situation or problem, the better you are able to deal with it. The data provided by evaluations gives you, his teachers and professionals more information by which to understand him, provide help and to alleviate his difficulties.

For many adults, the word "test" produces anxiety, tension and nervousness. We remember the tests we took at school or the ones we took to get a job or promotion. Tests used in evaluations are not used in a pass-fail situation. The child cannot fail. Children often enjoy the testing situation because they receive a great deal of individual attention. Some view the tests as games. Parents have told me their children asked to return to the office for more games.

Psychoeducational tests are designed to compare a child with thousands of other children the same age or in the same grade. Tests may give a personality description or an understanding of the child's behavior. By using this information, a professional should be able to determine why a child is having problems in school, why he acts or behaves in a certain way and what can be done about deficiencies.

Tests and evaluations give us a better understanding of the child. They lead to recommendations that help us deal with the child's problems or eliminate his difficulties.

If your child is evaluated, be sure you understand the results. The purpose of an evaluation is to give you more information to understand your child better. If you leave the conference more confused than when you came in, the evaluation was useless to you. Ask questions. If you don't understand what's said, assume the person giving you the result is not communicating them effectively, not that you aren't smart enough to understand them. Ask for the answers to be given in plain everyday language.

If your child is having trouble with schoolwork, fails exams, gets into trouble frequently, gets "held back" a grade or behaves unusually for his age, it's a good idea to have him evaluated. An evaluation will help your child and give you a better understanding of him.

When your child is evaluated, be sure that the individual or agency doing the testing is licensed, certified, approved by the state or has the proper credentials to provide the services you are requesting.

PART VII

BEHAVIORAL CONCERNS

CHAPTER 9

"He doesn't study or do homework like he's supposed to do," Irresponsibilty

Many of the children that I see who are having performance problems, receiving failing grades or are not performing to their potential are NOT due to academic or learning problems. They don't do what they're supposed to do! They do not do homework, study or complete projects. They fail to read assigned books, do reports, or bring the necessary materials to class. They don't bring all their books home. A fifth grader has to repeat the grade because of too many subjects failed. Another student has to go to summer school for two subjects. When the results of the evaluation indicate good intelligence and no achievement deficits, irresponsibility regarding schoolwork is often the cause.

Parents are often aware of this lack of effort and try to improve the child's responsibility regarding schoolwork by using a variety of rewards and/or punishments.

"If you get a B average the next report card I will buy you the video game you want."

"If your teacher tells me you did not do your homework this week, you will be grounded this weekend."

"You can't talk on the phone until your grades improve."

With some children this works, but for most it does not improve the child's responsibility regarding schoolwork. This is not because the discipline system is not set up right or is not appropriate. It is because this child's problem is not irresponsibility regarding schoolwork. It is irresponsibility in general/everything. The child is not doing his homework, but his room looks like a disaster area because his parents can't get him to clean it. He "forgets" to feed the dog. Never puts his bike in the garage, seldom hangs a towel up after he takes a bath, etc. If you focus on school only and do nothing to improve the other areas of irresponsibility, it will probably not work. You have to make this child more responsible in everything. School being one of several behaviors that are targeted.

Many parents tell me *"Hanging up the towel and cleaning the room are not that important when compared to school."* In general I agree, but when trying to change an entire behavior pattern they are very similar behaviors. The school has "classroom procedures" (Read chapter 2, do the ten math problems on page 35, bring the necessary supplies to class). At your house and mine we have "household procedures" (Hang up the towel after you bathe, get in bed for 9:00, put the dishes in the dishwasher after you eat). In the importance of the world, hanging up a towel and doing math homework is like day and night. However, they are basically the same behaviors because the child is doing what he wants to do, rather than what he's supposed to do in both situations. If you can't get your child to take a bath when you tell him, if you have to fight him to clean his room or brush his teeth, you probably will not be able to get him to do what he's supposed to do in school no matter what consequences are used.

When I talk to the parents about their child's behavior outside of school activities/work, they generally describe their child as irresponsible, lacking self-discipline or internal control, not doing what they are supposed to do. Parents' comments are varied.

"He's 12, but I still have to tell him to brush his teeth. I often have to bring him to the bathroom to be sure he does it."

"I can't trust her. She tells me one thing and does something else."

"He never cleans up his room. I have to force him to do routine duties, like take a bath. How many times do I have to tell him to do these things before he just does them without being told?"

"She's so irresponsible. I've told her when she says she's going to play at Paula's house, she must stay there. If she leaves, she's supposed to call me and tell me where she's going. However, she never calls. She just leaves. I usually don't know where she is."

"He's always losing things—books, pencils, sweaters."

In general, you can't believe what these children say. You may have difficulty depending on them to do things. They can't be trusted. They are often forgetful and frequently lose their belongings.

These children have a pleasure orientation because they do their own thing and take the easiest way. They do just enough to get by. Pleasure-oriented children see no reason to do things that are unpleasant to them. If you ask them to do something and they want to do it, they'll give you 100% of their effort.

If you ask them to do something—no matter how easy or small—that they don't want to do, it'll never get done. These children only do what they're supposed to when they want to. If it doesn't fit their needs, they don't do it. They often have difficulty following daily household routines (picking up toys, cleaning their rooms, taking a bath) or the daily classroom procedures (doing class work, turning in homework, completing other tasks). You must constantly remind them or force them to do what is expected.

How Responsibility Develops

There are three ways children acquire responsible behavior or self-discipline.

Born With "Good" Behavior

Some children seem to come to us with this behavior. They inherit it, and show it from a very early age. They're generally cooperative, do what they are supposed to do and even do things before they are told to do them. If you had this type of child, you wouldn't be reading this chapter.

Attitude Kids

The attitude develops first, then the behavior follows. You may tell a child, *"If you put your toys away, they'll be easier to find. By keeping track of the pieces of your game, you'll be able to keep it and enjoy it for a long time."* Or you may tell a child, *"If you hang up your new jacket, it'll last longer and look nicer."*

After hearing these reasons a few times, some children pick

up their toys, hang up their clothes and keep their rooms clean. It seems as if they develop an attitude first, and the behavior follows. I call these children attitude kids.

With these children, you can develop responsible behaviors by talking to them and establishing or changing an attitude. By giving them information, explaining things to them, being logical or getting them to see the situation from a different angle, an attitude develops. Their behavior follows. It's almost as if a light bulb comes on. You might say, *"You have to brush your teeth to prevent cavities. If you don't, you'll have rotten, ugly teeth."* The child brushes his teeth every night without you telling him again.

You might explain the importance of homework, why he shouldn't ride his bike on the highway, and the child behaves accordingly. *"Don't touch the pot on the stove. It's hot. You will get burned, and that hurts."* Or he could see his sister get injured by touching the pot, so he doesn't touch the pot. You probably wouldn't be reading this chapter if you had one of these children.

Behavior Kids

Behavior must be established first, then the attitude follows. Some children can be told many times to clean their rooms, but they still leave them messy. You could explain the cost of living, inflation and how many hours you had to work to buy their clothes to some children, but their jackets would still wind up on the floor. These children don't develop responsible attitudes from discussions with you. You must first establish the behavior and get them into the habit of doing something. Then the attitude follows.

Talking, reasoning, excessive explaining, lectures, yelling and screaming don't work with these children. This approach to developing responsible behavior in a child is as effective as asking a door to open by itself. They develop attitudes and responsible behavior by experiencing consequences.

What you do is more important than what you say. You can explain to this child all the reasons why he has to do his homework, get a good education, clean his room. He will probably understand and agree with 99% of what you say. However, the information or lecture goes in one ear and out the other. He will do what he wants to do. You will win the lottery before talking to this child will change his behavior. Talk is talk. It will not produce change. You're wasting your words talking with this child to try to change his behavior.

With the "attitude kid," a light bulb comes on (the attitude is established), and behavior follows. With the "behavior kid," the light bulb comes on, but it's very dim. It increases with intensity each time you are able to get him to perform the behavior or he experiences a consequence. The attitude develops gradually over time as he repeats the behavior.

The more you can get him to behave a certain way and something happens that he likes or doesn't like, the faster the attitude develops.

He must experience the consequences of his behavior. He must touch the pot to learn hot pots cause pain. It may be all right to explain why a child needs to do his homework, but the most important thing to this child is what will happen if he does it and what will happen if he doesn't. You might say, "*You've been giving me a hassle every night with the homework. You whine and complain. Every night the homework is done and you cooperate and are pleasant, you can stay up 30 minutes past your bedtime. If you give me trouble, you'll go to bed at your regular time.*"

This child doesn't have a lot of self-discipline, internal control or responsibility. He must develop it. He needs external controls and structure to develop the internal control. The more this child is on his own, in an unstructured setting where he must rely on his internal control, the more irresponsible behaviors will be seen. You'll also see irresponsible behavior in situations where the consequences are the same or where there is a lack of limits on his behavior.

Developing Responsibility And Self-Discipline

To develop self-discipline or the attitude of responsibility, you must first develop a habit in the child. Focus on the behavior. After developing a habit, hopefully an attitude will be established. The child will continue behaving in this manner. The techniques discussed below help a child develop self-discipline, independent behavior and responsibility.

Spell Out Rules And Consequences

Tell the child what you expect or want him to do. Tell him what will happen if he complies with your request and what will happen if he doesn't. Spell out the rule and consequence at the same time. This can be accomplished in three basic ways.

Natural Consequences

"I won't buy any more toys until you show me you can keep yours organized and put them where they belong." The natural consequence of not caring for toys is you won't be able to get any more.

Grandma's Rule

"You can't go outside and play until your room is clean and everything is put where it's supposed to go." You do what I want you to do, then you can do what you want to do.

Arbitrary Consequences

"I'm going to check your room after dinner. On the days it's clean, you can stay up past your bedtime. When it's not clean, you go to bed at the regular time." You pick a consequence that is important to the child and set up the rule.

These three methods of setting rules and consequences are discussed in detail in the chapter, Setting Rules for Behavior. These rules are the primary techniques used to develop responsible behaviors in children.

When trying to develop responsibility in children, most people focus on giving the child chores (making the bed, putting out the garbage, feeding the dog). This is fine, but it is not the main way children develop responsible behavior.

Chores usually involve consequences. If the child doesn't put out the garbage, he doesn't get his allowance. The reason chores are often used to develop responsibility is that predictable consequences follow the child's behavior.

When trying to develop responsibility or self-discipline in children, spell out the rule and the consequence ahead of time. Whatever happens to the child is a result of the child's behavior, no one else's. Responsible behavior can be developed frequently throughout the day by stating the rules and consequences before the rule is broken. By doing this, you put the responsibility for the child's behaviors on his shoulders.

By spelling out consequences ahead of time, you avoid random discipline. You avoid giving the child the impression others are responsible for what happens to him. Most parents are beautiful rule setters. They spell out rules very carefully and specifically. You may tell a child, *"You haven't been bringing all your books home from school. I want you to bring home the books you need for homework. Don't leave any at school."* This is a good rule. It is very clearly and specifically stated. What happens when the child breaks the rule? Then you decide what to do to him.

You decide the consequences after the rule is broken. When the child doesn't bring his books home from school, you tell him, *"I've told you to bring all your books home from school. Because you didn't, you can't watch the TV special tonight."*

You decide the consequence after the child breaks the rule. At 7:00 pm, the TV special is on, the child is in his room, angry at you and pouting, and feeling it's your fault he's missing the special. In a sense, he's right!

You could choose any consequence as a punishment. You could take his bike away, make him stay inside, miss baseball practice or anything else you decided. He feels you are responsible for what has happened to him.

If children are dealt with primarily in this way, it's difficult for them to develop responsibility. They feel what happens to them is your fault.

When trying to develop responsible behavior in children, spell out the rule and consequence ahead of time. You encourage the child to feel that whatever happens to him is because of his choices. He will feel responsible for his own behavior. In the above example, you could have told the child, *"When you bring home all your books, you can watch TV. When you don't, you won't be able to watch TV."*

When stated ahead of time, the consequence is within the child's control. He must be responsible for it. If he gets to watch TV, it is the result of his own choice. If he misses the special, it's his fault not yours.

Tie Consequences To Child's Behavior

When trying to develop responsibility in some children, it's best to tie everything to their behavior in the beginning. Set up a situation where the children earn rewards and pleasures, as well as punishments and disappointments. Spell out disciplinary measures ahead of time and tie all consequences to behavior. An example will make this point.

Suppose a family is watching TV when the mother suddenly says, *"Let's go get an ice cream."* They get an ice cream and the child enjoys it. Who is responsible for the pleasure he experiences? His mother is, because she decided to take him.

When trying to establish responsible behaviors in a child, try to relate everything to his behavior. In a case like the one above, you may designate some duty for the child before he earns the ice cream. It could be something important. *"If you clean your room, we'll get an ice cream. If your room isn't clean, we'll stay home."* Or it could be something relatively unimportant you ask the child to do. *"If you get the papers on the bed and bring them to me, we'll go get an ice cream. If you don't, we won't go get the ice cream."* Regardless of how it is set up, the child earns the ice cream. He is responsible for the pleasure, happiness and enjoyment he experiences.

Don't Assume Responsibility For The Child

Make your child responsible. If you force or make a child do his homework or you do it for him, you're more responsible for the work being completed than he is. The next night, you'll have to do the same thing again. The child isn't developing any responsibility or independent behavior. If you tie the child in the chair and make him do his homework, you'll get the homework done but the child is not developing responsibility. You'll have to go to college with him to be sure he does his work!

Suppose every morning you came to my house, woke me up, helped me dress and eat breakfast then brought me to work. I would be doing what I'm supposed to be doing—going to work every day. But what would happen to me if you weren't there one day? I probably wouldn't go to work because past habits have made you responsible for my behavior. The same thing happens when you stand over a child and force him to do what he's told. He doesn't feel responsible for that behavior.

A parent has been telling a child to clean his room, but it never gets done. Eventually, the mother gets fed up, drags the child to his room, stands over him and says, "*Clean this room. Hang up your clothes. Put the toys in the toy box. Make your bed.*" After 15 minutes, the room is finally clean.

A better way for this parent to get the room cleaned and encourage responsibility in her child is to spell out expectations and consequences ahead of time.

"*You can't go outside and play until the room is clean.*"

"*If your room is clean by the time we leave to go to Grandma's, we'll stop at the store and get some gum.*"

Put the responsibility on the child's shoulders. Avoid forcing a child to do what he's supposed to.

The same situation occurs when you allow your child to become dependent on you. You help the child to do things he can do by himself, or you do them for him. With younger children, this often involves self-help skills (getting dressed, taking a bath, feeding, cutting meat). With older children, it may involve picking up after them, keeping their rooms clean, waking them up for school, locating their baseball uniforms and equipment before a game. When this occurs, a child finds it difficult to learn independent, responsible behavior. It's easier to let Mom do it.

Children who are spoiled, who have their needs met for them by others or who often get their way have a difficult time developing responsible behavior. Avoid this type of parent/child interaction when trying to establish internal discipline or responsibility.

Make Consequences Different

Some children don't develop responsible behaviors because the same thing happens to them if they do the required task or if they don't do it.

"I'll be able to go to the movie Friday night whether I do my work in school or not."

"I'll be able to watch TV if I clean my room, but I can watch TV if I don't clean it."

If someone told me, "You can go to work and I'll pay you, or you can stay home and I'll pay you," I'd be fishing. I'd have to be stupid to go to work.

The same situation exists for a child who feels if he gets in a jam, he'll be able to manipulate his way out of the situation. Consequences will be the same if he cooperates or not.

Make consequences different if you expect to change behavior or develop an attitude of responsibility. If I go to work, I get paid. If I stay home, I don't. Be sure the child experiences different consequences for his behavior.

Lose A Battle But Win The War

It may be more important for the child to experience the consequences of his behavior than it is for you to get the task accomplished. You know a child loves to play outside. Tell him, *"You can't go outside to play until your room is cleaned."*

He says, *"I don't care. I didn't want to go outside and play. I'm going to watch TV."*

You think, *"What am I going to do now?"* The answer is nothing. The rule sticks. With this example, getting the room clean is actually the fourth thing you're trying to accomplish. The first is to make him realize there are different consequences to this behavior. Something will happen if he cleans the room. Something entirely different will happen if he doesn't.

The second thing you're trying to achieve is to teach the child he is responsible for his behavior. *"If you go outside to play in 2 minutes, 2 hours or 2 days, there's only one person in the entire world who's going to determine that. That's you. You're responsible for what happens to you. "*

The third thing you're trying to accomplish is to teach him you're going to do what he tells you to do. You're going to consistently follow through with consequences. The consequences depend on his actions. If he doesn't clean his room, he's telling you he doesn't want to play outside. You're going to follow through with what he wants. If he cleans his room, he's telling you he wants to play outside. You'll follow through with that. Getting the room cleaned is the fourth thing you're trying to accomplish.

Sometimes you battle with your child all day—homework, bath time, picking up. You try to win each battle by forcing the child to do what you want. If this is the case, you may be fighting the same battles until the child leaves the home to go to college. Although you win each battle, the child doesn't develop independent or responsible behavior. Sometimes it is better to lose a few battles but win the war.

A child refuses to take his bath. You tell him, *"If you're in and out of the bathtub by 7 o'clock, you can watch TV. If you don't bathe, you go straight to bed at 7. "* The child may refuse to bathe and go straight to bed. You may look at this as *"I lost. He won."* But it may be more important for him to experience the consequences of not taking the bath than for you to win the bath battle. After this happens a few times, he may be more responsive when you say, *"It's time to take your bath. "*

For some behaviors, it may not be that important if the child does what you ask. You don't die if you don't take a bath, do homework or clean your room. Experiencing the consequences today may get you more cooperation tomorrow. For some behaviors (those that are dangerous or may produce injury), you may have to control the child or get him to do what you request when you request it. However, most of the time you can forget about the battles and focus on the war.

Avoid Power Struggles

Don't get into battles or power struggles with the child if he refuses to cooperate. You tell the child, *"Go take a bath. "*

He says, *"I took one Thursday. I don't have to take one tonight."* Then you begin arguing, and a power struggle begins.

Avoid this when possible. Deal with him in a calm manner. Suppose I work for you, and you come in one morning and tell me, *"I want you to stay at work. Don't go home until you finish this paperwork."*

I respond by saying, *"I'm not going to do that. You can't make me. I refuse to do that."*

You wouldn't yell, scream or nag. You wouldn't tie me in a chair and make me do it or stand over me with a baseball bat and force me to work. You'd say, *"If you do the work, you're still working for me. If not, you're fired."* You'd imply you don't care if I do the work or not, but you're going to be sure one thing will happen if I do the work and something totally different will happen if I don't.

This same approach helps the child realize he is responsible. It helps avoid some problems described in this section.

Maintain A Business-like Approach

Some people will do things for you because of a relationship that has been formed or you have been nice to them. Other people would see this as a weakness that can be exploited.

Suppose you do ten favors for me. Then you ask me to drive you to pick up your car. I'm busy, or I don't want to take you, but ten flags pop up in my head. I remember the favors and how nice you have been to me. So I say, *"Come on, I'll take you."*

Another person may think he has put one over on the person ten times and say, *"No, I can't take you. I'm busy."*

You can pay some people to paint your house before the job is done, and you know the job will be completed. For others, you wouldn't pay them to paint the house until the job was finished. If you pay them before the job is complete, it would never get done.

Never say, *"I'm going to buy you this candy. Because I did, I want you to be good the rest of the time we're shopping."* The good behavior will last until the candy is eaten! Instead say, *"We're going shopping. I usually have to correct you many times. Each time I have to correct you, I'll give you a warning. If you don't have three warnings when we're finished, we'll get some candy. If you have three or more warnings, no candy."* The child needs the rules or expectations and consequences spelled out ahead of time. Consequences should occur after he fulfills the expectations. *"Even though you promise to cut the grass this afternoon, you'll receive your allowance after the grass is cut. Not before."*

Avoid Severe, Harsh, Long Or Big Consequences

Some children learn responsibility by repetition of consequences. It's better if 20 small consequences are experienced. Suppose you have a child who loves Saturday-morning cartoons. It is 7:30 am, and he's jumping on the couch and chair in the den. You go in the room and say, *"If you jump on the couch again, you'll have to go to your room for the rest of the morning. You'll miss all the cartoons."*

At 7:33, he jumps on the couch again, and you send him to his room for three or four hours.

This is not the best way to discipline some children. It works best with the "attitude kid"—the one you can talk to and reason with to produce behavioral change. The "attitude kid" will go to his room and start thinking, *"I missed my favorite cartoons. It's boring in my room. What I did was stupid. It wasn't worth it."* He develops or changes his attitude. The correct or expected behavior follows.

If you send another type of child to his room for three or four hours, he'll holler, cry or pout for about five or ten minutes. Then he'll play with his toys, find dust balls and make houses, count the dots on the ceiling, read or go to sleep. Big, long or harsh consequences don't make an impact.

For some children, it's better to say, *"If you jump on the couch or chair, you have to go to your room for three minutes."* He jumps, and you send him to his room for three minutes. After the time passes, he comes back into the den and jumps again. Send him back to his room for three more minutes. This procedure is repeated if he jumps again. For this child, it's better to send him to his room 30 times for three minutes than one time for three or four hours.

Big consequences don't significantly affect behavior. The more you can get a child to do something and something happens he likes or doesn't like, the faster the behavior will change and an attitude develop.

Another example is telling a child to do something. *"Go clean your room."* You repeatedly tell him to do it, but nothing happens after telling him 87 times. The 88th time you tell him, he still doesn't do it. You're really angry and give him a severe, long or harsh consequence. Rather than let something slide 88 times then come down with one big consequence, it's more effective to give some children 88 small consequences. You have to establish a cause-and-effect relationship.

Big incentives or rewards that occur after a long period of time don't work well with this type of child. In January you say, *"If you pass all your classes this year, we'll go to Disney World this summer."* Or *"If you don't get suspended again for the rest of the school year, I'll buy you a motorcycle."*

If you set up this type of long-term incentive for some children, the child will work like crazy for three days but rapidly slides back into his old behavior. Or he won't show any behavioral change until three days before the report card. Then he'll study 24 hours a day. For this particular child, it's better to get a weekly report from the school and base his privileges for each weekend on his performance at school. If there is a long-term goal, he can earn points toward the goal on a weekly basis.

Avoid Giving Sentences

"Go to your room. You're punished until you're 18."
"You can't use the phone for a week."
"You won't be able to play for the whole week."

These punishments work with some children but not others. Some children will go in their room and serve the sentence and come out and do the same thing again. Sentences are primarily given to change an attitude and to get a child to think differently.

Sentences work with the "attitude kid." Some children work better when there are goals or incentives. If you give these children a sentence, put a light at the end of the tunnel. They need a way they can work toward something. Example: *"Because you have been doing poorly in school, you can't talk on the phone this week. However, each evening if you do your homework and don't give me any trouble, you can talk on the phone that night."*

If all you give this child is a sentence, the only thing you are positive will happen is he won't talk on the phone for a week. Give him a sentence with a light at the end of the tunnel (a way to work out of the sentence), and you may get some homework completed.

Avoid Excessive Explaining, Lectures And Reasoning

Many parents talk, explain, reason or lecture too much. For some children, this approach doesn't help them develop better understanding of the situation or help them acquire responsible behaviors. A child may not accept explanations or reasons why he has to do something (homework, washing his face). 1, 100, or 1,000 explanations won't satisfy him or make him understand. The only thing that will please him is hearing what he wants to hear.

A child may come up to you and ask, *"Why do I have to study history? I'll never use it. It's stupid."* After many logical reasons and explanations, he still gives you a hassle. The only thing that will satisfy him is for you to say, *"Yes, you're right. History is stupid. Don't study for the test."* Sometimes the only reason that is necessary is, *"Because I said so!"*

Sometimes kids ask questions that don't have logical answers. Give me a good reason for, *"Why do I have to make my bed every morning if I am going to mess it up every night?"* There is none. The only answer is, *"I have the job. I pay the rent, electricity and phone, and I bought your furniture. You have to do it because I said so. You won't be able to watch TV when you come home from school until your bed is made."*

Model Responsible Behaviors

You are a very powerful role model for your children. They learn much, both good and bad behaviors, from watching you and seeing how you solve problems and deal with situations. If your child sees you acting in an irresponsible fashion or showing a lack of internal control, there's a strong probability he will learn this behavior. Show him responsible actions.

Chores

Many parents feel chores and duties around the house are a big part of developing responsibility. Chores are a way to develop responsible behavior. Giving a child duties around the house doesn't, by itself, develop responsibility. But it helps.

When giving a child tasks to perform around the house, state what you expect and what the consequences of failure will be. There are several ways to do this.

Allowances And Rewards

Allowance may be based on duties. A child gets an allowance of $1 a week. His job is to put out the garbage four times a week. Each time he does it without being told, he earns 25 cents toward his allowance. Whether he gets the full $1 or not is his responsibility.

Logical And Natural Consequences

The use of logical or natural consequences can be used by telling a child, *"This is our house. We are all responsible for what has to be done. Your father has certain responsibilities, your sister has duties and there are many things I have to do to keep the house running. If you do not hold up your end and do what you're supposed to do, someone else has to do it. When that happens, they use their time to complete your responsibilities. That means they will have less time to do things for you."*

Another child might like to stay up late to watch a TV program on Friday night. He's supposed to put his dirty clothes in the hamper by Friday night so you can wash them on Saturday morning. If this is done by 8:00 pm Friday night, he can stay up. If not, he goes to bed at his usual bedtime.

Your child's job is to cut the grass. If the grass is cut before 5:00 pm Saturday, he can use the car on the weekend. If it isn't cut, he has to find another means of transportation.

A child's duty is to feed the dog, but he never does it without being told. You may say, "*You don't get your supper until the dog is fed.*" The natural consequence of not being responsible is the child's supper is delayed, and he may get hungry.

Another child's responsibility is to clean the bathroom on Saturday. He may be told, "*If the bathroom is clean by noon, I'll drive you to your friend's house. If it's not clean by then, I'll have to clean it. Because that will give me more work and involve more of my time I will not be able to drive you. You'll have to walk to your friend's.*"

"*Your job is to put the dishes away. If you don't, I have to do it. I have less time to do my duties. So I'll have to stop doing something that I do for you. If I don't have the time because I'm doing what you're supposed to do, I won't be able to wash your clothes. You'll have to do that.*"

If the child can't perform duties and tasks around the house to help other family members and make things easier for all involved, then the other people in the family won't do things for the child.

Developing Trust

Most parents develop a lack of trust in a child because the child says one thing and does another. You can't believe what he says.

"*Do you have any homework?*"

He tells you no, but on Friday you get a note from the teacher saying he hasn't turned in half the homework for the week.

"*I'm going by Clark's house.*"

You call Clark's house. His mother says your child has not been there all day.

"*I'm going to a movie,*" but he goes some place else.

A lack of trust usually develops in several situations when a child lies or steals, lacks responsibility or is manipulative. If you can deal with or reduce these behaviors, you may be able to develop more trust in your child.

Here's an example I use frequently with children. "*Suppose you and I see each other every day. We go to school together or* *see each other every day because we live in the same neighborhood. Once a day I ask you to lend me a nickel or a quarter. I tell you, 'I'll pay you back tomorrow.' But tomorrow comes, and I don't pay you back. This goes on for 6 months, and I have not repaid you. Then I come to you and ask, 'Lend me $100. I'll pay you back tomorrow.'"*

I then ask the child, *"What are you going to tell me?"*

Most of the time, he tells me, *"I'm not going to lend you the money."*

I ask, *"Why?"*

The child usually says, *"Because you're not going to pay me back."*

Then I ask, *"Why?"* again.

The usual answer I get is because he doesn't trust me. I say one thing and do something else.

I then explain this is the same reason his parents don't trust him or question what he says.

Re-Establishing Trust

Three things must happen for trust to be re-established.

Ask for small things

They can't go to their parents and ask for big privileges. They can't ask to borrow $100 because they probably won't get what they request. They have to request small things. *"Could you lend me a penny?"* What is a penny? The child has to start out asking for small privileges or requests.

Grant the request

The second step is the parent must lend the money. You have to grant the child the request for the small privilege. If you never lend him the money or give the child a chance, you'll never be able to develop trust.

Do what you say

The third step in this process is for the child to do what he says he will do. The child might say, *"I'm going to Robbie's house. I won't go anyplace else."* To develop trust, you have to check to see the child has done what he said he would.

I usually tell the children, *"I know you manipulate your parents and lie sometimes. But when you're trying to build trust, you have to do exactly what you say you're going to do. By doing this, trust will develop, and they will allow you more privileges."*

Children who frequently ask or tell their parents, *"You don't trust me. You never believe me. Why do you have to check up on me? Why do you have to call Robbie's mother to see I am going to be at his house? Why do you have to check with the teacher to see if I have homework when I said I don't have any?"*

I tell the parents to respond, *"If I don't check to see that you've done what you said, there's no way I can trust you."* You must put the responsibility on the child's shoulders. If his behavior indicates he can be trusted, you can allow him more freedom or privileges. If his behavior does nothing to reduce your lack of trust, he can't have more freedom or privileges.

Developing Responsibility—Things To Remember

1. Many children do not develop responsible attitudes as a result of conversation or discussion. Communication is fine, but some children must first establish the behavior (get them into the habit of doing something), then the attitude follows. It isn't so much what you say, but what you do.

2. When trying to develop responsibility or self-discipline in a child, spell out the rule and consequences of his behavior ahead of time. This makes the child responsible for what happens to him.

3. After the expectations and consequences are clearly stated, the child might decide for the bad thing to happen. When this occurs he may try to blame others for what has happened. *"You're mean. You won't let me play. It's your fault I missed the cartoon."*

Tell him in words he can understand, *"It was your decision. It's your responsibility. I only did what you told me to do. You knew what was going to happen, and you decided to miss the cartoon."*

4. At first, the important thing in developing responsibility is

not completion of a task. It's important for the child to experience the consequences of his behavior and feel he is responsible for what has happened. You may tell a child, *"You can't watch TV until your room is clean."* The child doesn't clean his room, so you don't let him watch TV. At first, getting the room clean isn't as important as the child experiencing the consequences of his behavior (missing TV). Don't feel as if you lost because the room wasn't cleaned. You won because you made the child responsible for what happened to him. If you're consistent, responsible behavior will begin to emerge, and the room will be cleaned.

5. Avoid random discipline. Don't determine consequences after a rule is broken. Tie the consequences of the child's behavior to him. Make him responsible for his rewards and pleasures, as well as his punishments and disappointments. Pleasure or punishment must be tied directly to the child's behavior so he is responsible for the consequences of his actions.

6. Avoid power struggles and forcing children to perform duties and tasks. This doesn't lead to development of self-discipline and responsible behavior.

7. Avoid long, severe, harsh and big consequences. Rather than have 1 big thing happen, it is better if 20 small consequences are experienced.

8. Don't let a child become excessively dependent on you to perform tasks you know he can do. This type of parent-child interaction makes it difficult for children to learn independent, responsible behavior.

9. Meeting a child's every need, giving her everything she wants, letting her have her way and spoiling her often interfere with the development of responsible actions.

10. Giving a child duties or chores around the house doesn't by itself develop responsibility-but it helps.

Using Charts To Develop Responsible Behavior

A behavior chart is a formal method of keeping a record of your child's behavior. I find charts can be helpful in establishing responsible behavior. This chapter outlines how and why to construct them, types of charts and things to consider when you use them.

Setting Up A Behavior Chart
Analyze Behavior

The first step in developing a chart is to analyze the behavior to be increased or decreased. How frequently does it occur? Under what circumstances is the behavior seen? How long does it last? The chapter entitled, Deciding Which Behavior To Change, provides a review of this procedure. It is very important to analyze the behavior because this will determine what type of chart to use.

Identify An Important Consequence

The next step is to select a consequence that is important to the child. Most charts are based on reward and are set up in positive terms. A behavior chart also easily lends itself to a response-cost system of discipline.

Types Of Behavior Charts

The number and style of behavior charts available are limited only by your imagination. Several general types are described below. The type of chart you use is primarily determined from the information obtained when the target behavior is analyzed.

When Target Behavior Occurs Or Can Occur More Than Once A Day   Sometimes behavior to be changed is seen many times throughout the day (picking up toys, sassiness) Suppose your child never picks up her clothes or toys even after she has been told to do so. You analyze the behavior and find it occurs about 7 times a day. You might set up a chart similar to the one below.

Jason's Pick up Chart

MON.	TUES.	WEDS.	THURS	FRI.	SAT.	SUN.
☆	☆	☆	☆			
☆	☆	☆	☆			
☆	☆	☆				
☆	☆					
☆						
☆						
☆						

The week is divided into days, but each day is blank. Identify a reward. Next, tell your child, *"Each time I ask you to pick up something* (explain what you mean by this) *and you do it the first time I ask you, I'll put a star on the chart. If I have to remind you more than once, you won't get the star."* At the end of the day, week or whatever, she can trade in her stars for the reward.

When working with charts to change behavior that occurs more than once a day, do not include more than 1 kind of behavior on the chart. If you're working on sassiness, that should be the only behavior on that chart. If you want to work on another behavior, make another chart. It's best not to use more than two charts at a time.

When Target Behavior Occurs Or Can Occur Only Once A Day

If you're concerned with behavior that is seen infrequently or can occur only once a day (getting dressed for school, taking a bath, bringing books home from school, homework), the chart types described above are not appropriate. In situations similar to these, two different approaches could be used: verbal or written contracts and formal charts.

Verbal Agreement

A formal chart is not made, but a verbal agreement is made. This is usually used for only one behavior at a time. The child is told, *"On days you get dressed for school on time, you can have an extra dime to take to school. On days you're late, you get only the same amount you usually receive."* The child is asked to repeat the verbal agreement to be sure he understands it correctly.

"If you bring all your books home from school, you can stay up past your bedtime. If not, you go to bed at the usual time."

"When you leave your bike in front of the house and don't put it in the back yard, you won't be able to ride it the next day."

Written Contract

For some children, a verbal contract isn't sufficient. They forget all or part of the contract or disagree with its terms if they fail to live up to their part of the agreement. In these situations, it's best to formalize the contract by putting it into writing. A couple of examples follow.

Date_____

   I agree to put my bike in the back yard. When it is left in the front yard, I will not be able to ride it the next day.

Signed_____
Signed_____

Date_____

   I agree to have my room cleaned by 7:00 pm each night. If it is straight and clean at that time, I will be able to stay up 30 minutes past my bedtime. If it isn't, I go to bed at the usual time.

Signed_____
Signed_____

The agreement is spelled out on paper and both of you sign it. Then it is placed in a conspicuous place, such as on the refrigerator or on the door of the child's room. If the child follows or breaks the contract, the parent administers the appropriate predetermined consequence.

Formal Charts

   When a behavior occurs only once a day, the chart should include more than one target behavior but no more than three or four. An example follows.

   Three target behaviors are specified—getting dressed for school without help, bringing home all the necessary books to do homework and doing homework without a fight. Because the target behavior pertains only to school, the chart is based on 4 or 5 days instead of 7. The child is told how he can earn stars and X's, as well as what the stars represent and when they can be traded in. When using Charts, you must spell out the conditions—

what must be done to earn the reward (allowance could be based on completion of chores) and when the consequence will be given.

Tony's Chart (1st Week)

Getting ready for school	x	x	☆	☆	x
Bring all books from school	☆	☆	☆	x	☆
Homework without a fight	☆	x	x	☆	☆

Household duties and chores could alsobe included in this type of chart.

Jason's Duties

	Mon	Tues	Wed	Thurs	Fri	Sat	Sun
Making Bed	☺	☺	☺	☺	☺	☺	☺
Feeding Dog	☺	X	X	☺	☺	X	☺
Cleaning up after dinner	X	☺	☺	X	☺	☺	☺

I have described some general ways to set up charts, but there are many variations. Behavioral charts work better for younger children (10 and under), but they can be used successfully with high-school students. The procedures and principles are the same for any age group; only the consequences are different.

Why Use Behavior Charts?
The advantages of using behavior charts are discussed below.
Immediacy Of Consequences
The most important thing about reward and punishment is

not how large, expensive, harsh or severe it is, but how soon it follows target behavior. Behavior charts help you accomplish this because the behavior can be dealt with almost immediately.

Although the reward may be given at night (staying up past the child's bedtime), it can be meaningfully dealt with almost immediately by placing a star or an X on a chart at 9 am. A consequence that will occur on Saturday (a movie, a fishing trip) can be dealt with on a daily or hourly basis.

Charts Help You Look At Behavior Differently And Objectively

When you analyze and chart a behavior, you may see the behavior in a different light. The problem originally seen as extensive may no longer seem very significant.

Charting behavior also helps you see gradual improvement more easily. Earlier I mentioned that parents often look at a child's overall behavior, which causes them to miss gradual improvement. Problem behavior doesn't occur overnight. It develops gradually. Any improvement is also gradual, and behavior charts help you see this.

Charts Help You Be Consistent

Consistency is the foundation of effective child discipline. Charts help you follow behavior in a very consistent fashion. A chart placed on the refrigerator serves as a good reminder. Children often become involved in getting stars and working toward rewards and are quick to remind you if you forget.

Structure Provided By Charts Is Beneficial For Some Children

A child can see his chart, put his stars on it and become involved in working toward a reward. This is helpful for some children. Their involvement in charting their good behavior facilitates positive change.

Behavior Charts—Things To Consider
Make It Easy To Get First Rewards

When first using a chart, make it easy for your child to obtain the reward. Once she's locked into the system, expectations can be gradually increased. The best way to lose a child's interest in a chart is to have her fail to achieve the reward at first.

When starting a chart, make the expectations reasonable so the child can achieve the reward. When first beginning a chart, make the reward dependent on 20% to 30% improvement. The child who had 10 temper outbursts a day should receive the reward if he reduces the target behavior to an average of 7 or 8 a day and earns three or four stars. Each week the chart is used, expectations are gradually increased. During the second week, the child may have to show 45% improvement to get the reward, the third week 55% and so on. Never require 100% improvement for behavior that occurs frequently. Always allow some room for error.

How Long Should A Chart Be Used?

This depends on the individual child and the type of behavior you are dealing with. Use a chart for a minimum of 4 or 5 weeks after the behavior is no longer consistently present, though it may have to be used longer. One mistake parents make is they discontinue the chart too soon.

Once the chart has been in use for a sufficient period of time and the child is responding adequately, it can be phased out. This can be done in one of several ways. The child can be told he has done well and the target behavior is under control. Then you can use the chart to work on another behavior. Or you can start increasing the number of tokens the child must earn to receive the reward and try to interest him in behaving for the token rewards. Eventually you phase out the entire chart.

Another method is to ask the child if he wants to continue the chart if he is doing well. In many situations, you may notice the child losing interest in the chart. Then it can be discontinued. Try to avoid stopping before the new behavior has had a chance to establish itself.

Keep Chart Simple

Don't include too many behaviors on the chart or make it too complex. Once a parent called me to say a chart she was using wasn't working. I asked her what she had included on it. The list below was her response.

1.   Get out of bed when called.
2.   Get dressed for school on time.
3.   Brush teeth.
4.   Eat breakfast.
5.   Put school clothes in dirty-clothes basket.
6.   Homework.
7.   Come in from playing when told.
8.   Eat dinner.
9.   Clean up room.
10.   Take a bath without a fuss.
11.   Go to bed when told.

There were too many target behaviors on the chart. When this happens, two things could occur. First, the child will give up easily or not attempt the behaviors at all. In the above example, the child may have only gotten 15 minutes past his bedtime for all that work and felt it wasn't worth the effort. A child may also avoid projects that look too big or involve too much work. Secondly, when too many behavioral expectations are included in a chart, the child can easily manipulate the system. He can select certain behavior to perform, ignore the others and still receive the reward. Usually the behaviors the child avoids are the most important ones.

If charts are made too complex, the child may become confused. *"A gold star means this, while a blue star represents that. If you have 7 by Tuesday, this will happen. If you have 15 by Friday, this will also happen. However, you could combine the points you get this week with the ones you get next week, or you could add the ones from last week."*

After all this, the child is thoroughly confused. He says, *"Forget about this chart."*

Don't make the conditions of a chart too complex. Don't include too many behaviors on one chart. 3 or 4 target behaviors are enough.

Be Sure Consequences Earned Are Received

Psychologist: *"Mrs. A, tell me about the chart we set up to help Jimmy with his sassiness."*

Mrs. A: *"Well, it worked beautifully for the first 2 weeks. He showed about a 90% improvement; but the last 2 weeks he's back to the same old stuff."*

Psychologist: *"Jimmy, what happened? You were doing so well."*

Jimmy: *"The first week my mother told me I could go to the skating rink Saturday if I earned enough points. I got the points I needed, but she said she was too busy to take me. The next week was the same thing. I earned the points but couldn't go skating. So I figured what's the use."*

When a situation like this happens, you can't expect a chart to work for more than a short period of time, no matter how well it is constructed. Be sure to keep your part of the contract. If a child earns certain consequences, be sure he receives them.

Make Chart Positive

Most of the charts we set up involve positive consequences rather than negative. I feel this is a good rule to follow. Verbal or social reward (praise, hugs) should always be associated with behavior charts. When the child is placing his token on the chart and when he receives the final consequence, praise him. State descriptions of target behaviors in a positive manner. Don't use negative statements.

"Fighting with your sister ... "
"Messy room ... "
"Coming home late ..."

Descriptions on the charts should be positive.
"Getting along with your sister... "
"Clean room ..."
"Coming home on time . . ."

CHAPTER 10

"She doesn't want to go to school," School Phobia

Some children aren't too thrilled about going to school. Others refuse to go. They show reactions ranging from stubbornness, defiance and outright refusal to crying, fears, panic, physical complaints and nervousness. Some children show this behavior when they start school, but it may appear at any grade level. School avoidance or phobia is most common during elementary school years.

In most situations, the reason the child refuses to go to school has nothing to do with school! This becomes obvious to parents with a child who acts like this when they try to solve the problem by making modifications in the school setting.

Your child complains, *"The child sitting next to me hates me. The teacher is mean and screams too much. The school is too big or hard. The kids do not like me."* You talk with the principal and changes are made in the child's school environment (he is assigned a new seat in the classroom, changes teachers, moved to a lower-level class, given less work). Or the parent decides to take the child out of the school and place him in a new school.

Usually shifts in the school environment result in very temporary improvement (a week or so). Most of the time, very slight to no improvement is seen because the problem is usually not based in school but is part of the child. He starts a new school or changes teachers and is fine for a couple of days. Then the same behavior surfaces, sometimes even more intense than before.

Most of the time these children don't know what's wrong or why they feel the way they do. They are often worried, fearful, scared, confused and nervous. If you ask them a hundred questions (*"Is it the teacher? Are the kids being mean to you?"*) you'll probably get "*Yes*" to most of them. For every problem you solve by changing the situation at school, two more may develop. If the child volunteers a complaint about school and it is corrected, another one is apt to emerge in a few days. The primary basis of this behavior is a lack of confidence and/or a lack of independent behavior, which may result from several situations.

Separation Anxiety

Separation anxiety is present in many cases of school avoidance and refusal to attend. The child becomes nervous, tense, fearful or upset when he has to function independently or apart from his parents. Fear is not of school but of separation. The object of the child's excessive dependency is usually the mother. She is around more frequently, has been consistently available to him or has been the parent on whom he depends. However, excessive dependency could be directed toward the father or another significant person in his life (grandparent).

He may not let his mother go out of the house without him. Going to the store or to a meeting may become a chore. In other cases, the child doesn't let his parent out of his sight and must be physically in the same room, even the bathroom, most of the time. He may fear sleeping alone and needs to be in the same room with his mother to fall asleep. He may feel his mother is going to disappear or leave him if he goes to school or allows her out of his sight.

But if the child decides to separate from the mother, he can do it. A child comes over to play and they go outside. The child does not seem to miss his mother.

This child will usually promise you anything to get out of going to school or to get you off his back about going to school.

"If I let you stay home today, do you promise to go to school tomorrow?"

"If I buy you those tennis shoes you wanted, will you go to school tomorrow?"

The answer is almost always *"Yes"* or *"I'll try."*

The longer the time until the child has to go to school, the more confident he appears and the more promises he will make. On Friday night the child assures you he'll go to school Monday. But as Sunday night approaches, the apprehension, worry and concern increase. On Monday morning, it is full blown and the behavior seen the week before is back.

"What If?"

Many of these children are filled with thousands of "what if. . ." questions. Although his mother has never been late picking him up for school, every morning she hears, *"What if you're not there when school's over? What if you get in a wreck? What if I get sick?"* The child seems totally unsure of himself and needs constant reassurance.

These children also show more difficulty when it is time to go to school if they have been home for a while (after weekends, holidays, illness). Mondays are typically the most difficult, and Fridays are the easiest.

Most children are described by their parents and teachers as "good kids" who give very little trouble and don't exhibit behavioral problems at home or school. They tend to be cooperative in many other areas of their life. They usually do well academically and are good students. If you get the class work and homework from the teacher, they usually do it without a hassle.

By not attending school, they create other worries, concerns and apprehensions that interfere with them returning to school.

"What am I going to tell friends when they ask, 'Where have you been?' 'What happened?' 'Why did you miss school?'" "I'm going to be lost in class. I won't know what's going on."

"How am I going to catch up on all the notes, class work, homework?"

Because the dependency is on the mother and the problem is separation from her, this child will usually give less trouble to the father or some other relative. With the mother, he may get dressed without objection and not give trouble getting ready or leaving for school. When she drives him to school, the closer they get to school, the stronger the fear becomes. It is most intense when the child has to get out of the car, leave his mother and go to class. If the father takes him to school, he may show more trouble leaving the house than getting out of the car. If his mother is not home and his father is in charge of the morning routine, he may give little or no trouble.

The problem mainly centers around separation. The child may cry intensely or show extreme reactions when it approaches time for the separation or when you leave. But the behavior usually diminishes rapidly once you've gone. Only in the minority of cases will the child cry or show the extreme reaction for an extended period of time. When you get home from leaving your child at school and call to see how he's doing, you may hear, "*He calmed down as soon as you left. He's doing his work, and everything is fine.*" Believe them!

They're not telling you this to make you feel good and not worry.

Keep in mind when dealing with school phobia or fear that the source of the fear is often not school. Anxiety and fearfulness result from separation, lack of independent behavior and/or confidence problems.

Why Do Children Refuse To Go To School?

Most reasons children refuse to attend school focus on issues outside the school setting.

Trouble In School

With most children who refuse to attend school, problems lie outside the school situation not with the school. However, sometimes problems may exist at school.

These problems may center around the adults involved with the child in the school situation, the other children and academic or behavioral problems.

I wish I had a dollar for every time a parent told me, "*There's a personality conflict between the teacher and my child. The teacher doesn't know what she's doing. The principal's rules are stupid.*"

There are "squirrels" in every profession, and the teaching profession is no exception. Sometimes conflicts with the adults that the child deals with in the school setting may produce problems. Hopefully the professionals involved with the child will realize this and recommend shifting the child to another teacher.

Children who have socialization problems, get teased or picked on and don't have any friends sometimes refuse to go to school. The child may have a reputation and find it difficult to establish a relationship or break into peer groups. Because of these factors, school is not a pleasant situation and becomes something he may want to avoid. Socialization problems are also common with children who experience separation anxiety.

Other children refuse to attend school because they experience problems in the academic setting. They may have academic or behavioral difficulties, and school becomes a negative experience. They tend to avoid it. Although these children may show some behaviors described above, they usually develop physical complaints to stay home, skip school and flatly refuse to go. Or they have excuses for why they can't go to school (the teacher talks too fast, the child next to me keeps bothering me).

For children who have trouble with schoolwork, it's best to get an evaluation to identify the source of the problem. I often see children who show school avoidance and an evaluation sometimes determines that they have a learning problem. Once the problem is identified and steps are taken to remedy the learning deficiency, the reluctance to attend school may diminish.

Socialization Problems

Some children who experience difficulty with other children may show school refusal. Children who show dependency and separation anxiety also experience some socialization problems. But these are more a lack of appropriate skills. They aren't picked on by the other children or aggravated by them. The problems revolve around the fact that the child doesn't have many friends, doesn't interact well with other children and may be characterized as a loner. See the chapter that discusses socialization issues for a more detailed description of problems a child might have interacting with his peers.

Child Is In Control

The child is more in control than his parents. He can do what he wants when he wants for as long as he wants. He develops a disinterest in school and doesn't want to go. So he doesn't.

This may be the child who won't take "no" for an answer and does the opposite of what you tell him. He has a smart answer for everything you say. He's never happy, and nothing you do seems to please him.

The child is very manipulative. If you allow him to control the situation, he may decide not to go to school. The stubborn, strong-willed child and other personality types (pampered, spoiled, babied) are sometimes more in control than their parents. See the chapter that discusses children who are in control.

Dependency

Children who lack independent behavior often need assistance in problem solving and decision-making. They may have difficulty when they're required to deal with situations on their own or are separated from the person on whom they depend. Dependent children often show many of the characteristics of separation anxiety described in the preceding section. See the chapter that discusses a lack independent skills and how to promote more-independent behavior in your child.

Environmental Changes

Some children who experience changes in their environment show a decrease in confidence. They may be somewhat confused, insecure and uncertain. They may also become very dependent. They usually show the characteristics of the child with separation anxiety.

Changes could be major things, such as a divorce, separation, death of a parent or grandparent, birth of a sibling, moving to a new house, starting or changing schools, illness in the family. It could also be something that seems minor, such as the loss of a pet, different working hours of the parent, death of a distant relative, a friend moving out of the neighborhood, parental conflict, a shift in the daily or weekly routine.

Changes don't even have to be bad or traumatic. It could be a good or positive change, such as a mother quitting work, a father having more time to spend with the child, a move to a new house where a child has his own room. Something has changed in the child's environment and routine. With some children, this is unsettling and may produce school avoidance.

Dealing With Refusal To Attend School

Most problems require more than only manipulating the school setting. Modifications usually must be made in several areas of the child's life,

Try To Identify Problem

Talk with the child's teacher, principal, counselor or other administrative person about the problems your child has. See if you can identify a source. Look at your child's personality, your patterns of interaction with him, the way you deal with him and other environmental factors.

If the child is struggling in school or it appears he is having academic problems, an evaluation might be appropriate to see if he has learning difficulties. Even if you don't suspect a learning problem, it may be wise to contact a mental-health professional. The longer the behavior persists, the more difficult it is to deal with. I have found it much easier to deal with a school-avoidance problem when you catch it early.

Talk With School Personnel

If you feel a problem exists at school, talk with the appropriate person. If you feel the teacher is the problem, talk with her. If you don't get any satisfaction, talk with the counselor, vice-principal, principal or the next appropriate person. If the problem involves other children, talk with school personnel to see what can be done about it.

Treat Behavior In Matter-of-fact way

Don't use excessive punishment. Avoid criticism, embarrassment, yelling, guilt or similar methods. Don't use fear techniques to try to control this behavior,

"You're going to fail if you don't go to school."

"You're going to be 33 years old before you are out of high school."

"All your other friends are going to advance to the next grade, and you're going to repeat."

Work On Behaviors At Home

This is extremely important. If you can identify dependency in your child, work on developing independent behaviors. Don't pamper, spoil or cater to the child. Establish rules and spell out consequences ahead of time.

If confidence is a problem, use techniques to build it and reduce uncertainty and insecurity.

If there have been any changes in the child's life, try to stabilize the environment by being consistent, establishing routines and becoming predictable. Establish control. You must be in charge, not the child. Review the chapters that discuss the behavioral characteristics you are seeing in your child.

Increase Socialization

Many children who show school avoidance have difficulty relating to their age mates. Provide opportunities for the child to establish friendships and to interact with his peers. See the chapter that addresses socialization for additional suggestions.

Use Natural Consequences

If your child refuses to attend school because he doesn't feel well, tell him, *"The doctor said you can't watch TV, read or listen to the stereo because that will stimulate your brain and make you worse. All you can do is lie in bed in a quiet room."*

Don't punish the child for not going to school. But don't make it fun when he stays home. Restrict TV and other pleasurable activities.

Tell the child his job at this stage of his life is to go to school and do what he's supposed to do. Playtime, movies and having friends sleep over are privileges. If he doesn't fulfill his responsibilities, he won't have privileges. If he doesn't attend school, he won't be allowed privileges.

Get the class work and homework the child is supposed to complete that day and night. Have him complete it. Avoid using force or tying the child up and dragging him to school. This may be necessary at a later time. But initially set up consequences so you can get the child to choose to attend school.

Get Child To School

Try to get the child to school, even if he doesn't attend any classes. It's better if he's in school sitting in the principal's office or in the cafeteria than at home. The longer he stays at home, the more intense the fears and dependency become. Try to get him to school, even if it's for short periods.

Leave As Soon As Possible

If you take him to school, don't hang around or linger. The longer you stay, the more difficult the separation. Most teachers are aware of this problem and various methods of dealing with it. Speak with the teacher and develop a plan of attack. Leave as soon as possible—even if the child shows intense reactions.

Try To Get Father Involved

If the mother is primarily dealing with this situation, I often suggest the father get involved and take the child to school or deal with the separation at the home. Many times dependency is specifically related to the mother. The child often gives the father less difficulty.

Work On Gradual Change

The child's anxiety, worry, fear or lack of independent behavior may be too intense for him to handle a whole day of school. Many times we try to set up a situation where the child identifies the most preferred subject and have him attend school for that subject. In other situations, we might have him attend only the homeroom or first period. After he attends that period, he can call the parent to come get him. If he wants to stay, he can stay for another period.

School avoidance doesn't usually change overnight. Gradual change is what is sought. The first 50% of any behavior is the hardest to change. Concentrate your effort here.

If your child refuses to stay in school all day, every day, work on him staying for one period. When he is successful and feels comfortable with one class, make it two (usually in about a week or two). Then require three periods. Getting him to stay half the day is hardest. If you can get him to stay until lunch, the second half of the day is fairly easy.

Concentrate on small improvements and change rather than totally eliminating the school avoidance.

Use Positive Consequences, Incentives And Rewards

In the example used above, you may set up a reward system based on the child's school attendance. For every period he attends school during the week, he earns points. If he gets so many points, he may be able to go skating or have a friend sleep over.

Identify things that are important to your child, and use those as incentives. You may also want to use normal activities. If he and his father go fishing every Saturday, he might have to attend a certain amount of school to earn this privilege. If what you ask the child to do is very small (attend school for one period) and the incentive is important, you may get the child going to school. Once this process is started and the child is in school, even for short periods of time, the fear and worry start to diminish and need for dependency is decreased.

Many chapters in this book are indirectly related to the treatment of school avoidance. Review the chapters that pertain to your child's personality characteristics and behaviors for suggestions on how to deal with behaviors and situations that might contribute to a refusal to attend school.

CHAPTER 11

"My child does not pay attention and can't keep still," Attention Deficit Disorders

Although characteristics of this disorder have been described as early as the late 1930's it is currently being written about and seen as a reason for children's behavioral and school problems more frequently than ever. The over diagnosis of Attention Deficit Disorder (ADD) and Attention Deficit Hyperactivity Disorders (ADHD) is a major concern for many professionals who deal with children. It seems that half of the referrals to my office have concerns pertaining to ADD/ADHD. However, many are not "true" ADD/ADHD. I am not going to present as much information on this topic as I did in previous books because there is a wealth of information available. The interested reader can contact the Association for Children and Adults with Attention Deficit Hyperactivity Disorder (CHADD) at 8181 Professional Place. Suite 201, Landover, MD 20785 to get additional and accurate information regard this.

Characteristics Of ADD/ADHD

How active should a child be? How restless, distractible, talkative, impulsive, stubborn? What is normal overactive behavior? Generally, normal behavior is behavior that doesn't interfere with a child's ability to cope with his environment or get along with others. See the chapter on What Is Normal? to help determine if your child's behavior is within normal limits.

Symptoms Of ADD/ADHD

Although there are various causes of these behaviors and they appear in a variety of areas, the symptoms generally fall into three areas. It should be kept in mind that the child does not have to show all three of the characteristics. There could be one or two. In addition the behavior(s) do not have to be observed 100% of the time.

Activity Level

More than the average child in his or her age group, the child fidgets or squirms when he sits, is unable to consistently remain seated for a period of time, frequently goes from one thing to another, often runs when he should be walking, often cannot remain still when watching TV, gets out of his chair during meals, is described as busy, never stops talking, etc. Although not as frequent, some of these children are "hypoactive." That is, they show a decreased level of activity. They often are described as being in "slow motion." They talk slow, get dressed slow, ride their bike slow, etc.

Attention Span

When compared to other children the same age, the child appears distractible, has a short attention span, has difficulty following a series of directions, forgets easily, daydreams, has trouble concentrating, etc. Some children are also "over focus." That is, they will fixate on things and it will be hard to get their attention. A child may focus on his pencil in school and block out everything else that is going on in the classroom. They may over focus when watching TV and it will be hard to get his attention.

Impulsive Control

More than the average child in his or her age group, this child appears impulsive, acts before he thinks, does not weight consequences, his "mouth over loads his brain", etc. One young child told me, *"I'm trying not to talk, but my mouth keeps talking!"* indicating problems in impulsive control. *"I'm trying to be good, but I can't help it!"* is something else that is frequently said. In this area the child could also have a "short fuse" in the sense that he gets easily upset, irritated, mad and/or has a temper tantrum. The "short fuse" could also appear as a sensitive child whose feelings are easily hurt or who cries easily.

Characteristics Of ADD/ADHD

Below is a list of characteristics of these children. The majority of statements were obtained from parents and teachers. I divided the characteristics into six areas. Only a few or many of the characteristics may appear in a given child.

Motor behavior—Symptoms include:

1. High activity level
2. Unusual amount of energy
3. Excessive activity
4. Restless
5. In constant motion
6. Fidgeting
7. Inability to keep still
8. Goes from one thing to another
9. Never stops moving
10. Inability to sit still during meals, TV
11. Inability to keep his hands to himself
12. Over-talkativeness
13. Nervousness
14. Unable to sit still for any length of time
15. Clumsiness
16. Poor gross motor coordination
17. Poor fine motor coordination
18. Accident-prone

Attention and Concentration—Symptoms include:

1. Short attention span
2. Poor concentration
3. Daydreams

4. Easily distracted
5. Inattentiveness
6. Easily bored
7. Short interest span
8. Rushes from one activity to another
9. Inability to maintain attention
10. Frequently changes activities
11. Inability to listen to a story or take part in a table game for any length of time.

Impulse control—Symptoms include:

1. Acts before he thinks
2. Daredevil behavior
3. Low frustration tolerance
4. Poor planning and judgment
5. Flies off the handle easily
6. Inability to control himself
7. Temper outbursts
8. Acts without thinking
9. Gets upset easily
10. Poor foresight
11. Low boiling point
12. Poor organization

Emotions—Symptoms include1

1. Unpredictable
2. Moody
3. Poor emotional control
4. Feelings easily hurt
5. Impulsive, then remorseful
6. Cries easily
7. Fearless
8. Becomes overexcited and more active in stimulating situations
9. Has good and bad days
10. Difficulty in coping with environmental changes

11. Reckless
12. Uninhibited
13. Dr. Jekyll-Mr. Hyde personality
14. Can tell when he wakes up what kind of mood he's in and what kind of day he'll have
15. Poor self-concept

Relationships with others—Symptoms include:

1. Stubborn
2. Disobedient
3. Inability to accept correction
4. Hard to discipline
5. Defiant
6. Refusal to take "No" for an answer
7. Inability to listen
8. Resists controls by adult
9. Negative attitude
10. Sassy
11. Independent
12. Extroverted
13. Poor peer relationships
14. Often gets into fights
15. Bossy with children
16. Difficulty when playing with more than I or 2 children
17. Attempts to control peers
18. Overexcitable in normal play
19. Socially bold and aggressive
20. Easily led by peers

School—Symptoms include:
:
1. Gets out of seat
2. Speaks out of turn
3. Daydreams
4. Disturbs others
5. Makes disruptive noises

6. Sloppy
7. Disorganized
8. Messy
9. Forgetful
10. Inability to work well alone or in groups
11. Works best in 1-on-1 situation or when you stay on top of him
12. Can't stay in seat
13. Poor conduct
14. Failure to follow or confusion of directions
15. Academic trouble
16. Poor grades
17. Inability to keep mind on work
18. Doesn't complete task
19. Can't finish work in a reasonable amount of time
20. Can't stay on one task
21. Poor penmanship
22. Wastes time
23. Difficulty retaining information

Difficulties in these areas

Most ADD/ADHD children show some difficulty in all six areas. It's important to realize a child doesn't have to have characteristics in all or even many of the above areas to be called ADD/ADHD. It is not uncommon for a child to have more problems in one area than another.

All ADD/ADHD children do not have coordination problems. One ADD/ADHD child may be able to sit and remain in his desk all day but can't concentrate for more than 30 seconds at a time. Another child may have good concentration but constantly fidgets, squirms and can't remain in one place long enough to attend to the task. A child may be overactive and get along well with his peers. Each ADD/ADHD child is an individual who presents his own distinct picture. If you still have doubts or feel your child's activity level differs from the average, contact your child's doctor or a mental-health professional who primarily deals with children. They will be able to help and give you some information and answer your questions.

Causes Of Problems With Activity Level, Attention Span And Impulse Control

To say a child has ADD/ADHD implies that there is a "physical problem/chemical imbalance" and that he cannot control his behavior. The primary and best method of treatment for this disorder is medication. However, many children who show problems with activity level, attention span and/or impulsive control do NOT have a "physical problem or chemical imbalance" and the behaviors are due to other factors/causes. I am very conservative when it comes to medicine and children. I want to be very sure I rule all other factors before I consider medication. Some professionals do not do this and will diagnosis ADD/ADHD after a 15-minute interview with the child and parent. This is the reason this disorder is over-diagnosed.

Most children who present problems in activity level, attention span, and/or impulsive control do not show a clear-cut picture. That is, there are several factors that could be contributing to the child's behavior. The behavior could solely be due to environmental/personality factors, or due to a combination of behavioral factors and physical components. The behavioral components must be dealt with first before the extent of the physical components can be determined and the need for medication is recommended.

Let me use an example of two children in a classroom setting who look exactly the same to make the point. Both children do not complete their work, daydream, look out the window, get out of their desk, talk, blurt out answers, etc. The first child is looking out the window instead of looking and listening to the teacher because he can only focus on the teacher for 90 seconds and then he is distracted by something going on outside. He does not finish his work because he has enough control to focus on his work long enough to finish half of the work and then something else catches his interest. He blurts out answers to questions before raising his hand because the answer comes out his mouth before his hand gets above his shoulder. This child can't control or help himself and the behavior is related to physical factors. The second child is looking out the window because it is more fun looking at the birds and cars than to listen to the teacher. He does not finish his work because he perceives it as boring and something he does not want to do and "blows if off" or does half of it. This child blurts out answers because he wants to be the first one to answer or the center of attention. This child can control himself. He doesn't want to, hasn't learned to or is not in the proper environment to develop self-control or discipline.

Lets say we have a child who shows problems with activity level, attention span, and/or impulsive control. When we look at it some 20% of the problems are related to physical factors (the first child) and the remaining (80%) is related to environmental/ personality factors (the second child). If this child is started on medication before anything else is done, the medication will address only part of the problem and will not be effective. Usually in this case, the dosage of the medicine is then increased! This usually is also not effective. All other factors should be ruled out before medication is considered.

I have been a consultant for the Jefferson Parish Public School System for over 25 years. I provide supervision and consultation for some of the school psychologists employed there. A psychologist might tell me *"I observed Johnny in the classroom and he doesn't look like an ADD/ADHD child."* My response usually is *"I've been doing this a bunch of years and have written two books on this subject and I don't know what an ADD/ADHD child looks like. Could you tell me what they look like?"* There is no one test, checklist, observation, question, etc. that can be done to determine if a child is truly ADD/ADHD. The evaluation is usually over a period of time and involves providing the parents with effective methods to deal with their child's behavior, teacher consultation, family therapy or other interventions. This is done to determine how much of the behavior is within the child's control and how much is not. After a period of time a determination can be made. I could write about effective and ineffective evaluations for pages, but I won't. I will next briefly discuss some environmental and personality factors that will produce problems with activity level, attention span, and impulsive control that mimic ADD/ADHD.

Ineffective Behavior Management/Personality Characteristics

When ineffective or inconsistent management techniques are used by parents or there is inadequate discipline in the home, some children may develop problems with activity, attention and impulse control. Some children can avoid unpleasant duties and responsibilities or manipulate others to have most of their needs met.

Because of faulty management, other children "call the shots" at home. They have more control than their parents.

These children usually determine when they go to bed, if they take a bath, what time they come in from play, when and if they will do their homework.

Other children are "spoiled" because they get what they want. At home, they do not listen, appear moody, get upset easily, do not settle down when warned and show a number of the ADD/ADHD like behaviors.

Some children are stubborn, strong-willed and want to do what they want to do, when they want to do it. Management techniques that work well with most children do not work with these children. They have to be dealt with differently. If not managed correctly they may show problems with self-control/discipline, responsibility, and other behaviors that mimic ADD/ADHD.

The child who is overly dependent on the parent or the parent that does "too much" for the child (dress him, bathe him) may show a lack of independent work habits in the classroom. As long as you stay on top of him or "make him do it" he does fine. However, as soon as the teacher leaves his desk, he's counting the dots on the ceiling, playing with his pencil, etc.

The anxious, depressed, or worried child may have trouble concentrating in the classroom. The manipulative child who frequently "beats the system" does not develop internal control or responsibility.

Some problems with attention, activity and impulsive control are a result of the way the child is managed, an attitude he develops, patterns of behavior he has learned and/or personality characteristics. See the chapters that pertain to the above situations for more detailed information.

Environmental Factors

Some children need more consistency, external control, boundaries, structure and predictability in their environment than others. When this does not exist some problems with attention, activity and impulse control may develop. Some of the situations described above produce a lack of structure in the child's life. For example, if the child is in more control than the parents, there are no effective boundaries or limits on his behavior because he is "calling the shots."

A lack of parental supervision could also result in these behaviors. This could be the child who is unsupervised and allowed to "run the streets" or the parent is physically present but does not place limits on the child. Parents who have difficulty getting themselves in control or "getting their act together" will certainly have troubled placing structure in a child's life.

These behaviors will also be seen in chaotic environments where there is of violence, conflict, unpredictability, abuse, trauma, etc. Divorce, separation, remarriage, birth of a sibling, death and other environmental changes may also produce these behaviors.

ADD/ADHD

Without getting technical or using scientific terminology, I will briefly explain how problems in activity level, attention span and impulsive control relate to ADD/ADHD. As mentioned above behaviors that are associated with this disorder stem from a chemical imbalance or physical/neurological factors. The brain is comprised of "ON" and "OFF" switches. If I want to sit down for an hour, I turn off the "get up" switch and it stays off. The overactive child sits down for dinner and is told *"If you do not get out of your chair while we are eating more than twice, you can have your favorite dessert when we are finished eating."* He really wants the dessert so he turns off the "get up" switch but after a short period of time it turns on by itself and he is out of the chair. When he is reminded about the dessert, he turns it off again, but after a few minutes he is out of the chair again. This situation is repeated several times during dinner and he is very disappointed when he does not get the dessert.

A mother is washing clothes and tells her son to go get his dirty clothes in his bedroom and bring them to her. He turns on the "go get your clothes" switch and proceeds to his bedroom. On the way to the bedroom he sees a spider on the wall in the hall. The "go get your clothes" switch turns off and the "follow the spider" switch turns on and he is walking down the hall following the spider. After about ten minutes of his mother waiting for him, she calls for him, but there is no answer. She starts looking for him. Hearing water running in the bathroom she goes in there and finds him playing with the water in the sink and asks, *"What happen to the dirty clothes?"* He says, *"Oh, oh, I forgot."* And then runs and gets the dirty clothes. He was not defiant or refusing to do what she asked. He forgot. Not because he had a bad memory, he got sidetracked/distracted. Another switch turned on and the "get your clothes" switch turned off without his knowing.

Most children have a chemical in their brain that allows them to sit still, pay attention, think before they act, etc. These children do not. It would be like me telling you *"Stop your hair from growing and I will buy you a house, a car, a boat and a condominium in Florida."* I do not care how hard you try I am not going to spend a nickel because you physically cannot control that behavior. It is not that the child cannot control the behavior at all. It is that he cannot consistently control the behavior most of the time. This is why medication is the treatment of choice. It replaces what the child is lacking.

Behavioral concerns related to this disorder are usually identified early in the child's education, usually before fourth grade. Often as the child grows, the behavioral patterns change. The younger children show more activity problems and the teenagers show more impulse control problems. Both have attention difficulties. It used to be felt that most children will "outgrow" this by puberty. However, current research indicates that this disorder is often present till the late teens or early twenties. A small portion of these children will continue to have similar problems in their adult life and will require interventions.

Other Situations

In a number of situations, problems with activity, attention and/or impulse control exist with other conditions or disorders and are part of that condition and have to be treated differently (e.g., a different type of medication then is used with ADD/ADHD may be needed). In other situations, ADD/ADHD coexist with other disorders and can be treated as ADD/ADHD. A few examples follow.

Anxious or depressed children, those who worry or show obsessive-compulsive characteristics often have problems with attention. Early Bipolar Disorders are sometimes misdiagnosed as ADHD. Activity attention and impulsive control are often seen in children with depressed levels of intelligence, Tic Disorder, Tourette Syndrome, Asperger Disorder, Pervasive Developmental Disorder, Post-Traumatic Stress Disorder, and significant emotional problems.

Often the medication that is used with ADD/ADHD children is tried first in the above situations. If it works, it will be continued. If it does not, a different type of medication may be needed to improve the behaviors.

Mental Health Interventions

Individual therapy, family therapy, counseling, parental workshops and meetings, counseling for parents in effective techniques of child management, teacher consultation and providing interventions to the school are the primary methods to deal with the behavioral components of activity, attention and impulsive control problems. ADD/ADHD families could also benefit from some of the above interventions.

Parents must be involved in the counseling or psychotherapy. If I see a child one hour a week, his parents and teacher(s) have him the other 167 hours. If I can provide the parents and teachers with effective methods to deal with the child the rest of the week, the probability of success in changing the child's behavior greatly increases. In a sense, the parent and teacher becomes the child's "therapist." Be actively involved in your child's treatment.

Counseling and psychotherapy should be geared toward the parents because the parents are with the child more. If they have some specific techniques to deal with the child's behavior, change occurs faster. If the child's problem involves school, the teacher should become involved. Other significant caretakers (nursery school, aftercare program, grandparent, relatives) should become involved in the treatment plan.

Medication

Medication is the treatment of choice of ADD/ADHD, but most parents and professionals don't like to give medication before other things are tried. I agree. I usually set up a management system with parents to deal with behavior before considering using medication. If techniques are implemented and overactive behaviors continue, some of the specific techniques outlined above can be tried. If all the non-drug methods are used correctly and are unsuccessful, then it is appropriate to consider medication.

Use medication with one of the methods of treatment described above, specifically counseling for parents in effective techniques of child management. Different drugs are used to treat different types of overactivity. Medication, especially at first, should be used in conjunction with some type of mental health intervention, usually providing parents with effective techniques of child management, teacher consultation, and providing interventions for the school to implement in the classroom.

Stimulant medications, such as Ritalin, Ritalin-SR, Dexedrine, Cylert, Concerta and Adderall, are the drugs most often used to manage the behaviors associated with ADD/ADHD. Some medication works the opposite in children.

The above medications are stimulants. If you took them, they would make you overactive. But it "slows down" a hyperactive child. If you give a hyperactive child a tranquilizer or drug that would slow you down, it usually increases his activity level.

Medications used with these children are not tranquilizers.

The drugs are stimulants that activate certain parts of the brain or produce the chemicals that are lacking. By doing this, the child has more control. By having more control, he can sit, attend and concentrate for longer periods of times and think before he acts. If you take any child and give him one of the medications mentioned above, one of four things will happen.

Medication will "calm him down"

He will be less active and able to concentrate and attend to things for longer periods of time. He will be able to control himself better. Most symptoms will decrease, and he will show a positive improvement. If this occurs, you know he is ADD/ADHD and the dose is adequate.

Nothing happens

The child doesn't show any significant change. The child may be ADD/ADHD but is not receiving enough medication. The dose needs to be increased.

Child appears drowsy

The child acts as if he's tired and may fall asleep when watching TV or when he sits still. When this occurs, he probably is ADD/ADHD but receiving too much medication.

Child may become more active

If this occurs, the child is not ADD/ADHD. Discontinue the medication.

Child's dosage

Do not increase or decrease the dosage of your child's medication without consulting his doctor. If the second, third or fourth reaction occurs, contact your child's doctor. You can usually see one of the above results in 1 to 7 days after the child starts taking the medication.

Most physicians give the child the minimal amount of medication. The effects are observed. If there are no positive results, the amount of medication is increased. When you first give the child medication, keep in touch with his doctor. Most medication is given for school problems and is primarily given during the school hours. It is necessary to get reports from the child's teacher(s). Tell the teacher(s) when the child starts the medication. Ask them to report any behavioral changes immediately.

Parents' Questions About Medications

Most parents who give children medication for ADD/ADHD have many questions regarding the drugs and their effects. Some of the questions have been answered, but below are some typical questions asked by parents, along with brief answers.

Is there a risk of drug dependency in later years?

No. Years of clinical experience and research have failed to reveal an association between medical use of stimulants in the young child and later drug abuse.

What should I do if he has to take other medication for a sore throat, cold, allergy?

Consult your child's doctor. Some medications can be taken with other drugs; some cannot.

Will the child be "doped up"?

The child will not be "doped up." The medication seems to activate a part of the child's body and give him more control so he can sit longer. His concentration and span of attention increase and he should show more impulsive control.

If I give him medication to improve his school behavior and performance, do I have to give it to him on weekends, holidays and during the summer?

Ask his doctor. Some physicians require the child to take the medication all the time. Others suggest that the child be on the medication only when in school.

How long do the effects of the medication last?

For Ritalin and Dexedrine the effects usually "wear off" in three to four hours. For this reason, a child taking these drugs usually takes a dose in the morning and a dose at lunch. The entire school day is covered. If the child's overactive behavior is a concern at home, the child may also take another dose when he comes home from school. The effects of Cylert, Concerta, Ritalin-SR and Adderal are longer lasting, about 4 to 8-1/2 hours. A child on this medication usually receives one dose in the morning.

What is a minimal dose of medication?
This is different for different children and usually depends on the medication the child is taking.

Are there any side effects with these medications?
Loss of appetite and inability to fall asleep are the most common side effects. Most children become tolerant of these side effects within the first week or two of treatment.

Other side effects, which occur less frequently, include mild stomachaches and headaches, and increased "tension" behaviors including nail-biting, eye-blinking, sensitivity or moodiness. Tourette Syndrome has occurred in rare instances. When these occur, medication may have to be changed. If side effects continue, contact your child's doctor. These are short-term effects of the drugs. There is little research evidence of long-term risks of stimulant medication.

There are suggestions of a period of growth suppression. But over a long period of time, the loss of expected growth is made up. Information at present supports a delay in growth rather than a suppression of it.

When will I know if the medication is working?
Sometimes you can tell within a few hours after giving the child the medication. It may take a week to see the effects of Ritalin, Adderall and Dexedrine. Improvement may not be evident until the third or fourth week with Cylert and Ritalin-SR.

Does medication interfere with healthy psychological development or handicap the child emotionally?

No. Medication gives the child more control, reduces the negative attention he receives and enhances satisfactory psychological development.

Other Treatment Approaches

"Fads" to treat ADD/ADHD come and go because they lack the scientific data to back their claims that they are effective methods of treatment. When I first wrote a book pertaining to this in 1983, a diet and nutritional approach was the treatment of that time for ADD/ADHD. In that first book, a considerable amount of space was devoted to this. This book has been revised twice and the amount of space devoted to "other methods of treatment" has significantly decreased because of a lack of research evidence to support their claims. Since that time, a number of diets (e.g., removing sugar, avoiding food coloring and additives), relaxation and biofeedback training, food allergies, health foods, etc., have been proposed as causes or methods of treatment of ADD/ADHD. However, none have had research data to support their claims. Look on the Internet and you will find a variety of cures/treatments. However, be careful because the Internet does not tell you what is fact, fiction or a "rip off." Consult your child's pediatrician when considering alternative methods of treatment. He or she may provide additional information and advice.

While there seems to be some relationship between what a child eats and ADD/ADHD, research is limited.

Attempts are being made to gather additional data. A child's body chemistry as it combines with certain food is very individual thing. Adding or eliminating certain chemicals in one child's diet may work for him but not for another child. Some parents have told me a diet produced significant improvement in reducing their child's activity level. But it seems for every parent I've heard report positive results, a large number have told me diet didn't improve their child's behavior.

The fads come and go with numerous claims of success, but I haven't seen enough research or positive results from the people

I come in contact with to make me a firm believer. However, I do not like to see children on medication and usually try every other alternative before I recommend drugs.

When parents ask me, "What about other types of treatment?" I believe some of the approaches may be worth a try. Gather as much information as you can about any treatment approach before trying it or spending any money. Consult your child's doctor for further information and advice.

CHAPTER 12

"The Teacher Say's He's the Class Clown"

Many parents and teachers feel like the class clown is doing what he's doing because he does not get enough attention. While this may be true in some cases, most of the time this is incorrect. Some children who get too much attention look very similar to children who do not get enough attention. There are a number of explanations for the class clown's behavior and several factors must be considered when trying to change this behavior.

Causes And Cures
Attention
While this is the exception rather than the rule, some children want to be the center of attention because they do not get enough parental attention. The solution to this is fairly simple—increase parental or the amount of attention this child receives.

Children who are spoiled, children who entertain their parents, those who are in more control than their parents, and/or those who have few limits placed on their behavior often develop an attitude that the "world revolves around them." They are sometimes bossy, controlling and want to be the center of attention and they usually are. This behavior sometimes transfers to the classroom and the result is a class clown. Before changing this behavior in the classroom, it must be change at home.

Socialization Difficulties
This generally occurs in two situations. Some children lack age-appropriate socialization skills. They do not know "when to hold them and when to fold them." They don't discriminate between play and work situations. They don't know when "to

stop" or when "enough is enough." Because of a lack of social skills, they "don't know how to act" in certain situation. Therefore, inappropriate, unusual or weird behaviors are often seen in social situations. Sometimes these children attempt to be the class clown. These children are usually not readily accepted by their peers because of their socially inappropriate behavior.

The other situation occurs in the child who possesses appropriate social skills, but does not have many friends or does not feel that he "fits in" or is part of a peer group. These classroom behaviors are attempts to be accepted by the social group and/or to establish friendships.

In both of the above situations, the first attempt in changing this classroom behavior is to increase socialization experiences outside of school. This is done to help teach the child more appropriate ways of interacting with his peers and/or to develop friendships. Involvement in sports, clubs, scouts, karate, dancing, etc. will give the child an opportunity to meet other children his age. The activity itself (being on a baseball team) will give the child some additional opportunities to develop social skills. However, this can be significantly increased by inviting children to the house or to a fast food restaurant after practice. Opportunities to socialize can be created by inviting children from school to your house or an activity (going to a movie).

Getting a kid more involved with other children, by itself, will sometimes improve social skills. Some of the time it will not if that is all that is done. Let's say you have a child from school over to your house. The children go play in the back yard for a couple of hours. However, the whole time your child is playing he is acting silly or doing or saying inappropriate things. This will not increase age appropriate skills or establish friendships. Instead it will reinforce inappropriate behavior and the "friend" may not want to come back to your house.

Instead of just inviting a child over to play, we set up a "supervised socialization experience" in an attempt to change this behavior. Before the child comes to your house you would tell your child, *"You know how you act silly when Scott comes over."* Explain exactly what you mean by silly. *"Every time you act silly.*

I'm going to give you a warning. If you stop behaving that way, it will not be a warning. If you keep it up it is a warning. When it is time to bring Scott home and you do not have three warnings, we will stop at McDonald's on the way to Scott's house. " In this way, we create a situation to help the child change his behavior.

See the chapter that discusses making friends for more information.

Confidence Problems

It is said that many comedians are shy people who lack confidence. I don't know how true this statement is, but many class clowns have confidence problems. Therefore, the way to indirectly deal with this type of class clown is to strengthen confidence. See the chapter that discusses this for more details.

Establish A Home-School Communication System

Once attempts have been made to indirectly deal with the class clown's behavior, it can be directly dealt with by establishing a communication system with the teacher(s). You would talk to the teacher(s) and target a few behaviors that need to be changed. Then establish a home-school communication system. See the chapter that discusses this for more detailed information.

CHAPTER 13

"She Thinks She's an Adult," Lack of Respect for Authority

Some children are 5 years old and think they are 37. They feel equal to adults and do not respect authority. They either have an attitude or just don't listen or pay attention to what adults say. This is a big problem in our overall society and obviously often produces major problems in school. These are either angry kids, one's who have not learned to comply with authority, who have not had appropriate models, have impulse control problems and/or have strong willed personality characteristics.

Causes And Cures
Models
Children learn a great deal from modeling the behaviors of others. The way you handle conflicts and problems and deal with authority is apt to be imitated by your children. If you, the child's uncle, his best friend's dad or his favorite professional basketball player has no respect for authority, your child may show similar behavior. If a father has no respect for the child's mother, the child may go to school and show a similar disrespect for the female authority there.

The old saying, "Don't do as I do, do as I say," is ineffective in dealing with behavior. If your child is having problems in this area, first look at yourself and the child's immediate environment to see if these behaviors are being modeled there. If these behaviors exist, you must eliminate these before the child's behavior can be corrected. Models who show disrespect for authority can also be found in cartoons, movies or TV programs. Peer groups, "gangs" or singers that promote disrespect for authority also serve as models.

Parents who blame the teacher or school for their child's problems teach the child to question or disrespect authority. Parents who talk in front of the child about how incompetent the teacher is or those who "run interference" for their children teach a lack of respect. You must show a respect for authority in front of the child if he is to respect authority.

Spoiling, Kid's In Control

Spoiling is a troublesome word because most parents don't like to hear other people call their child spoiled. It's usually OK for a parent to say, "My child is spoiled." Most people define this child as one who has everything or gets anything he wants. They usually define spoiling in terms of material things. Parents buy the child a great deal. This may be true in some cases, but there is much more to spoiling than buying a child material things. A child could have every toy imaginable and not be spoiled, while a child with few material possessions could be very spoiled.

Spoiled children manipulate their parents to get what they want (staying up late, going outside to play after they have been told no). The child is in control. He has no respect for his parent's authority and often this lack of respect generalizes to other adult authority (teachers, principals, coaches).

A general description of the spoiled child is one who is more in control than the parents. Control may involve material things, but more often it includes a variety of behavioral activities. There is usually a lack of effective discipline or parental control. The child is allowed to do his own thing, get what he wants and has a great deal of control over his environment.

Parents must be in control. I'm not talking about control by force or a dictatorship. I mean control that involves setting rules and being consistent with consequences. I discuss this in great detail in the section on Methods and Techniques.

In order to develop respect for authority, the consequences of his behavior must be related to his actions and consistently enforced.

Whatever happens to a child should be related to his behavior.

A child goes shopping with you. You tell him, "If you're bad in the store, you won't get a candy." The child is bad and gets the candy. The child would have to be stupid to listen to the authority and this teaches a lack of respect for what adults say. The more a parent sets rules and consequences and consistently stick to them the more respect the child will have for authority.

Spoiled children and those who are in more control than their parents are usually irresponsible because they do what they want to do. A responsible person usually has a healthy respect for authority because they do what they are supposed to do. Therefore, an indirect way to help develop respect for authority is to teach them responsibility. See the chapter that discusses this.

Angry Children

Children with underlying anger often have trouble with authority figures. Authority says "black" and the child's initial response is "white." By reducing the anger in the child and/or getting him to express these feelings appropriately, cooperation with authority can be improved.

The child can handle these feelings in several ways.

1. Your child can express his feelings appropriately. "I don't like getting hollered at every time I get a bad grade."
2. He can keep his feelings to himself and say nothing.
3. He can express his disapproval indirectly through passive aggressive behaviors, such as stubbornness, sassiness, mumbling under his breath doing just the opposite of what he is told.
4. He can acknowledge his anger directly through physical actions, such as biting or attempting to hit the person whom he perceives as the source of anger.
5. He can displace his feelings to a less-threatening person or to an inanimate object. A teacher reprimands a child in the cafeteria. When she leaves, the child starts pushing one of his classmates. A child fails a test and breaks his pencil.

Some ways of dealing with anger get the child in trouble with authority, while others do not. The next sections discusses methods to reduce the build up of anger and getting the child to express these feelings more appropriately.

Stubborn, Strong Willed & Pleasure-Oriented Children

When I graduated from college, I was young, very idealistic and thought I knew everything. I believed the environment was the factor in determining and shaping behavior and personalities. Since then, I've aged, and I hope I've gotten wiser. I realize there's a lot I don't know. I've also developed a greater respect for the effects of heredity on personality characteristics.

Environment and the way you deal with your children can shape personalities and develop behaviors. Some children's personalities can be seen at a very young age. This is often true of the strong-willed, pleasure-oriented child. Even at a very young age, these kids think they are an adult and show minimal respect for authority.

These children are independent, stubborn and want to do it their way. They'll buck the system every chance they get. They want to do what they want, for as long they want, when they want.

A strong-willed, pleasure-oriented child is primarily concerned with satisfying his own needs and wishes. He's more concerned with the pleasure he derives from his behavior than any punishment. He may know he's not supposed to do something and will be punished if he does. But if it's fun, he'll do it and worry about punishment later. He starts doing what he pleases and disregards rules and responsibilities imposed by others. He is more concerned about what he wants to do than what he's supposed to do or what's going to happen if he doesn't do what he's supposed to do. Obviously, he often has significant problems with authority and in the school environment.

If you ask him to do something, no matter how difficult, and he wants to do it, it'll be done. If you ask him to do something, no matter how small, and he doesn't want to, it's like trying to run through a brick wall.

These children are usually very skilled manipulators or con artists. Their mission is to "get over" or "beat authority" and are quick to manipulate people and events to satisfy their own needs and wishes or to avoid unpleasant duties and responsibilities. The manipulation is pleasure-oriented because he wants something, but someone or something is preventing him from getting it. He knows what he has to do to get around what blocks him so his needs will be fulfilled.

Although these children can be polite, charming and affable when it is to their advantage, they often have problems with authority or those in a position of supervision or direction over them. They are often rebellious, stubborn, oppositional and resistant. People they give the most trouble to are usually their parents.

Dealing with the strong-willed child

Problems with authority are accentuated in this child because the methods of discipline and behavior change that work well with most children do not work with this child.

Punishment does not work well with this child as the main method of discipline because he usually does not have a fear of authority and will not behave to avoid bad things happening to him. He's more concerned with how much fun he is going to have, what's in it for him and what I want to do. Reward is a much better consequence for this child than punishment. He is more motivated by "hanging a carrot in front of him" than "standing behind him with a baseball bat." See the chapters that discuss reward and punishment.

These children need consequences. Talking, explaining, reasoning, lectures, etc do not work with the strong willed kid. For other children you can explain to them the need to do homework and they'll do it. You can explain the same thing to the strong willed child. He'll understand it, agree with you and tell you what he thinks you want to hear. Then what you told him goes in his right ear and out his left ear and he'll do what he wants to do. You are going to win the lottery before talking to this child changes his behavior! It's not what you say, it is what you do that will change the behavior. Rather than an explanation on the importance of homework it would be better to say, "If you finish your homework you can get on the computer. If not, no computer tonight." Big, long consequences do not work well with this child. A lot of little consequences are better than big ones.

The pleasure-oriented does not readily accept "No" as an answer. He's good at enticing authority into power struggles, screaming matches, contests and battles. Avoid this by all means. Deal with him in a very business like or matter of fact manner. See the chapter on Setting Rules for Behavior for more information.

Look at the school environment

Is some things going on at school or related to school that is making the child frustrated or angry? Is he being teased, isolated socially, struggling with school work, spending too much time on homework, constantly in trouble at school, etc.? If nothing can be identified, try to change it. See the sections that pertain to problems related to the above.

Models

Earlier in this chapter I talked about how models influence a child's behavior. Review that section for more information on dealing with this problem.

Avoid random discipline

This is disciplining after a rule is broken. From random disciplining, the child feels others are responsible for what has happened to him. Anger is apt to develop. To avoid the buildup of anger by random discipline, see the chapter on Setting Rules for Behavior.

Avoid excessive negative attention

This involves several concepts, but primarily centers on the use of negative consequences or punishment. Don't use punishment as the main method of control. Eliminate verbal punishment, such as yelling, putting a child down, name-calling and excessive criticism.

Use reward as a disciplinary tactic. Emphasize the child's successes, accomplishments, achievements and good behavior. Pay more attention to normal good behavior-when the child brushes his teeth after being told once and so on.

Being on a child's back most of the time may result in a buildup of anger and aggressive behavior.

Avoid power struggles

Avoid power struggles when possible. At times, it may be better to have the child experience some consequence of his behavior than to win the battle. Even if you win each battle, you may wind up losing the war. See the chapter that pertains to developing responsibility for more information.

Look for change and try to stabilize the environment

Children who experience environmental change, especially divorce, separation and remarriage, may develop underlying anger. The anger and resentment that results from the changes may be expressed in other ways.

Try to identify the changes and stabilize the environment.

Get the child to express his feelings through more appropriate methods.

Avoid excessive restriction

Some children are overprotected, excessively restricted and not allowed to be like other children their age. This develops feelings of anger. They want to do things that others do but are prevented from doing so. Sometimes you have to look at your child's peer group and age mates to decide what is too much restriction.

Communicate aggressive feelings

Encourage your children to express their negative feelings to you-what makes them angry, what we do they don't like and what do they disapprove of. Encourage them to express their sources of anger and their opinions. If a child expresses these emotions appropriately, don't view this as sassy or disrespectful. Your child asks for permission to visit a friend, but you say no. He tells you, "You never let me go to Jeff's. Every time I make plans with him I can't go."

If these feelings are expressed in a normal tone of voice and the child is actually trying to communicate the way he feels, listen and try to understand his emotions.

This is an appropriate expression of anger and should not be reprimanded or punished. Allow the child to complain, disagree or disapprove, provided he does not do so in a sarcastic, nasty manner. Allowing a child to yell, curse or be sassy isn't teaching him to communicate his emotions effectively.

Impulse Control Problems

Children with impulse control problem frequently act before they think. Their "mouth overloads their brain" and may often tell a teacher or principal what's on their mind and then realize what they said after they said it. See the chapter on Attention Deficit Disorders for more information on impulse control problems.

Teenage Behavior

Adolescence used to occur around 13, 14 or 15 years of age. Because of many factors, today we see the emergence of teenage behavior at 10 and 11, and sometimes even a little earlier.

Adolescents are looking for independence, an identity and to break away from their parent's "control." They know everything and the adult world is stupid. The emergence of normal teenage behavior brings with it defiance for and the questioning of authority. These children change significantly when it comes to cooperation and compliance when typical teenage behavior emerges. Ask a parent of a teenager or a teacher that teaches this age child.

For more information in this area I suggest that you get my book, Keys to Parenting Your Teenager, that is published by Barron's Educational Series.

CHAPTER 14

"They Tell Me He's Immature. What Does That Mean?"

Immaturity

Maybe you've noticed I seldom use the word immaturity. I avoid this word as much as possible because it means many things. There are several general areas of immaturity. According to the dictionary, "immature is defined as lacking complete growth or development. This can occur in a variety of different areas.

A parent may tell me, "My child is immature." Or "The teacher suggested he repeat a grade because he's immature." The first questions I ask are, "What did the teacher mean by immaturity? What exactly is the child doing that makes her feel he's immature?"

To change or deal with any behavior, it must be specified by stating it in detail not in general terms. Before it can be determined if a child would benefit from repeating a grade because he is immature, we have to know exactly what the problem is. Some immaturity is a "time based" and will get better in a year. Other immaturity is "learned" and will not get better with the passage of time. Other things need to be done. To modify any behavior, it must be defined in exact terms not in vague generalizations. There are some general areas where lags in development may occur. Let's look at some of these.

General Areas Of Immaturity
Physical Immaturity

This is a lag in the development of a physical skill. The child may be 7 but shows physical development in one area or several like a 3-year-old. This may occur in coordination (fine or gross) or in specific skills necessary for learning (ability to follow directions, processing information a child hears, processing information a child sees).

Some delays in physical areas may not significantly impact on a child's life. If a child is deficient in gross motor skills, he may not be able to hit a baseball or ride a 2-wheel bike very well. Other areas of physical immaturity, such as an inability to remember the sounds of words or follow verbal directions, may significantly affect the child's life. These deficits affect school performance. See the chapter that pertains to learning problems for more information.

Academic Immaturity

This relates to lags in the development of academic skills. Physical immaturity may have an impact in this area, and some of the above deficits may affect academic skills. A lag in fine motor coordination may interfere with the child's ability to copy from the board or complete required seatwork in the specified time.

Although the child is 8 years old, his hand-eye coordination may be like a 5-year-old's. It is like taking a kindergarten student and having him do the written work required of a second or third grader.

Another academic lag results from a poor foundation. You may have a child in fifth grade with reading skills only developed to a third-grade level. He has difficulty in school. This poor foundation could be a result of many factors, such as a lag in physical development of skills necessary for learning, absences from school, not doing required homework or class work or ineffective teaching. Regardless of the cause, the end result is the same-the child is below his grade placement in academic skills.

Deficits in intellectual function may also result in academic lags in development. If a child's level of intelligence is in the low average, slow learner or lower range, he may be behind in school, even though he's working to his capacity. A child may be in fifth grade and working up to his intellectual potential but is only achieving at a mid-third-grade level. See the chapter on Intelligence for more information.

Social Immaturity

Lags in this area result in an inability to get along with or interact with children in the same age group. The child may be able to relate very well with adults, older children or younger children, but has difficulty relating to his age mates. He does not know how to relate to his peers, or he uses inappropriate methods to interact.

A child who primarily plays with much younger children may develop immature methods of relating to and dealing with his age mates. Children who are overprotected, restricted or dependent may relate to others in an immature manner. An eighth-grader may show the social skills of a fifth grader.

There are many causes of social immaturity. See the chapter related to making friends for more detailed information and methods to improve the child's social interaction.

Emotional Immaturity

Lags involve emotional reaction to situations, frustrations and problem solving. A 10-year-old may become upset and cry whenever he is frustrated. The 5-year-old continues talking baby talk. A 12-year-old whines when she doesn't get her way. The child does not show the emotional development of his age-mates.

Emotional immaturity results in similar situations that produce social immaturity. A child who is babied, pampered, overprotected or dependent may show these behaviors. See the chapters that have information regarding this.

Behavioral Immaturity

The child shows behaviors that are not appropriate for his age. This may occur in several different areas.

Some children don't show the level of responsibility most of their age mates demonstrate. They may lose their belongings, not complete class work and have trouble cleaning their room. In general, they don't show as much self-discipline or internal control as they should. Review the chapter that discusses developing responsibility behaviors.

Other children don't show an appropriate attention span or activity level for their age. They may be easily distracted, can't keep their mind on what they're doing, fidget in their chair, not be able to sit still or show other lags in the areas of attention and ability to stay still. See the chapter on Attention-Deficit Disorder for further discussion.

Behavioral immaturity is also seen in children who lack independent behavior. They may need a significant amount of one-on-one attention to perform in school or to complete tasks. As long as the teacher is standing over them, they do the work. If independent work is required, the child usually doesn't complete the task. This behavior may also be seen when children have extreme attachments to their parents or have difficulties in making decisions or functioning independently. See the chapter relating to independent work habits for methods and techniques to improve this type of immaturity.

Children who are overprotected, pampered or babied may also show some behavioral immaturity. This may involve thumb-sucking, soiling, bed-wetting, daytime accidents or similar behaviors.

Many areas overlap. When someone describes your child as immature, have them specify exactly the behaviors the child exhibits that indicate a lack of development of age-appropriate skills. Before making any other decisions, you must know exactly what you are working with.

Some behaviors improve with time; others get worse. Others do not change. If immaturity is seen in the academic setting and there are concerns about having a child repeat a grade, then it's important to identify the type of immaturity he is showing. In some situations, repeating a grade will help; in others, it won't. See the chapter on "Should My Child Repeat the Grade?" for more information.

CHAPTER 15

"I'm Sick and Can't Go to School"

Some children have a variety of physical complaints or ailments on Sunday night or in the morning before it is time to go to school. Others get sick at school and request to come home. When a child voices recurring physical complaints or concerns, take him to a physician to see if there is a physical reason. If results are negative, the reason may have a psychological basis. Many bodily complaints, illnesses and pains don't have a physical basis. These include headaches, dizziness, stomachaches, nausea, muscle aches, sore throats, vomiting and stomach or chest pains. When complaints are seen that have no physical reason, they may have a psychological basis.

To say a child's headaches or chest pains are the result of psychological causes does not mean he is faking them or not experiencing pain. It means a physical reason doesn't exist. If you had a hard day and develop a headache as a result of the tension you experienced, you have a psychologically induced headache. This doesn't mean your head doesn't hurt or you're faking. It means a physical reason for your pain does not exist.

Children's physical complaints based on psychological tension fall into this category. When a child has a headache before school or a stomachache just before a big test, it's probably not the result of a conscious choice by the child.

Physical complaints with a psychological basis do not always show a pattern and cannot always be related to a specific event. They may occur in a random fashion or when they seem least likely to occur. A child who doesn't get headaches in school may complain about them while watching cartoons in the afternoon. Or the stomachache that occurs in school may also appear on weekends.

Some children show physical symptoms during a period of calm when the child is not under pressure. If you can't identify a specific physical pattern behind the child's complaints, they may be psychological in nature.

There are several reasons why physical complaints occur that have no basis in physical disorders.

CAUSES
Somatization

This refers to psychological conflicts or frustrations expressed through the body. Some children express their psychological conflicts by physical complaints; others do not.

Physical symptoms and pain may represent psychological frustration, anger or insecurity. This may result from ambiguous, fluid and changing environments, such as an inconsistent home situation, a divorce or separation when the child is torn between both parents, a situation where the parents don't agree on methods of dealing with the child or any unpredictable environment.

Children also release psychological problems through their bodies when they have built up anger, resentment and hostility toward others they can't express. These bottled-up emotions are expressed through the body. Frustration in particular is a major psychological cause of physical symptoms.

School is a very frustrating situation for children who are having academic or behavioral problems. The child who is failing school, not meeting parental expectations, may have to go to summer school, spends four hours each night on homework, etc. is under a great deal of pressure. Another child might be experiencing socialization problems at lunch time, getting his name on the board ten times a day, does not complete his class work, etc. and is frustrated because of this. These experiences may result in physical complaints in an attempt to avoid the negative situation.

Manipulation Or Avoidance

Some children use physical symptoms to avoid unpleasant

duties, responsibilities or situations. Some children fake pain to avoid school, tests or chores. Most physical complaints used as manipulation or avoidance result from unconscious processes.

The child doesn't plan to have the headache to avoid school. He really experiences pain and has not consciously decided to use an avoidance maneuver. Physical complaints usually occur while the child is at school. They are used to avoid stressful situations by returning home. The child escapes punishment and unpleasant responsibilities.

Attention

When children are sick, they usually receive a significant amount of positive attention. Parents tend to be easier on them, give them their way and wait on them.

Some children learn one way to get positive attention is to be sick. Physical symptoms occur because the child desires positive attention and affection.

Modeling

Some parents model physical complaints to their children. A mother frequently has headaches, a father uses physical complaints to avoid situations or grandparents emphasize physical problems. There's a strong probability that children exposed to these models will develop similar behavior.

Most of the time parents attribute this to heredity. But when children show physical symptoms similar to those of their parents, they result more frequently from a learning process than from heredity.

One-Trial Learning

Sometimes when a child is sick or has physical complaints, he may later develop similar symptoms. He learns there are considerable benefits from being sick. Consequently, symptoms appear again.

Faking

Although this doesn't occur as much as most parents think,

some children fake physical symptoms to gain advantages, as mentioned above. Keep in mind most children do not fake sickness. Their pains and aches are psychologically caused and unplanned. They experience the pain, but the symptoms don't have a physical basis.

Dealing With Physical Complaints

Stop physical symptoms from working to the child's advantage. If a child receives a significant amount of attention for headaches or avoids unpleasant duties or situations, physical complaints may continue. If they fail to provide secondary gain, they usually decrease. There are basically two ways to accomplish this.

Natural Consequences

This involves using natural consequence of a behavior to deal with the problem. If a child is sick, he must see a doctor. Most children dislike that.

A child frequently wants to come home from school because he has a headache or upset stomach. Tell him, "The doctor told me when you are sick, you have to stay in bed. You can't watch TV, play or read because that stimulates your brain and makes your headache worse. If you come home, you'll have to go to bed. What do you want to do?"

Your child feels ill in the morning and doesn't want to go to school. Tell her, "If you feel that bad and can't go to school, you also have to miss dance class this afternoon to stay home and rest."

By using natural consequences, you set up situations in which the advantages of being well outweigh the advantages of being sick. If the physical complaints have a psychological basis, they'll begin to diminish. Use this procedure for all causes of physical complaints described above.

A child was referred to me because she had been hospitalized twice for dehydration resulting from excessive vomiting. Medical test results were negative both times. When this child didn't get her way, she started gagging then vomited. Although several other methods were tried, the following procedure produced the best results.

One Sunday afternoon, her parents decided to take her and her brother to the movies. The children each wanted to see a different movie. When the parents decided to attend the show the brother selected, the little girl started vomiting. The parents treated it very matter-of-factly and gave the girl a towel. They told her to get in the car and take the towel. "If you feel you have to throw up, do it in the towel." On the way to the show, she gagged a few times but didn't throw up. After this was used a few times, the excessive vomiting was eliminated.

A teacher I worked with used a similar procedure to deal with a young child who vomited in the classroom. She told the child, "It's OK if you want to vomit in class. But if you must vomit, do it over there. Then wash your face, come back and clean it up." After this, the child vomited only once in the classroom. The behavior did not reappear.

Ignoring

By ignoring excessive physical complaints, you withdraw all attention from the behavior. If a child frequently complains of stomachaches, ignore them. Don't respond to his excessive complaints. Another way to ignore a child's excessive ills or pains is to remove parental attention but deal with the behavior.

A question frequently asked by parents is, "How do I know the child isn't really sick?" Most parents and teachers who deal with a child on a daily basis can tell when a child is sick because his mood changes, and he isn't as active or alert. He's not himself. Depend on your knowledge of the child's total behavior to determine the basis of his complaints. If he's sick, you'll know it.

Reduce Influence Of Models

When a significant person in the child's life (mother, father, grandparents) shows excessive concern and talks a lot about sickness or illness, there's a probability the child will model this behavior. Avoid discussions about physical problems in front of a child who shows excessive physical symptoms.

Provide Structured, Predictable, Consistent Environment

Some children who experience a changing, ambiguous or inconsistent environment develop physical symptoms. This often occurs in the case of a separation, conflict between parents or similar disruptive situations.

Use Rewards And Charts

When excessive physical concerns are seen in children, behavior charts and positive consequences can be used to correct the behavior.

I once worked with a 10-year-old who constantly said, "I think I'm going to throw up. I'm dizzy. My stomach hurts." This happened every 30 minutes at school and at home.

His mother set up a chart dividing the day into time periods of 30 minutes each. She told the child, "I'm going to set the timer on the stove. If you don't complain about being sick by the time the bell rings, I'll put a star on your chart. If you complain, I'll put an X on the chart."

The child liked to go hunting with his father, so stars on his chart were traded in for shotgun shells to be used on the weekend. As the child became involved with the chart, the time period was increased (he had to go 1 hour without complaining before he would receive a star, then 2 hours). After using the chart for about 5 weeks, the behavior significantly decreased.

Look For Areas Of Difficulty

If a child's physical complaints form a pattern, they may represent an attempt to avoid frustration, failure, difficulty or situations he feels he can't deal with. When this pattern occurs, look beyond the physical symptoms.

A child who gets sick in the morning or complains of illness on school days but not the weekend may be having trouble with schoolwork, his teacher or schoolmates. Another child may show physical complaints only on the days he has a Boy Scout meeting. Further investigation might reveal the child isn't getting along with the other children at the meeting, one of the kids may be teasing him or he can't do what is expected.

When physical complaints occur and an area of difficulty can be related to them, try to eliminate the source of discomfort or difficulty before dealing directly with the pain, illness and aches.

Counseling And Psychotherapy

When physical complaints are symptoms of an underlying psychological conflict, the above methods may not significantly reduce them. When this occurs, the child and family require professional intervention (individual or group therapy, counseling, family therapy). Consult your child's doctor for aid in identifying an appropriate mental-health professional.

CHAPTER 16

"It's a Hassle Getting My Child in Bed at Night so He'll be Ready for School the Next Day."

Just as getting up in the morning and ready for school can produce hassles in some families, going to bed at night can produce an equal number of problems. Many parents dread nightfall because a variety of behaviors that produce difficulties revolve around bedtime.

Your child just may refuse to go to bed "No, I want to watch TV, let me stay up longer" he may try to prolong going to bed. At bedtime he tells you, "Let me tell you what happen in school today." Because you want your child to feel like he can talk to you, you say "OK". Then he goes into a 30-minute discussion of every event that occurred in school that day.

Your child goes to bed readily but once in bed he comes out of his room twenty times. " I need a drink of water." "I forgot to kiss you." "I have to go to the bathroom, etc."

Your child may show fears or not want to sleep in her own room or bed. She may not be able to go to sleep unless someone lies with her. She may want to sleep with you. "I'm scared when I go to sleep by myself."

A child can display other behaviors to delay going to bed, to get him out of his room or you into his room many times before he actually falls asleep. Several things can be done to make this daily activity a lot easier and reduce problems.

Causes Of Bedtime Problems

Habit

The child has not established a habit of sleeping in his own room or by himself. Parents have allowed him to develop other nighttime routines, such as falling asleep while watching television or sleeping with them.

Manipulation

Some of the above behaviors are used to manipulate parents in order to stay up later.

Irresponsibility

Many children who buck their parents when it is time to go to bed often have trouble with many daily routines (coming in from playing, taking the bath). This behavior is just one of many non-compliant, irresponsible behaviors.

Child In Control

Children who are in control often show this type of behavior. They are more in control of the environment than you.

They don't want to sleep in their own beds. Being able to sleep elsewhere or to be able to stay up as late as they want is just one of several behaviors indicating parental lack of control.

Fears

Some children who have nighttime fears have problems going to bed.

Dependency

Children who have not developed overall independent behaviors and who rely heavily on their parents often have trouble at bedtime.

Environmental Change

Shifts in the environment may produce feelings of uncertainty, insecurity and dependency in children. Some children who have experienced a divorce, separation, death of a parent, continuous parental conflict or other changes may have difficulty going to bed.

School Problems

The child who is having academic, behavioral or social problems in school may show some problems with bedtime because when he wakes up he'll have to go to school.

Dealing With Bedtime Problems
Establish A Set Bedtime

A child who goes to bed at different hours every night is more likely to give you trouble than one who has a set bedtime. Perhaps you have a child who goes to bed at 7:30 some nights, 8:30 other nights, 10:00 on other nights. He is giving you trouble about going to bed. He's apt to give you less trouble if you specify a set time when he must be in bed every night.

What Time Should A Child Go To Bed?

There is not a set answer to this question because it varies for every child. How much sleep your child requires depends on his activity level during the day, his physical makeup and many other factors. You could consult your pediatrician or a child-development book. Try to get an idea of how many hours of sleep a child requires at certain ages.

It's probably best if a child goes to bed before you so you and your spouse have some time alone. Younger children should go to bed before older children. This can be part of the general seniority system set up in your household. You should be in more control of your child's bedtime than he is.

Have Child Sleep In His Own Bed

Many children sleep with their parents, siblings or on the sofa in the den rather than in their own bed. Some mental health professionals feel serious problems can arise from children sleeping with their parents. I don't think this behavior in and of itself-in most situations-is detrimental. However, I'd bet most children who sleep with their parents are in more control than their parents are.

I often view this behavior like many others a child shows. Refusal to take a bath, not coming home when told or other behaviors indicate the child does what he wants to do rather than what he's supposed to do. For these reasons, I feel the child should not sleep with his parents.

A child who sleeps with his brother or sister or is allowed to fall to sleep on the couch may develop habits that will be difficult to change later.

If the child is in more control than you, one method to deal with this bedtime problem is to try to establish control in many areas of the child's life-not just bedtime.

If you can get more cooperation from a child at mealtime, homework time, coming in from play and other routine activities, it is easier to get the cooperation required at bedtime.

In trying to change this specific behavior, look for gradual improvement. You're trying to get a child back in his own bed because he's sleeping with you every night. Set up a system so the child can select one night out of the week when he can sleep in his own bed. Let's say this is Friday night. Tell him if he wakes up in his bed Saturday morning and didn't come to your bed during the night, Dad will take him to eat breakfast at a fast-food restaurant.

You don't want to say, "If you sleep in your bed all week, we'll go fishing on Saturday." The odds of the child doing that are slim to none. Look for gradual improvements. If you can get the child sleeping in his own bed one night a week, then move to two nights, to three and so forth.

Keeping The Child In His Room

When some children are sent to bed, they come in and out of their bedroom several times. They forgot to tell you something, they have to get a drink or they have to go to the bathroom. With all this activity, they have difficulty going to bed. Another situation similar to this is the child who calls out for his parents to come in because he forgot to tell them something or has to be kissed good night.

In dealing with situations similar to these, tell the child he has 2 chances to come out of his room to get a drink of water and go to the bathroom. If he comes out of the room no more than twice, the next night he may be able to stay up a little bit past his bedtime. Or you could use some other reward that is important to him. If he comes out of his room 3 times or calls for you more than twice, he doesn't get the reward. Look for gradual change in this behavior.

Another situation is when your child wakes up during the night and comes to your bed. This may occur once, twice or several times during the night. When this occurs, return him to his bed. Establish a situation similar to the above. If he is coming into your bedroom 5 times at night, try to reduce it to 4, then 3 and 2.

A similar behavior occurs in a child who is put to bed but continues to play and doesn't stay quiet. He has trouble going to sleep. This occurs very frequently in overactive children. Usually, if you can get him to lie quietly, he will fall asleep readily. But the problem is he doesn't remain quiet. Tell the child, "I'm going to set the timer on the stove. If you can lay still and be quiet till the bell rings, I'll come in and read you a story."

Start setting a timer at a very low time interval-say 30 to 45 seconds. After a few times, gradually increase the time interval. As the child lies quietly for longer periods, he is apt to fall asleep.

Deal With Fear

If fear or other anxiety is associated with bedtime, you may need to deal with this first. See the chapter that discusses school phobia to get some ideas on how to handle fears.

Be Consistent

Say what you mean, mean what you say and follow through with what you tell the child. If the rule at your house is every night you come in our bed we'll put you back in your bed, it should be followed every time the behavior occurs. Be consistent with bedtime and consequences associated with the behavior. Don't let the child manipulate you and "beat the system."

Look For Gradual Change

Don't try to change the behavior all at once. If a child refuses to go to bed every night, it's ridiculous to say, "If you don't give me any trouble this week, you can have a friend come over to play Saturday."

Try to change the behavior gradually; the first 50% of the behavior is the most difficult to change. Once you get a child cooperating 2 or 3 nights of the week, the remainder is fairly easy to accomplish.

Don't Foster Dependency

This involves two general areas. One is having to lie with the child so he goes to sleep. The other pertains to the child who can only fall asleep in your bed then must be moved to his own bed.

Try to avoid developing rituals or other nighttime routines that foster dependency. Some children who show dependency tend to be overall dependent children. A child may be dependent for many other behaviors, such as dressing and bathing. Bedtime is just one of many behaviors. Try to establish independent behaviors in many areas of the child's life. See the chapter that discusses independent behavior for more information.

Use Positive Consequences

Try to stay away from using punishment, yelling, screaming or similar negative behaviors to deal with bedtime problems. Try to stay calm and set up rules and consequences ahead of time. Use positive consequences or incentives to deal with the problem. "People that go to bed in time get to stay up 15 minutes past their bedtime tomorrow"

Stabilize The Environment

Some children who have experienced significant changes in the environment show bedtime problems. More structure, predictability and consistency need to be established.

See If Problems Are Occurring In School

Try to determine if a behavioral, academic or social problem exists at school. If one exists, take the necessary steps to eliminate it.

CHAPTER 17

"My Child is Being Teased By the Other Students" Dealing With The Bully and Making Friends with Others

There is a saying, 'the only things in life you have to do are to pay taxes and die." For most, you could add, "getting along with people" to that list.

Dealing with others is a significant part of your life. The same is true for children. The child needs to learn how to appropriately relate to his peers and how to deal with other children who are aggravating or intimidating him. Problems in this area are related to two general situations. This first results from development of ineffective or inappropriate methods of problem solving or interacting with others. The second relates to a lack of socialization or lack of the development of the age-appropriate skills necessary to interact with peers. I'll discuss some of the causes and ways to deal with socialization difficulties.

Aggressiveness, Fighting, Name-Calling And Similar Behavior

Aggressiveness with other children may be seen in two general ways. The first is physical, such as hitting, pinching, pushing, shoving, biting. The second is verbal, such as name-calling, sarcasm, flip attitude, putting down others, cursing.

When I see children showing these behaviors, I look in several areas.

Models

Developing a behavior from seeing someone else acting that way is a powerful form of learning for children. If you use physical punishment (spankings) or threats ("I'll get my belt if you don't pick up your clothes"), you're teaching your child to become aggressive when people don't do what you want them to do. If you control your child because you are bigger and can intimidate and overpower him, the child is learning similar behaviors to deal with his peers. A sarcastic, hollering, screaming parent may develop similar behaviors in his child.

I've seen many children who call their mother names, have fits, punch holes in walls and become violent like their father. They didn't inherit these characteristics-they learned them!

If you want to eliminate certain behaviors in your child, be sure you don't model the same behaviors at home. The old saying, "Do as I say, not as I do" doesn't work. Children do as you do, not as you say.

If you tell your child to fight, to not let others pick on him and convey this method of problem solving, he is highly likely to show this behavior.

Other models children imitate may be found in their peer group, on television or in the movies. If your child belongs to a peer group where violence and a flip attitude are condoned, this may be the reason for the behavior.

If your child's play involves fighting, guns and aggressive behaviors, he may use this in other situations as a method of problem solving. Children who watch a lot of violent cartoons or movies and are somewhat obsessed with the characters may also develop this pattern.

Underlying Anger

Children with a significant amount of underlying anger may release this anger through aggressive behaviors with other children. This underlying anger may result from many factors. These may include parental conflict, school failure or frustration, changes in the environment, conflict at home.

Spoiling/Control Children

Spoiled children often develop problems because they are more in control than you. They may develop a very self-centered approach with their peers and want to control them. The bossy, domineering attitude that characterizes their play is often the primary reason for the difficulties they experience in relationships with other children. They need to be the leader, take control and tell everybody else what to do.

This behavior/attitude may be an attempt for the child to structure the environment. He wants to be in control and call the shots. "I'll pitch. Jeff, play first base. Jason, you catch. Preston, play outfield." This child is bossy; this usually upsets the other children. Friction, conflict, fighting and arguing usually occur. This is often followed by rejection from the other children.

Lack Of Age-Appropriate Social Skills

Some children have difficulty with others because they have not had the opportunity to develop appropriate skills. This occurs in several different situations.

Lack Of Experience

Some children don't know how to play with others because they haven't had the opportunity to learn. Although children are in school 6 to 7 hours a day, they only have about 30 to 40 minutes to socialize (before school, recess, lunch, after school). If the child goes to school, comes home and stays inside or there are no other children in the neighborhood, your child may not develop appropriate skills.

Playing With Younger And/Or Older Children

Children who don't play with children their own age may develop inappropriate skills. If the majority of their play involves children significantly different in age, problems may arise. If a 9-year-old primarily plays with 3- and 6-year-olds, he is probably dominating the play and learning these social skills and/or immature methods of interacting with others.

If a child plays with older children, he may develop passive patterns of interaction because he is being dominated. Or he may become aggressive because he needs these skills to compete with older children. A younger child interacting with older children may also be exposed to attitudes, conversations and behaviors he shouldn't be seeing or hearing. When he gets with children his own age, he may feel uncomfortable and out of place. Or the skills he learns may cause him to be rejected by his peers.

It's important for your child to play with children his own age. He'll be able to learn age-appropriate skills. A child with socialization difficulties may need more contact with children his age than he gets in school.

Adult Interaction

Children who spend a lot of time with adults or interact with them more than their age mates may not develop age appropriate socialization. These children are often 7 years old going on 23. They talk like adults, are concerned about adult things and worry about adult things. Because of the skills they develop, they often have trouble playing or interacting with children their age.

Overprotection

If you restrict, overprotect, pamper or baby your child, he may have trouble interacting with others. If a child stays in the house and isn't allowed to play with others, he won't develop interpersonal skills. If he isn't allowed to sleep at his friend's house, go to the movies or play, he may show lags in development of social skills. He can be described as immature.

If every time a friend asks you to do something, you have to make up an excuse because you know you can't do it, the friend stops asking. Look at your child's peer group, ask other mothers of similar-age children to get an idea of what is appropriate and inappropriate protection and restriction.

Dependency, Insecurity, Lack Of Confidence

Children who are highly dependent on their parents sometimes have difficulty separating from them. These children would often rather stay close to their parents at home than to play with other children. Some children also develop dependency on their siblings.

Dependent behavior, as well as other situations, leads to insecurity, a lack of independent behavior and a lack of confidence.

This makes it difficult for the child to assert himself, socialize, deal with unfamiliar situations and meet new friends.

More dependency develops and the child's negative view of himself strengthens. The dependent child's patterns of interaction are often described as immature.

Personality Types

Some personality characteristics by themselves may result in socialization difficulties. This is especially true with the shy, introverted, withdrawn child. The "man of few words" is usually in the background in most social situations, doesn't meet new people easily, has difficulty maintaining verbal interaction, doesn't initiate conversation and usually responds to questions with I- or 2-word answers. These children have trouble establishing and maintaining relationships.

Often I get a referral of a child like this. The mother or father says their son or daughter is exactly like they were as a child. Or their child's personality is very similar to their own present behavior (no friends, a loner, introverted).

The Manipulative Child

The manipulative child may have some difficulty maintaining close relationships because he often has a self-centered approach to his environment. He is more concerned about his needs, wishes and wants than the feelings of others.

Others have difficulty depending on or trusting a manipulative child. These children are extroverted, talkative and often very popular. But most of their relationships are very superficial. On first meeting this person, he is likable, and initial friendships are formed easily. However, once you become more familiar with him, you realize he is not dependable or trustworthy and is mainly concerned about himself. It's hard for others to maintain close, long-lasting relationships with an individual with these personality characteristics.

Genetic Factors

The environment affects and shapes some personality

characteristics, but genetic factors are heavy contributors to behavior. Sometimes you have to work around the basic characteristics and look for improvement but not change. The shy child may always be shy but not to the extent it interferes with his life or socialization.

Emotional Difficulties

Some children with significant emotional problems have difficulty relating to people. They maintain emotional distance from others and have difficulty establishing and maintaining relationships. Their behavior or attitude is often seen as unusual or weird, and other children tend to stay away from them.

Sibling Conflict

Most siblings argue, disagree and fight. To what extent it becomes a problem depends on how frequently it occurs and how it disrupts the family or household activities.

High Intelligence

Sometimes children with levels of intelligence very significantly above average have difficulties in socialization.

Dealing With Socialization Problems

Increase Socialization

The way you learn to deal with and relate to people is by being with them. The major way to deal with socialization problems is to have your child interact with other children who are his age and preferably the same sex. Minimize playing with siblings, younger or older children and time spent with adults or in solitary activities (in front of the TV or computer). You don't want to eliminate time with siblings, younger or older children and adults. Just be sure the majority-at least 51% of time in social interaction outside school is spent with children his age and the same sex.

Some children's interests are not the same as children their age, and this minimizes interaction. A 9-year-old boy may not like sports but is more interested in art, music or computers. Get the child involved in clubs, camps and activities that place him with children of similar interests. This way friendships may easily be formed because of common concerns and goals.

Have your child get the phone numbers of the children in his class, on his baseball team or in school clubs. Invite children to the house to play. Invite another child to come with you if you go to the zoo, to eat pizza or go fishing. Meet other parents in the class, karate class or scout troop. Have other children sleep at your house. Get your child more involved with children his age.

There are many types of socialization experiences:
1. Piano lessons, karate and classroom environment are situations in which other children are involved. But there is very little interaction between the children.
2. Baseball, soccer, gymnastics and dancing are activities where there is adult supervision and a directed activity. This allows for more interaction between the children.
3. Scouts, youth activities at church and 4-H are activities with adult supervision and direction. These enable more opportunity to interact.
4. Inviting children to the house for a few hours, taking a child and his friend to play miniature golf and having your child visit with other children are situations that allow for the most socialization experiences.

The socialization experiences toward the bottom of the list afford more opportunities for social interaction. Focus your energy on these activities.

Decrease Inappropriate Models
The other day the mother of a preschool child called me. He was hitting, punching and pushing in school. Her child had been doing fine since we'd started working with him. I asked her if anything had changed. She said no but mentioned he wouldn't listen that morning. His father pulled his hair, shook him and slapped him.

It drives me crazy when a parent tells me every time their child gets in fight at school they get a spanking. If I handle my anger by punching holes in the wall and my children start doing the same, they didn't inherit those qualities. They learned the behavior as a method of problem solving.

If you have an aggressive child, minimize control by force and intimidation. If your child hollers and screams at others or is flip, negative and sarcastic, don't use these methods to deal with him.

If you are shy, introverted and lack confidence, don't model these behaviors in front of your child. Try to increase appropriate methods of problem solving. Model effective behavior.

Create Social Situations

If you have a child who is aggressive, shy, doesn't share or fights, create situations to decrease behavior and promote more appropriate behaviors. When faced with a problem, most people reach into their bag of tricks and come out with a solution.

When the aggressive or withdrawn child reaches in his bag of tricks, he keeps coming out with the same solution or an inappropriate method of problem solving. Try to increase his bag of tricks and give him alternate techniques to deal with situations.

Suppose you have an aggressive child who fights, doesn't share and argues. Invite one of his classmates over to the house for a couple of hours to play. Before his friend comes over, tell the child, "You know how you and Clark fight and argue. Each time I see that kind of behavior starting, I'll give you a warning. If it stops, fine. If it doesn't, it'll be counted as a warning. If you don't have 3 warnings when it's time for Clark to go home, we can stop at the park and feed the ducks. If you have 3 or more warnings, we won't stop."

A child who cries as a method of problem solving has a child over after school on Friday. Tell him, "Wayne is coming over after school and staying until 6 o'clock. I'll break the afternoon into 6 parts-3:00 to 3:30, 3:30 to 4:00, 4:00 to 4:30, etc. and put it on a piece of paper. I'll put the paper on the refrigerator. Each period of time that passes that you don't cry or whine, I'll put a check. If you cry, I'll put an X. For every check you get, tonight we'll play 3 minutes of that game you like."

By using these techniques, you attempt to get the child to try other methods of problem solving and increase his bag of tricks.

Start With One Child

When trying to create social situations and getting your child to effectively interact with other children, start with one child. Sometimes problems occur or are more intense when the child plays with more than one playmate. Some children play fine with one child. When you add one, two or three, problems occur.

Reduce peer problems by restricting the number of children he plays with at one time. Allow him to play with only one child. Introduce other children gradually.

Limit Time He Plays

When you're trying to increase a child's socialization, limit the amount of time he plays with others. Rather than have a child initially come to the house for 4 to 6 hours, let the child come over for 1 hour after school. Or have the child come over 30 minutes to play before going to the movie or out for pizza.

Sometimes having your child play with another child for long periods of time may defeat the purpose. The interaction may start out positive and end up negative. He may be able to play fine with another child for 30 to 45 minutes, but after that, he has difficulties. If your child shows this pattern, or you try to establish friendships, limit play periods to the length of time he can handle. Two 45-minute play periods with a 30-minute break may produce significantly fewer problems than 90 minutes of play.

To determine how long a play period should be, look at the individual child and analyze his play. See if there's a pattern to the conflicts. As the child becomes successful in his interactions, increase the time spent with other children.

Import Children; Export Your Child

Some neighborhoods don't have children of the same age, or you may not want your child to play with the children who are his age. Bring children to your neighborhood, or export your child to other areas. In the past, the neighborhood school allowed the child to meet many children around his neighborhood. Today, schools may draw children from all areas of the city. Or the students attend the school because it's close to the parent's place of employment.

Get phone numbers of the children in your child's class. Involve him in clubs, sports and activities at playgrounds or schools in the neighborhood. Although the children who become involved in the activity may not be within walking distance from your house, they may live in the neighborhood. Make friends with the parents of children in your child's class and other children your child interacts with, such as the ball team or his karate class.

Reduce Interaction With "Undesirable" Children

You may not want your child to play or interact with some children. The best way to do this is not to restrict his play with a certain child, but try to increase his socialization with other children. If there is only one other child your son can play with and you tell him he can't play with that child, that's difficult to handle. However, if there are 10 children to play with, restricting play with one child is easier. Your child may be able to see more clearly the negative characteristics in the "undesirable" child as his socialization increases with other children.

Sometimes you have to restrict interaction, but generally try to build new relationships. Your child only has so much time to socialize. The more children involved, the less interaction he will have with one child.

Strengthen Self-Confidence

If the child's difficulty with other children seems to be related to a negative self-concept or a lack of confidence, take steps to build a more positive self-image and confidence. See the chapter relating to confidence more information.

Avoid Pampering And Spoiling

Children who fail to develop independent skills or who do not develop age-appropriate patterns of interaction may experience problems with other children.

Work Around Personality Characteristics

Some children seem to be born shy or with personality characteristics that may interfere with their ability to maintain and/or establish effective relationships with others. You may not be able to change the characteristics significantly, but they can be modified so they won't produce significant problems.

Treat Emotional Problems

If the child's peer problems are resulting from significant emotional problems, counseling may be the best way to deal with it.

Psychotherapy And Counseling

This treatment may be helpful for any children experiencing socialization problems. If you try the above methods and the child still has trouble, consider counseling. There are various types of therapy. Look for certain things when selecting a therapist or counselor.

Ask around. If you start hearing a name frequently and people say good things about the person, you may want to consider him or her. Ask the child's teacher or pediatrician. Call your local mental-health center and ask for a referral.

Dealing With Teasing And Bullying

Some children have difficulty with other children because they are victims of teasing, ridicule, and name calling and other verbal or physical assaults. Children that are picked on are usually the ones who do not have many friends, do nothing about the teasing, are shy, lack assertiveness and/or do and say strange or weird things.

For the children who says or does unusual things, we would try to modify these behaviors. Some of the suggestions in the section Methods and Techniques will give you some information on how to do this.

For the child who does not have many friends is usually alone on the playground, with the adults or playing with younger children or those of the opposite sex. These behaviors make them an easy target for teasing. For the children who do not have many friends, you should increase socialization with children roughly their age and of the same sex, especially children who attend their school. Previous sections of this chapter discuss ways to increase socialization. For the shy or dependent child or the one who lacks assertiveness we would try to build his confidence and change the behaviors that may be causing the problems. See chapters that pertain to this for more information.

For the child who does nothing when teased, etc we try to get him to go through a three-step procedure to deal with this situation, this is described below.

Try to Change Yourself

What is the child doing that contributes to the teasing? What can the child change in himself that might stop the name-calling? How is he responding to those who make him the target?

If he cries every time he's called a name, he might want to stop crying and make a joke of the teasing or come up with something funny. I saw a young girl who was teased because she was overweight. When called names, she got upset and ran after the child who called her a name.

One day she decided to respond to another child who called her elephant by saying, "Yes, I might get a job in a circus." After using this and several other lines, the kids stopped bugging her and went on to tease someone else. She stopped giving them what they wanted.

It's easier for me to change me than for me to change you. Sometimes by changing me, you will change. It is easier for your child to change himself than other children.

Look closely at how the child responds to other children. Give him alternate ways of responding that may produce the opposite reaction of what he is currently doing. He may have to ignore if he reacts, or he may have to react if he is ignoring. If the child makes several changes in himself and nothing has significantly changed, it is time to move to the next step.

Try To Change Others

The child could communicate his feelings to the other children.

206 The Parent's Guide To Solving School Problems

"I wish you would stop calling me names."

"It hurts my feelings when you do that. I wish you'd stop."

If this doesn't work, try to get the child to go tell someone in authority-his teacher, principal, the teacher on yard duty, counselor, baseball coach or some other appropriate person. By communicating the problem, the adult may be able to intervene and correct the situation.

If these techniques don't work, try this.

"If you call me another name, I'll knock your head off!" I'm no proponent of aggression, control by violence or fighting. But there comes a time when you may have to stand up for yourself, and this may involve a fight. However, this is the second-to-last thing I suggest-not the first.

Usually the child who is teased is basically a good kid in school and almost never gets in conflicts or fights. I usually suggest the child tell the principal, teacher or someone else, "I tried this, this and that. I've even asked you to help me with this, but nothing has helped. I told Chad this morning if he calls me another name, I'm going to punch him." The child may not win the fight, but the one doing the teasing may choose someone else to tease who'll give him less trouble. If this is tried without significant improvement, the last step is suggested.

Avoid The Situation

If every time a child goes to a particular part of the playground or neighborhood he gets teased, maybe he should stay away from that area. Escape or avoidance of the situation is a method of dealing with the problem if any of the other techniques have been tried. Sometimes a child develops such a reputation at school that he can't shake it. In these situations, a change of school might be warranted if all other methods fail.

CHAPTER 18

"He Won't Bring Home Notes, Books, Assignments and Tests"

Most children learn quickly if they don't write part of the assignment, they'll have to spend less time on their homework. They'll have more time to play. If they "forget" a book in school, they won't have to study that subject. If a test paper with a failing grade or a bad note from the teacher gets lost, they won't get yelled at or punished. If they lose or "forget" to show a detention until 2 minutes before school on Monday morning, they'll probably be able to play all weekend.

"Mom, a band of gypsies attacked me on the way home from school and took my science test. I don't remember what grade I received."

I often see children a day after they received their report cards. They have "forgotten" the grades they got. Many kids use these behaviors because they work. Other kids are disorganized, distractible and genuinely forgetful. Still other children have trouble in this area because they are irresponsible, lack self-discipline or can't function independently.

Causes

It Works
Many children continue to engage in these behaviors because they get away with it. It's more to their advantage not to bring home the required books than to bring them home. The child may see the situation as, "If I bring home my math book, I'll have

to do homework. It'll cut into my playtime. If I leave it at school, I'll have more time to play." The consequences of leaving the book at school are much better than those of remembering to bring it home.

The first thing to do in dealing with this type of behavior is you have to stop it from working. Don't let the child get away with it. Make the consequences of his behavior different. The consequences of showing you a math paper at night are better than showing you a math paper in the morning 2 minutes before the bus arrives to take him to school. See the chapter on Setting Rules for Behavior for more information.

Negative Attention Or Punishment Centers Around Schoolwork

If every time I sit down to do homework you yell at me or criticize me, I'm apt to forget what I had for homework or not bring the necessary books home. If I know a failing test gets me restricted for a month, I might lose it.

If your child frequently forgets, loses or doesn't bring home school-related work or materials, look at your method of discipline. If discipline primarily involves negative attention or restrictions, use other methods of discipline. See the chapters on Reward and Ignoring for additional types of disciplinary tactics.

Attention-Deficit Disorder Or Hyperactivity

Children with attention problems and/or increased levels of activity forget because of their inability to concentrate and their distractibility. They may have difficulty following directions and tend to be disorganized. See the chapter on this disorder for more information.

Dependent Children

These children have a great deal of trouble functioning independently and rely heavily on others for aid and guidance in problem solving, decision making and daily functioning. If your child has some difficulty in this area and shows these characteristics, try to develop an overall level of more independence and self-reliance in many areas of their life. See the chapter that discusses dependent children.

Lack Of Responsibility Or Self-Discipline

Children who are irresponsible in many areas of their life usually show the same behavior in their approach to school related activities and work. Try to develop an overall level of responsibility in these children. See the chapter that discusses this.

School Not Important

Adults realize the importance of education and how doing what you're supposed to do in school directly relates to this. Children don't have the same beliefs. Some children could care less about school and take school as seriously as you and I take Saturday-morning cartoons. They don't care if they receive an A or an F, 0% or 100%. They see school as something they must put up with until it's no longer necessary. For this child, try to develop other incentives to get him to perform the necessary task regarding school.

What Can You Do?

Assignments

A common statement made by some parents is, "The teacher says he's doing poorly because he isn't prepared for class and doesn't do all his homework. I don't know what he has to study or what he has for homework. When I ask him about it, he tells me he finished it at school or has completed everything he has to do."

To help a child do the required assignments, you must know what he has to do to see that it gets done. With some children, this is no problem. But with others, it's a daily mystery. There are several ways to deal with situation. Below are some suggestions.

An Assignment Book

Provide an assignment book. Have the child write down all the assignments as they are given by the teacher(s). At the end of the period or day, he brings the book to the teacher(s). The teacher writes a name or initials through the assignment. Be sure the teacher marks the assignment so the child can't erase or change what is required. If the child doesn't have any homework or assignment, he should write "no homework" and have the teacher also initial that.

Using this procedure, which requires only a few seconds of the teacher's time, the child is responsible for the entries and having the teacher sign it. This procedure provides exact information about the work to be done each night.

Often when I discuss this with a parent, he tells me he tried this method. The teacher agreed to be involved. However, the child forgot or didn't get the assignments signed by the teacher. I usually ask the parent, "What happened to the child when he didn't get the assignment signed?"

In most cases when the system didn't work, the parents did nothing. I then tell them, "The child would have to be stupid to bring it home signed because that would mean he'd have to do the work. By not getting it signed, he didn't have to do the work. The consequences of getting it signed were more to his disadvantage than to his advantage."

If you use this type of system, establish one consequence for getting the assignments signed and a different consequence for not getting it signed. You could establish appropriate rewards or negative consequences for bringing or not bringing home the assignment properly signed. On the days when the assignment is brought home signed, the child might earn extra play time or TV time. When he doesn't, the child does not earn the extra privilege. Or use negative consequences. When assignments are signed, the child can watch TV or play. If they aren't signed, he doesn't watch TV or play.

Home-School Communication System

This is similar to the system described in the chapter about communicating with teachers.   It can be established to monitor the child on a daily or weekly basis. By using this system, you can tell if the child is doing the required assignments.

Look At All Work

If a child tells you he completed a certain assignment in school but the teacher tells you he isn't doing the required assignments, establish a general rule. He must show you all completed work; nothing is to be left at school. If something is left in school, you must assume he didn't do it. This means he has to do it again at home. You must see all completed assignments for them to be considered completed.

School Programs

Some schools have programs established where children who do not complete the required assignments stay in at recess or after school to complete the required work. If your school has such a program, utilize it.

Teacher Sends Home Incomplete Work

In some situations, have the teacher send home on Friday all the work or assignments that weren't completed during the week. Establish a work time for the child on Saturday before he goes out to play or watch cartoons. The child learns he will have to do the assignment. He can do them when they are supposed to be done, or he can complete them when he should be playing.

Too Much Negative Attention

See if there is an excessive amount of negative attention centering around homework time. If there is, the child may be avoiding the homework to avoid the hassle or negative attention. Try to create a calm, positive atmosphere centering around homework. See the chapter on Homework for additional information.

Help Him Be Organized

If the child is disorganized, distractible, dependent and irresponsible, try to develop and improve these behaviors in other areas of his life.

Don't Assume Responsibility

Don't assume responsibility for getting the child's assignment. Don't go to school and copy the assignment off the board or have his older sister go in the classroom and copy it. Don't call a friend who has a child in class to find out the assignment. Have the child make the phone call and find out. Or have him go back to school to copy the assignment off the board.

Stop Behavior From Working

Establish consequences that are different for completing and bringing home assignments and other consequences for not doing these required tasks.

Tests And Notes

One school year I got a call from my oldest son's teacher. She told me he was doing poorly in math. It was a surprise to my wife and me. I asked the teacher, "How can that be? He's getting good grades on his tests." The teacher told me this wasn't true and he had failed about half of the math tests he had taken during the grading period. I hadn't seen them.

When I questioned my son, he said he had lost the tests or had put then in his desk and forgotten to tell us about them. We weren't seeing the bad test papers so we didn't know of his poor performance or that he needed help in certain areas.

Some children don't bring home notes from school, whether good or bad, or other communications from the school regarding PTA meetings, penny parties, skating events. Several procedures can be used to increase the probability you will see more of the tests and notes coming from school. Let's look at a few of these.

Reduce Negative Attention

Reduce the negative attention given to poor test grades or bad notes from school. Reward good performance and good notes rather than punishing poor grades and notes indicating misbehavior.

Use Behavior Charts

Set up a behavior chart, and put it on the refrigerator. The child can earn points for every test or note brought home from school. He will receive more points for A's than B's, etc., but he will receive points for all test papers, even a failed one. Points are given for all notes that come home from school. Notes indicating good behavior provide more points than those indicating misconduct or notes involving a general communication from the school regarding the penny party or early dismissal. Points the child earns can be used to receive a reward or other desired activity or thing.

School Policies

Some schools have a policy; they require children to have all test papers signed. Other schools have only failing grades signed. Still others do not require the parents to sign any test papers.

If your child is not bringing home tests and notes, talk with the teacher. Establish a system so you sign all your child's test papers or notes. You, the teacher and child are then aware of the fact every test must be signed by you and returned to school for the teacher to see it. It's best to set up different consequences for when the child brings the paper home to be signed and entirely different consequences if he does not bring the paper.

Celebrate Passing Grades

Make a big deal about all your child's passing grades. Post them on a bulletin board so everyone can see or on the front of the refrigerator. That way grandparents, relatives and friends can see them and make positive comments about the test grades.

Books

Some children don't bring home any books; others only bring home the books in subjects in which they don't have any homework. They forget to bring home the required material to complete the homework or assignment. Techniques similar to the ones discussed above can also be used in this area. Here are a few additional ideas.

Bring Home All Books

The child who forgets the appropriate books maybe required to bring home all of his books every day from school. Set up consequences for bringing home all his books. Other consequences can be set up for days he doesn't bring his books. After he does this for a while, you may allow him to bring home just the appropriate books.

Set up a situation where he can play or watch television when the appropriate books come home and he is not able to engage in the activity if he forgets a book. If he has trouble remembering again, have him bring home all his books.

Know His Schedule

If you know your child has a spelling test every Thursday or a science test on Friday, set up a situation where he receives a point every time he brings home the science book or spelling book. Points can be traded for a treat.

Extra Work

A child who doesn't bring home books may be given an option. On days he has homework and doesn't bring home the required book, you will give him work to do. The work will be twice as much as he would have to do if he brought the books home from school. If the child's homework is 10 math problems and he doesn't bring the book home, you might give him 20 problems to do.

Another Set Of Books

You might get another set of books from school. Tell the child if he brings the appropriate books home and does his homework, a consequence will happen. If he doesn't, you'll have a book handy. He still has to do his homework but an entirely different consequence will happen. Create a situation in which leaving his books in school does not allow him to get away with not doing the homework. Make it to his advantage to bring home the required materials.

CHAPTER 19

"Homework is a Nightmare"

Some parents are happy to have the summer end so the children are back in school. Others dread the end of summer because school means grades and homework. For them, school brings arguing, fighting and repeated attempts to have their child do his homework, study for a test and make adequate grades.

Getting children to do their homework is a never-ending battle for some parents. I have provided some suggestions to make this job a little easier. Some other chapters under the section on Methods and Techniques will give you additional tips.

Establish A Routine

Children who do homework after school on some days, after dinner on others or late at night at other times are more likely to give you trouble at homework time than children who do homework the same time each day. Establish a time each day when homework is done (after school, after dinner, before watching TV at night, 5 o'clock). Stick to it.

Try to establish a routine regarding how your child does his homework (have the child do his most difficult subjects first, study before doing the written work). The method depends on the individual child. What works with his sister may not work with him.

Establishing a routine may help your child learn to be organized. Discuss what needs to be done and ways to get it done. A calendar, list or visual of the routine may make sense out of jumbled assignments and may make them seem easier.

When Should Child Do Homework?

A question I am frequently asked is, "When should I have my child do his homework? As soon as he comes from school? Should I let him have a break to play first?"

There is no standard answer. Some children can go out to play then come in to do the required work. Other children who get excited and stimulated by play find it impossible to calm down and study effectively. The answer depends on your child. Use the method that works best with your child.

Some children complain strongly about doing homework after coming home from school if they can't play first. Tell your child, "You can go outside and play today before doing your homework. If you come in when I call and don't give me any problems about the homework, tomorrow you can play before you do the homework. If you give me trouble and I have to fight you to get the work done, tomorrow you'll do it first then go play."

Put the responsibility of when homework is done on the child. He decides when it will be done. If he goes out to play and then homework runs smoothly, he's telling you, "I can handle this. Let me go play first tomorrow." If he gives a lot of trouble, he's telling you, "I can't handle this. Make me do my homework before I go play."

For a child who attends after-school care or goes to grandma's house, try to get him to do his written work before you pick him up. Some grandparents and after-school-care programs have homework time set up. They work with the children to see some homework is completed. Other programs do not, and the child is on his own. If this is the case, it may be better to let your child play or watch TV and do homework later.

For others, you might want them to get some work done. For them, and children who go home and are on their own until a parent gets home, use something different. Identify an appropriate incentive and tell the child, "When I pick you up or come home from work, you receive a point for every written assignment completed correctly and neatly. For every point you get, you can stay up 10 minutes past your bedtime." Or "You have been wanting Chris to sleep over on Friday night. If you have 10 points by

Friday, he can sleep over."

For some children, it may be best to break up the homework period. They work 13 minutes before they go out to play and another 13 minutes before they get their snack. Other children may require three separate work periods. This procedure is good for children who have short attention spans.

Where Should Child Do Homework?

It depends on the child. Minimize distractions. Avoid watching TV or listening to the stereo while doing homework. Some children can do their homework at the kitchen table with others. Others do better when working alone or in their room. Try several different locations or situations. Use the one that works best for your child.

How Much Time Should Be Spent On Homework?

It depends on the school he attends and how much homework is given. Check with your child's teacher to get an estimate of how long the homework should take. Problems arise in this area when 20 minutes of homework takes 3 hours or the child comes home from school and does homework until it's time to go to bed. Several situations contribute to problems in this area. Let's look at some of these and methods to deal with them.

Some children spend 3-1/2 hours trying to get out of 13 minutes of homework. They try to avoid homework instead of doing it. Children may show this type of behavior in other areas of their life.

Some schools send home classwork to be done as homework if it isn't finished in school. If your child's homework takes many hours to complete because he didn't do his classwork, something needs to be done to get the class work completed in school. Set up a home-school communication system.

Attention Problems May Cause Child To Take Longer

Overactive children and/or those who have problems with attention and concentration may take a long time to do homework. They can't sit still or they don't have enough control for sustained attention. Make attempts to decrease the child's level of activity and increase his attention span. See the chapter on Attention Deficit Disorders for techniques to will help accomplish this.

Academic Problems

Children who have academic problems may require more time for homework. This occurs in several different situations. The school may be too different for the child. A child with average intellectual ability has difficulty in a school geared toward above average children. The low average child may have difficulty keeping up in an average school. A child who has a poor foundation, a learning disability or a specific developmental lag may also have to spend an excessive amount of time on homework.

In these cases, the school may have to make adjustments for the child (less homework, less written and more verbal homework, put him in lower-level class, place him in a reading lab or resource room). Or you may need to look for another school. See the appropriate chapters for more information.

Use A Timer

Use a timer or set a specific time when homework has to be finished. Identify an incentive, and estimate how long it will take to do the homework. Maybe you estimate 30 to 40 minutes. Set the timer on the stove for 60 minutes. Tell the child, "If you finish all your homework by the time the bell rings and it's neat, we can play your favorite game tonight. If not, we won't play."

Another method to use to reduce homework time on weekdays is to talk with your child's teacher. Tell her you're going to set a time limit for homework. After a certain period of time, you'll shut it down and not allow your child to do any more. The child will experience whatever consequences the teacher or school has set for no homework. Or the child has to do all the homework he didn't complete during the week on Saturday morning before he watches cartoons or goes out to play.

Your child seems to be putting forth an effort with homework and studying, and it still takes a long time and/or he has trouble grasping the material. It may be wise to have him evaluated to see if a learning problem exists or another school might be more appropriate.

A child who spends an excessive amount of time doing homework may feel like school is his whole life. He's involved with school the entire time he's awake. He can't maintain this pace for long-neither can you. He'll burn out, shut down and lose motivation. Do something quickly to change this situation!

Don't Foster Dependency

Try to develop independent homework behaviors. For some parents, homework means sitting with their child the entire time to get the homework done. If they're not physically close while their child works, nothing happens. Although it's good to help your children with homework, it isn't necessary for the child to become excessively dependent on you to do it.

If you develop this habit, you may have to continue indefinitely. You also run into a lot of trouble if you have two or more children who require this. Children dealt with this way may also show a lack of independent behavior in school. The teacher may say, "If I'm standing right over him or it's a one-on-one situation, he does fine. However, if I give him some independent work, he doesn't finish it."

In some instances, sitting with the child can serve as the reward. Your child has 10 math problems for homework. Usually you have to sit with him to get them done. Tell him, "I have something to do. Do the first 2 by yourself and I'll sit with you while you do the rest." After a week, require him to do 3 or 4 math problems before you sit with him. The amount of work can be increased every few days.

Many children who show dependent homework behavior lack independence in many areas of their life. Don't foster dependency in other areas. Require more independence. See the chapter related to this for additional suggestions, for additional suggestions. Another way dependency is developed around homework is when the child manipulates you. You provide the correct answers or do the work for the child. Don't do this!

Avoid Excessive Negative Attention

Some children try to put off homework because they receive negative attention at that time. Homework time for some children means their mother gets upset or they get hollered at, criticized or slapped. They try every trick they know to prevent this from happening.

Most parents become too emotional when helping their children with schoolwork. They get upset, frustrated and lose control. The learning situation becomes a negative experience for parents and children. This is the main reason parents don't make good tutors, even if they are teachers.

Although it's easier said than done, try to deal with homework in a calm, matter-of-fact way to reduce the amount of negative attention the child receives. Deal with the child and his various behaviors in a positive way.

Don't Force Child To Do Homework

If you have to battle the child every night or fight with him to do homework, negative attention builds up on this activity and behavior. If you have to tie the child in a chair and make him to do the work, you may get the homework finished each night. But nothing is done to develop any responsibility or self-discipline.

If this is the procedure you use, you'll have to do it every night-probably until the child finishes school. If you are more responsible for the child doing his homework than he is, you're in for trouble. Put the responsibility on the child. Set rules and consequences and enforce them consistently. See the chapter that discusses responsibility.

General Techniques To Deal With Homework

I have provided a few examples of how the concepts discussed in the section on Method and Techniques can be applied to homework.

Some Behavior Carries Its Own Consequences

"Go do your homework. It should take 30 minutes to do if you apply yourself. If you fool around, it'll take 3 hours. That means you'll have less play time."

"Your sister and I are going to Grandmother's house at 7 o'clock. If you finish your homework, you can come with us. If you aren't finished, you'll have to stay home with your father and finish it."

Do What I Want, Then You Can Do What You Want To Do

"You can't go outside and play until homework is done."

"You can watch TV when you complete your work."

"Homework must be done before you go to baseball practice."

Set Expectations Using A Consequence That Is Important To Him

"If you do your homework without complaining or giving me a fight, you can stay up past your bedtime. If you give me trouble, you'll go to bed at the same time."

"If you finish your homework by 7 o'clock 3 of the next 4 nights, on Saturday we'll get those handle grips you've been wanting. If you don't, we'll try again next week."

Work On Other Behaviors

Many children who show trouble with homework show similar behavior in other areas of their life. Try to develop other behaviors (independence, cooperation, responsibility, self discipline) to help produce more cooperation and less hassle at homework time.

CHAPTER 20

"It's a Problem Every Morning Getting Her Up and Ready for School"

Some children have problems during school, even before they go to school. The morning routine of getting up, ready and dressed for school produces headaches in some families. Hopefully, some of the information below will make the morning run smoother at your house.

Types of Problems
Getting Out Of Bed
This child appears to be in a comma when you try to wake him. He doesn't hear the alarm or hears it, turns it off and goes back to sleep. You frequently hear "five more minutes" and have to call him twelve more times. He may get out of bed and go back to sleep on the floor or the sofa in the den. It's a fight to get him out of bed in order to start getting ready for school.

Routines Are A Hassle
Once out of bed, the morning routines start-brush your teeth, comb you hair, get dressed, come sit at the kitchen table, get your books together so you can leave for school, etc. This child fights all the morning routines. He complains, whines, talks back and it is a battleground in the morning.

Routines Are Passively Resisted
This child also has trouble with the morning routines, but he is not "in your face" and openly resisting doing what he is told. He doesn't complain, etc. He doesn't listen and just does what he

wants to do. You tell him to go get dressed and he complies and goes to his room. Ten minutes later you check on him and he is playing with some trucks or watching cartoons on TV. You tell him to brush his teeth, comb his hair, etc. and you find him in the bathroom playing with the water and nothing has been done. Although he does not actively resist the parental request, he just "does his own thing" in the morning and getting ready for school is a problem.

Refuse To Go To School

For some children this problem starts at night, especially on Sunday night, when you hear, "I'm sick," "I don't feel good," etc. "I'm not going to be able to go to school tomorrow." Others show this in the morning before school. Still other children complain the whole time they are getting ready for school "I want to stay home," "I don't see whey I have to go to school five days and only be off two days," "School is stupid," "My baby brother does not have to go to school, why do I have to?" etc.

Other kids just flat out refuse to get dressed and ready for school. Say "I'm not going to school today" or show a great deal of anxiety, fear or nervousness when it is time to go to school.

Causes And Cures

No Set Routine

Children that go to bed at different times every night, stay up late or determine when they go to bed may have trouble getting up in the morning. This is especially true of older children. Kids should have a set bedtime. Establish a bedtime and consistently stick to it. See the chapter that discusses getting children to bed at night.

Lack Of Responsibility

Often times children that give trouble getting up and dress for school in the morning battle their parents on many daily routines (doing homework, cleaning their room, taking a bath). These kids want to do what they want to do rather than what they are supposed to do. They are generally irresponsible. Rather than only attacking the morning routine and trying to make the child cooperative and responsible at that time, you would want to develop overall responsibility with most routines. Getting ready for school in the morning would just be part of trying to make the child more responsible in general. See the chapter that discusses developing responsible behaviors.

Lack Of Independent Behavior

Dependent children have to have people standing over them and make them do what they are supposed to do. They want people to dress them, tie their shoes, etc. Therefore, they have trouble with the independent behavior that is required for a successful morning routine. Don't assume responsibility for this child by "making" him get dressed, etc. Try to develop more overall independent skills in many areas of his life, (homework, cleaning his room), including the morning routine. See the chapter that discusses independent behavior for more information.

Kids In Control

Children who are in more control than their parents usually have trouble complying with parental requests because they are the authority! This often involves most daily routines. If your child is "calling the shots" you need to get in control. .

School Problems Exist

For children who experience behavior, social or academic problems, school becomes a negative situation. Like most of us, children tend to avoid situations that produce negative. If your child is having difficulty reading, is being teased every day at lunch, having daily behaviors problems in the classroom, etc, he may not want to get up or dressed in the morning to go to this negative situation. Try to identify any problems so they can be corrected in order that school can become a more positive experience.

Attention Deficit Disorder

Children who have attention span problems or increased levels of activity are easily distracted, get side tracked, go from one thing to another, and/or have trouble finishing activities they start. You send your child to his room to get dressed. He goes with no problem, but as he starts to put on his socks he noticed a toy under the bed that he has not see in two weeks. He starts playing with the toy. Fifteen minutes later you go in his bedroom and he's got one sock on, his underwear on his head and has barely started getting dressed. See the chapter that discusses Attention Deficit Disorder.

School Phobia

It is not that these children do not want to go to school. They are afraid to go to school! More correctly, they are afraid to separate from their parent because of a lack of confidence in their ability to function independently. These children must be dealt with differently than the above children. Review the chapter that discusses techniques on how to deal with this child.

Use Consequences And Behavior Charts

Positive and negative consequences can be used to modify this behavior. "If you're dressed and ready for school by 8:00 we'll have time to stop and get a donut on the way to school." People who give me trouble in the morning getting ready for school will not be able to play video games after school."

Natural consequences can also be used, but they have to be important to the child. For some children you can say, "If you miss the bus, you will not go to school today" and this would be very upsetting. Another child would not get dressed in the morning until he's 18 and didn't have to go to school any more.

"If you miss the bus, I'll take you to school and you'll owe me a taxi fare of $5.50. You will pay me back the money by doing these ten chores. I will not give you any money for anything until you pay me my money back."

"I'm leaving for 8:00. People that are dress get in the car dressed. People that are not dressed will get in the car too at the time and get dressed on the way to school."

"Get dressed when you want. I'll take you to school when

you ready. You'll be tardy and have to deal with your teacher and principal." When using this consequence, be sure you tell the teacher what you are doing. Most schools assume that a child being tardy is the parent's fault. In addition, the school can set a consequence (detention, staying in at recess and doing the work that was missed) for being tardy. See the chapters on Setting Rules For Behavior, Reward And Punishment for more information on using consequences to deal with this behavior.

Behavior charts can also be used to improve the morning routines. The chapter on responsibility discusses the use of behavior charts.

CHAPTER 21

"My Child Has Low Self-Esteem," Confidence Problems

Some children's lack of confidence causes school difficulty. While for others, difficulty in school produces confidence problems. These children are also describe as having low self esteem, always feeling guilty, sensitive, tending to give up easily, having a feeling that other children are better than they are. These statements are reflective of a negative self-concept or a lack of confidence.

Development of a Poor Self-Concept

Self-image and self-concept refer to how you feel about yourself, what you think about yourself and how you see yourself when compared to others. When a negative self-image exists, the child sees himself as possessing more negative qualities than positive traits. Many other problems may also emerge as a result. This type of situation usually develops when more emphasis is placed on a child's faults, failures and misbehaviors than on his successes and accomplishments.

Suppose a circle represents your personality when you are born. Half is comprised of positive qualities-things you can do as well or better than other people. The other half is comprised of negative qualities or skills-things you can't do as well or things other people do better than you.

Let's say you can cook-that falls on the plus side. I can't cook very well, so in my circle this skill would fall on the minus side. However, I know something about refinishing furniture; that falls on the plus side of my circle. You don't know anything about furniture refinishing, so for you this skill is a minus. You could go on listing skills and abilities and placing them on the plus or minus sides of the circle.

Although you have many skills that are superior to mine, I have an equal number of abilities superior to yours. When we look at the overall comparison, we find you and I are basically the same in terms of our value, worth and competence. What makes us different is that we have different skills in different areas. The same situation exists for children.

When a situation exists where more emphasis is placed on negative traits than on positive ones, a negative self-image develops. This can happen under several conditions.

Attention To Misbehavior

A negative self-image may develop if more attention is paid to a child's misbehavior than to his appropriate actions. Suppose a child does 50 things in a day; 25 are good and 25 are bad. The child gets positive attention for 2 of the 25 good behaviors and negative emphasis on 24 of the 25 bad ones.

Good behavior is overlooked because it is expected. If the child is doing what he's supposed to, no one says anything. But if he does something wrong, you're quick to condemn. A child is supposed to make his bed. He does the job for 6 days but forgets to make it on day 7. When is attention given for bed making behavior? The day the child fails to make the bed.

Excessive Punishment

Excessive negative attention can also occur when a great deal of punishment is used on a child. Negative consequences tend to place emphasis on bad behavior and overlook good behavior. A child brings home a report card with 3 A's, 2 B's and 1 D. Most of the attention is for the poor grade, with little emphasis on the good grades. You tell a child if he gets a detention he'll be grounded for the weekend. The child gets a detention. When he comes home, he gets a lecture, is punished and receives a great deal of attention for the misbehavior. If he had not received a detention, he wouldn't have gotten punished. And he would not have received any attention for good behavior! Punishment places emphasis on "bad behavior."

Personality Characteristics

Children who have academic difficulties or certain personality characteristics receive more negative attention than others. Students who have trouble with schoolwork experience frustration, failure and emphasis on their negative traits more than children who have few academic problems. A child who is "hyperactive" must be corrected (don't touch that, keep still, be quiet, sit down) more frequently than a child without these behavioral traits. The strong-willed child doesn't listen as well as other children and has to be corrected more frequently.

Expectations Exceed Capacities

If expectations exceed capabilities, your child will fail more frequently than succeed. Some parents expect a 6-year-old to act like a 12-year-old. The child has average intelligence, and his best is represented by C work in school. But his parents expect A's and B's. When this happens, the child will fail to meet the expectations. If behavioral or performance expectations are set above the child's capabilities, he will fail and receive unnecessary negative attention.

The negative emphasis is due to direct attention to minus personality characteristics. Parents, teachers and peers don't have to accentuate the negative behavior for a poor self-concept or a lack of confidence to develop. It can be an indirect result of situations similar to those described below.

Overprotection

Suppose I have someone who works with me. Every time I'm asked a question, I turn to him for the answer. He tells me what to say, then I tell the person who asked the question what to do. This continues for several months. One day, the person on whom I have depended doesn't come to work. The phone rings, I answer it and I'm asked a question. What do I do now?

I would probably tell the person to call back because I'd feel

I couldn't handle the problem by myself.

Children who are dependent, overprotected, spoiled or rely heavily on others to do things for them are often faced with this same situation. Parents who sit with their children and "make them" do their homework, do their work for them, protect them from consequences, blame the school for their child's problems, etc often contribute to the child low self-esteem. They feel as if they can't handle problems. The I can't is accentuated, and the negative side of the personality is emphasized. A poor self-image and a lack of confidence may be apparent when this child is required to function apart from those on whom he has depended or those who have protected them or ran interference for them.

Significant Change

Situations that involve significant change (separation, move, change of school) and inconsistent, fluid environments put the child in a position where he doesn't know where he stands. These may indirectly produce an emphasis on negative personality characteristics. The child may feel insecure. He doesn't know if what exists today will exist tomorrow. He has no assurance things will remain the same. And he can't predict his environment. He feels as if he can't handle certain situations. A lack of confidence is apparent.

Regardless of the origin of the negative emphasis, when it happens, certain personality changes occur.There is a gradual change in how the child sees himself. The positive side of his personality decreases, with a corresponding increase on the negative side. He tends to view himself as made up of more faults, failures and mistakes than of successes, accomplishments and achievements. He sees his peers as more capable, effective and competent than he is. He generally lacks pride in himself and his accomplishments.

If you view this process as the action of a scale what you see happening is the child sees the negative side as a very large pile of rocks, while the positive side of the scale has very few. Once the scale tips off-balance (a negative image develops), something must be done to swing it back to where it should be-balanced (equal number of weak and strong points).

The Child's Attempt To Deal With A Poor Self-Concept

Everyone tries to keep their scales balanced. The first way a child with a poor self-image attempts to do this is to pile more rocks on the positive side. At first he will seek out situations that produce positive attention. This child tries hard to do good and gravitates toward things where he experiences success, gets pats on the back or feels a sense of accomplishment. If he's having trouble in school, he'll try harder. Let you go over his work on the way to school. Do extra studying and go to a tutor easily. He may also become involved in karate, baseball card collecting or any person, event or activity that produces positive attention. Often this approach to strengthening confidence produces good results.

However some times it does not. To get positive attention, a child may develop inappropriate or bad behavior, such as being the class clown, talking excessively or constantly demanding attention and approval from the teacher. Or he may get involved with a marginal or unacceptable peer group because he feels comfortable and equal with this negative group of children.

If the first attempt piling rocks on the positive side does not balance the scales, he will then try to avoid getting any more rocks on the negative side. He tries to avoid situations that may produce failure, frustration, criticism or mistakes-or any situation that accentuates his weak points.

The child may avoid competition or any win-lose situation. If he does compete, he is usually a poor loser because he can't bear to come in second. If the child with a poor self-image starts something that becomes difficult, he may give up easily. He would rather not try something than to try it and fail. He doesn't like new situations and avoids going places or doing things where he isn't sure of himself.

He won't try things where success is doubtful. This avoidance may involve lying. But the behavior is usually geared toward staying away from anything that may accentuate his inadequacies. You usually interpret this behavior as a lack of confidence. If every time a child sits down to do homework with his mother, it results in a screaming match. He'll avoid homework. If every time he tries to do math, he's frustrated and doesn't understand what he's supposed to do. He'll leave his math book in school or won't write down his math homework assignment. For this child, it is better for his confidence scale not to study for a test and fail it (in this situation, he's lazy, irresponsible) than to study hard for it and fail it (in this situation, he's inadequate).

If you punish, criticize, reprimand or do anything to stress a weak point, a child with a poor self-concept often reacts significantly. You may not mean anything serious by your comments, but it provokes a major reaction. A child is doing homework and you very calmly say, "Don't do it that way. Why not do it this way-it'll be easier." The child violently reacts to the suggestion.

A child raises his hand in class to answer a question, but the teacher calls on someone else. A child with a negative image may feel the teacher doesn't like him. Or you may bring home something today for the child with the poor self-concept and nothing for his brother. The next day, you bring home the same thing for his brother. On the second day, the child with the negative image complains, "You always get something for him and nothing for me. You like him better." The child looks for things in his environment that confirm the way he feels about himself.

How A Poor Self-Concept May Be Expressed

Behaviors described above result from a child trying to balance his scales or to overcome negative emphasis in his personality. The child may also adopt one or a combination of the behavioral styles described below. It's his way of dealing with a negative self-concept.

Accepting What He Feels Environment Is Saying

If the child feels he's trying his best, but it isn't good enough, the environment is unpredictable or he doesn't know how to perform properly. He may accept what he feels the environment seems to be telling him, "I'm trying my best, but I still don't know what's happening. I'm getting more negative attention. There must be something wrong with me. Maybe I'm useless, bad, worthless and inferior to others."

The same effect occurs if you are called stupid. You start thinking you are stupid and begin acting that way. If your faults are pointed out frequently enough, you begin thinking you have an excessive number of them.

Children who have accepted negative from the environment are often shy, somewhat withdrawn, timid and show an obvious lack of confidence. They tend to belittle themselves and may appear unhappy and dissatisfied.

Masking Inadequacies

Another way children deal with a negative self-image is by trying to mask their inadequacies and faults. They try to present a front showing only positive qualities. If I had a negative image and used this method to deal with it, I would communicate to others I am the greatest. I would say, "I have the best house. My children are never bad. I send them to the best school money can buy. I never make mistakes. I'm never wrong."

I wouldn't admit to any inadequacies. I'd present a front of total competence. What I'm actually telling you is I feel as if I have numerous faults. But I am not going to let you see any of them because if you see one, you'll know what a bad person I am and won't like me.

Children often respond like this when they have a negative self-image. They must have the best bike, electric train, shoes or bigger, more-expensive things than others. They don't admit to mistakes and don't accept responsibility for their own behavior.

Someone else is always at fault. They quickly blame others for their mistakes and always have a string of excuses to justify their behavior.

Pleasure-Oriented

A third way children deal with a poor self-image is to tune out the environment. They become more concerned with their needs and wishes than the wants, desires and rules of others.

If a child encounters a changing or unpredictable environment, he may feel he doesn't know what he has to do to be good or to get positive attention. If he is in an environment that places great attention on his mistakes, he may feel his best isn't good enough.

In both these situations, some children act as if they think, "I don't know what I have to do to get positive attention or to please other people, so the heck with them. But I know what pleases me and makes me happy. So I'm going to do that."

The pleasure-oriented child is primarily concerned with satisfying his own needs and wishes. He responds to the environment accordingly. He is more concerned with the pleasure he derives from his behavior than the punishment that may result. He may know he isn't supposed to do something and will be punished if he does. But if it's fun, he'll do it and worry about the punishment later.

If you ask him to do something and he wants to do it, it will be done. If you ask him to do something and he doesn't want to do it, it is ignored. It may seem as if this child acts before he thinks, but this isn't true. He behaves this way because he is more concerned with what he wants to do than with what will happen to him.

These children are quick to manipulate people and events to satisfy their own needs and wishes or to avoid unpleasant duties and responsibilities. The manipulation is pleasure-oriented because the child wants something that someone or something prevents him from getting. He knows what he has to do to get around what is blocking him so his needs will be fulfilled.

Although he can be polite, charming and affable when it's to his advantage, he usually has problems with authority or those in a position of supervision or direction. Children who are pleasure-oriented are often rebellious, stubborn, contrary and resistant.

In school, a variety of problems are often characterized by an inability to follow classroom procedure. This child does only what he wants to do in the classroom. The teacher may say, "Take out your reading book, and turn to page 33." The child doesn't feel like doing it, so he takes out some paper and starts drawing. He may also daydream, be inattentive or overactive. It seems this child has not developed any internal control, self-discipline or responsibility because he doesn't follow classroom procedure.

He does what he pleases when he pleases. This behavior pattern produces significant problems in school.

Changing A Poor Self-Image And Building Confidence

To eliminate a negative self-concept, to build confidence and to make the child feel better about himself, you must reverse the process that produced it. More attention must be given to the child's successes, accomplishments and positive personality characteristics than to his failures, mistakes and misbehaviors.

The plus side of the personality increases, with a corresponding decrease on the negative. The child's self-confidence improves. There are several ways to accomplish this process.

Using Reward

When I tell parents to take the emphasis off of what a child is doing wrong and place it on what he's doing right, they often misinterpret my recommendation as reluctance to discipline the child. To the contrary, this child needs a great deal of structure and discipline. But minimize negative consequences. Use reward as the primary means of providing structure. See the chapter on Reward for a detailed discussion of how this can be accomplished.

Attending To Everyday Positive Behaviors

Sometimes when I tell parents we want to strengthen the child's self-image and build his confidence by attending to his successes, I hear, "We already do that. When he brings home a good grade, hits a home run or wins the science fair, we praise him."

These parents are saying anytime something major happens, the child gets positive attention. How often do these things happen—once a week, twice a month, 3 times a year?

Major accomplishments happen infrequently. How many interactions do you have with your child daily? It could be 30, 100, 200 or 400. If most of these are negative, the positive events that happen once a week or twice a month aren't going to offset the negative buildup.

Although you want to attend to your child's major successes, you can accomplish more by paying attention to his daily good behavior because it occurs more frequently.

A major way to increase confidence and positive image is to acknowledge normal everyday behavior. Look for daily good behavior and praise the child when it occurs. It may be making his bed, helping you set the table, going to bed when told, picking up his toys, doing his homework or saying thank you. By looking at such behavior, you can increase the amount of positive attention the child receives each day. This will produce change.

Have Realistic Expectations

Behavioral and performance expectations should be in line with the child's capabilities so he can experience success, approval and other forms of positive attention. If you expect him to get A's and B's when he is capable only of C's or expect him to act like a 14-year-old when he's only 8, the child is certain to fail. He'll experience unnecessary negative attention.

Provide Structure And Consistency

Lack of confidence, uncertainty or poor self-image seen in some children may result from an inconsistent living situation or an environment in which significant change has occurred (separation, divorce, birth of a sibling). In these situations, try to provide a predictable, structured environment to make the child feel more secure and confident.

If the lack of confidence and poor self-image primarily results from the family's inconsistent, overprotective or spoiling approach to the child, see the chapters that pertains to these concerns.

These chapters provide suggestions on how to structure the environment to alleviate these problems.

CHAPTER 22

"My Preschool Child is Biting Others!"

Biting usually occurs in children under 4 or 5. Whether it's a concern and how it should be dealt with depends on the age it occurs and under what conditions. It is very common for 1 to 2-1/2-year-olds to bite because they are teething. After 2-1/2, conditions under which biting occurs should be explored.

The majority of children will "out grow" this behavior and the overall picture it is not that big of a deal. However, if you are a parent, teacher or school that has a child who bites, it is a major concern. Many years ago when everybody was not suing everybody, this is a behavior that preschools dealt with frequently. Today when lawsuits occur as frequently as days that end in "y", biting other children could be the basis of a lawsuit and often produces panic reactions in school administrators and owners. Aggressive behaviors, biting included, are the primary reasons why children are asked to leave preschool.

Causes
Method Of Problem Solving
If the young child gets along fairly well with others and seems happy but bites someone when he gets into a conflict or fight, it may not be of any concern. If the behavior occurs infrequently and it seems to be one method the child uses to solve problems, don't put a great deal of emphasis on this behavior. However, if it occurs frequently, it is much more of a concern.

If the child seems unhappy and/or bites others for no apparent reason, this may be of more concern.

Excessive Negative Attention

Some children bite if there is a significant amount of punishment, negative attention, correction, hollering and similar kinds of interaction in the home. There is too much negative discipline.

Lack Of Socialization

Some children who haven't had much opportunity to interact with other children may show this behavior when interacting with others.

Environmental Change

This behavior may occur when there has been some environmental change. It may involve significant change, such as a divorce, separation or a move to a new house. Or it may involve confusion, change and ambiguity resulting from less significant changes, such as parental conflict, different working hours of the parent, changes in routine.

Lack Of Emotional Closeness To Parent

Biting is sometimes seen when the child doesn't have enough quality time with you. This usually happens with the mother. The child doesn't spend enough time with you in fun activities, such as reading stories and playing together. Some conditions exist that prevent emotional closeness to the parent.

Child In More Control Than Parent

Biting of adults and/or children is often seen in children who are in more control than their parents. When they are not first, someone does or says something they don't like or generally when things do not go their way, they bite.

Dealing With Biting In Young Children

Don't Model The Behavior

If a child bites you, don't bite him back. This is an inappropriate way of trying to reduce the behavior. Don't model the behavior you are trying to eliminate in the child.

Avoid Being Bitten

In very young children, the best way to deal with the behavior is to avoid being bitten. Don't allow her to bite you or place yourself in situations where biting can occur.

Develop Socialization Experiences

Have the child interact with other children. Place her in situations where she is not alone or primarily involved with adults. Get her with children her own age.

Increase Quality Time With Child

Try to set aside some time in the day that result in quality interaction between your and your child. Play with him, read stories or go outside and get involved in some type of activity with him.

Be Consistent

Say what you mean, mean what you say. Don't tell him anything you can't or don't want to do. Follow through with everything you say you're going to do. Deal with the biting in the same way every time. You may remove him for a short period of time, place him in the corner, say, "No," or something similar, depending on the age of the child. Do the same thing each time.

Use Positive Consequences

Depending on the child's age, rewards for not biting could be used. Give praise and positive attention for interaction with age-mates or adults when biting is not observed.

Communicate With The Teacher

Establish a home-school communication system to deal with this behavior. See the chapter that discusses this. If the behavior occurs randomly (if the child seems to bite others for no reason or at any time), target the biting itself and try to change it directly. If the biting can be predicted (when a child wants a toy and he won't give it to him, when he's not first, when he doesn't get his way), you might want to target the behavior precedes the bite in an attempt to change the biting indirectly. For example, sharing, compliance with authority, taking turns, etc. and try to change it. If a child learns to share or cooperate with authority, the need to bite is reduced.

Take The Child Out Of Control

Children who are in more control than their parents often use biting as a method of problems solving. Often times this behavior is significantly reduced when the parents gain control and are "calling more of the shots" than the child.

CHAPTER 23

"Someone Has to Stand Over Him and Make Him Do His Work" Lack of Independent Skills

A lack of independent functioning effects children in school in two areas. In one situation, the child when required to functioning independently or apart from the person they depend on, shows significant nervousness, anxiety, worry and sometimes fear. They may show excessive crying, and/or panic attacks when it is time to leave the house or car to go to school or when they must remain alone at a birthday party. Often this child has trouble attending school and shows similar behaviors when it is time to separate from the parent. This was discussed in detail in the chapter on refusal to attend school. I will concentrate in this chapter on the other situation.

When some children are required to act independently they may look lost and act as if they don't know what to do. They lack independent skills and must have people near them to make them perform. If left alone doing homework, they daydream and/or are unable to complete tasks. In school, attention problems may be evident. The child is unable to do independent seatwork. If the teacher stands next to him or works with him on a one-on-one basis, performance is fine. At home, the only way the homework can be done is to sit next to the child or tie him in the chair and make him do the homework.

If independent behaviors are required, the child appears not to know where to start and seems confused about what to do. These children may seem passive, confused or lack age-appropriate behaviors. They may be unable to dress themselves, bathe themselves or do things on their own. They rely heavily on other people to do things they should be doing (getting their clothes ready for school, packing their books, reminding them to take their lunch money to school).

This type of dependent child usually doesn't show an emotional reaction when dependency is not available or they are required to function independently. They don't perform or complete the task. They may appear to be "space cadets."

Causes And Treatment
Genetic And Heredity

Some very-young children want to bathe and dress themselves. They resist you if you want to do things for them. Other children would let you dress them until they are 35 years old if you wanted to do it.

Some children seem to be born with the ability to get others to do things for them. They have a passive approach to the environment and allow others to do for them rather than do it themselves. They think, "Cutting my meat at dinner, wiping myself after I go to the toilet and dressing myself all require energy, effort and work. If I don't do it, someone else will do it for me-so why put forth the effort?"

If your child is like this, don't foster the dependency. Don't do things for him that he can do himself.

Attention Deficit Disorder

Children with attention span problems or increased levels of activity often show a lack of independent work habits and have trouble getting things done because then can't stay focus, are easily sidetracked and/or have difficulty staying still. This child may have enough control to stay focused on his math work to finish half of the twenty problems.

After ten problems he gets distracted and starts looking out the window, etc. You have to "stay on top" of him to get him to complete his work. See the chapter that discusses this disorder for more information on this child.

Learning Problems

The child with reading problems may lack independent skills

or not be able to follow directions when engaged in this activity. The child who is "behind" in school may also appear "lost" in the classroom because he does not understand the material.   The child with writing or perceptual motor problems has trouble with paper and pencil tasks. Writing is difficult. It takes a long time to write. They have trouble copying from the board, etc. Because of these factors they may have trouble working independently when you put a pencil in their hand.

A fourth grader is actively involved and participating in a teacher directed activity regarding the discovery of America. The teacher is asking, "Who discovered America?" "How many ships did he have?" "What were their names?" The child is paying 100% attention, raising his hand to answer questions, etc. However, when the teacher says "Write a paragraph about what you think would have happened if Columbus would not have discovered America," the child who was an active participant a few minutes ago starts playing with his pencil, counting the dots on the ceiling, looking out the window, etc., and does not complete the task.

The above child's problems and lack of ability to work independently occurs when he has to write. Children who have learning problems, are behind in school, do not understand the material, have trouble following directions, etc., also have similar problems. See the chapters related to specific academic problems and weaknesses for more information.

Overprotection
Overprotection may involve several different reactions to the child, such as pampering, spoiling, babying, excessive attention and restrictions. Overprotection occurs in three general situations.

Doing Things For Him That He Can Do For Himself
Doing his homework, dressing him, giving him a bath, talking for him when others ask him a question, feeding him. I've even seen situations where a parent of a 7-year-old wiped his behind every time he went to the bathroom. If this occurs, imagine in how many other situations this parent did things for the child.

Get a book on child development to see at what ages your child is capable of performing certain tasks, such as tying his shoes or caring for himself at the toilet.

Children of parents who react like this are usually seen by the other kids at school as "mama's baby, a sissy, a weinie, a nerd."

Dealing with your child this way doesn't allow him to develop independent behaviors. It will also interfere with his peer relationships. Many times children in this category also sleep with their parents and are treated as if they are much younger than their actual age.

Protecting The Child From Consequences

Some parents run interference for their children and don't allow them to experience the consequences of their behavior. This occurs in several different situations.

The child who forgets his lunch money at school or his books at home has a parent who brings the book or money to school. The child who waits until the last minute to do a book report has a parent who will do it for him.

I have seen children who have been in six schools by third grade. The reason they have changed schools is because they had a poor teacher, an ineffective teacher, a teacher who screamed and hollered, a crazy principal, etc. This parent makes excuses for the child; the child is never wrong. It's always someone else's fault.

These parents have difficulty accepting problems or deviations in their child's behaviors and continually find excuses to project blame elsewhere.

Your child needs to experience the consequences of his behavior to develop independent behavior, responsibility and adapt and adjust to adulthood. It could be natural consequences, such as not eating if he forgets his lunch money or not being able to do homework if he forgets a book in school.

Or it could be other types of consequences.

"The mornings you are dressed and ready for school without my help, we'll stop and get you a donut on the way to school. If I have to help you, we won't stop and get a donut."

Doing things for a child who should be doing for himself, not finding fault in your child and projecting blame to others, and protecting him from experiencing the consequences of his behavior result in problems.

Restrictions From Normal Activities

Some parents won't buy their child a bike because he may fall down and hurt himself. They won't let the child play in front of the house or go to a neighbor's house without the parent being there because he may be kidnapped. This may also include a restriction from activities, clubs or sports other children are involved in.

These children spend a lot of time in their home away from other children. Independent skills are not developed. There is a high probability they will become excessively dependent on the parents, and age appropriate social skills will not develop.

Get an idea of what children in your neighborhood are doing. What is acceptable behavior and restrictions for children your child's age? Allow your child to do the normal things most children do. Get him involved with other children. Let him be a child.

Mother Is Too Close To Child

This usually occurs when the mother shows an excessive or abnormal attachment to the child. Her life revolves around the child. This usually occurs in three general situations.

Parental Conflict Or Absent Father

In some situations where there is parental conflict and the mother and father do not get along, the mother may center her life around the child. Everything is done with the child. In some situations, the mother becomes the child's playmate. This also happens in first-born children when the mother doesn't work and a great deal of time is spent with the child.

In most separations and divorces or in single parent households, the child spends more time with the mother than the father. In other situations, the father isn't home because of work or involvement in other activities. In these situations, the mother is the one who tends to do things with and for the child.

Dependency may develop in these areas. In addition, the child may lack male models.

Get the child involved in activities with other children. Suggest the father spend more time with the child. If the father isn't present, another male role model should become involved. Try to promote more independent behavior. Don't become the child's playmate. Emotional closeness to your child is something that is very positive, but you can go overboard. Don't promote dependency by having your child's life primarily revolve around interaction with you.

Symbiotic Relationship With Mother

The mother bonds with the child in a very close relationship. She gets a tremendous amount of satisfaction from the child being dependent on her. The mother becomes the child; anything that happens to the child indirectly affects the parent. It's almost as if the child and parent are one person and cannot be separated. This abnormal relationship usually results from some emotional problems on the parent's part. If this is the case, counseling for the parent is certainly recommended.

Parent(s) Believes Child Has A Problem

This could be a physical, social or other related problem. A dependency develops because the parent must help the child or run interference for him.

Emotional closeness to your child is a positive part of parenting. But if it goes overboard, problems are certain to occur.

Lack Of Confidence

Children who have a negative self-image tend to see others as more capable and competent. Sometimes a lack of confidence will make the child avoid situations where he may fail. If he's not absolutely sure on how to do a math problem or the answer to a question on his science homework, he won't attempt it or wait for someone to give him assistance. This child may have trouble functioning independently. Dependency on others becomes a safer situation.

To alleviate dependency, try to strengthen your child's confidence and help him to develop a positive self-image. See the chapter that discusses confidence for more information.

Punishment Or Negative Attention Are Primary Discipline Methods

The major method of control of the child is through fear. Some children are hesitant to function independently for fear mistakes may be made and discipline will follow: The less I do, the less chance I take.

The probabilities of failure and negative attention are minimized. See the chapter on Reward and Punishment for additional information.

Communicate With Your Child's Teacher

If your child's lacks independent work habits in the class room set up a home-school communication to reward complete work, paying attention or whatever independent skills the teacher feels need to be improved. See the chapter related to this.

Work On Overall Independent And Responsible Behavior

Usually the child who you have to stand over to do his homework is the same child you have to fight to get him to clean his room, pick up his toys, take a bath, etc. You have to "make" him do a lot of things, just not schoolwork. Also work on these other behaviors. See the chapter pertaining to responsibility for more information.

PART VIII

ACADEMIC CONCERNS

CHAPTER 24

"Am I Expecting Too Much," Grades

For some parents, high grades in school are a must. Others just hope their child receives passing grades. Parents make some mistakes about grades and school performance.

Consider Intellectual Ability

Some parents expect too much from their child in terms of grades. About 50% of all children have average intellectual ability. Their learning potential is in the average range. For half the children in the United States, doing their best means C-level work. However, many parents view a C as an unacceptable grade and demand A's and B's. If you took 100 children and placed them in a room, you'd find 50 of them have average intellectual potential, 25 are above-average and 25 are below average.

Suppose you have no idea of a child's intelligence. If you assume he's average, you have a 75% chance of not overestimating his ability. However, if you expect above-average intellectual ability, you have a 25% chance of not overestimating his ability. If you were a betting person, you'd have a better chance to win if you expected average work than above-average work.

But most parents expect and sometimes demand above average school performance from their children. They don't accept C-level work.

There's nothing wrong with being average. If C-level work was unacceptable, schools wouldn't have grading systems that indicated above-average, average and below-average work.

See the chapter on Intelligence for more information regarding this.

Same Performance

Another mistake some parents make is to expect the same performance all the time. Everybody has trouble learning something and makes a mistake. No one is perfect. A ninth grader was expected to get straight A's on her final report card to go on a summer trip. She didn't and wasn't able to go. She told me she had some trouble understanding algebra and didn't do well in that subject. Her inadequate report card showed all A's and a B in algebra!

Allow your child some margin for error. Look at the child's overall performance. He may like a particular subject and get an A or a B but get a D in another subject. The remaining grades are all C's. Rather than place a lot of negative emphasis on the D, look at the child's overall average performance.

There are some periods in a child's life when his grades may drop. In the lower grades (first and second grade), it isn't that hard for an average child to overachieve and receive all A's or mostly A's and a few B's. As the child progresses in school it may be more difficult to overachieve and the A-B student may become a C student around third or fourth grade. His decrease in grades may not reflect a problem. It may show it is more difficult for this child to overachieve. Grades now reflect his average ability.

In preadolescence or adolescence, grades may also show decline. The 8-, 9- or 10-year-old may have a 3-pound bag with 3 pounds of activities to put in it. The seventh, eighth or ninth grader still has the same 3-pound bag, but now he has 23 pounds of activities to put in it. At this age, important things are talking on the phone, the opposite sex, going out, looking good and going to football games. You can only put so much in a 3-pound bag. Grades and schoolwork are usually placed on the bottom of the list of important things to do. Grades may decline.

Don't Make Time Period Too Long

Another general mistake some parents make is trying to improve their child's grades over too long a period of time. Most schools have grading periods of 6 or 9 weeks. Often disciplinary measures are put into effect until the next report card. For most children, this is too long, and several problems are apt to arise.

Let's say you have a child who failed two subjects because he wasn't prepared for tests and didn't turn in the required work. You tell him, "You have to spend 2 hours in your room each day doing homework and studying. You won't be allowed to go outside and play until your grades improve."

If this means till the next report card or 4-1/2 weeks until progress reports are issued, several things may occur. This child will probably go sit in his room each day and daydream, draw, play with something, count the dots on the ceiling or do anything but study.

Secondly, when long punishment is used to improve grades, one of two typical patterns results. Some children work very hard in the beginning and keep at it for about 2 or 3 weeks. But because there is no immediate reward, they give up, go back to their old ways and grades don't improve. Other children play around during most of the punishment period and work very hard only the last week or 2 before the report card. This last-minute burst of studying doesn't improve overall grades, and they remain punished. They actually feel punished for working hard, based on the principle of immediacy of consequences.

The most important thing about a reward or a punishment is it follows the behavior you're trying to control. Whatever behavior occurs immediately before the consequence is the one that is affected by punishment. Because of this principle, don't use methods that continue until the next report card.

When working with grades, set short-term goals. Deal with the situation on a daily or weekly basis rather over a long period of time. A home/school communication system can be established to monitor the child's behavior or performance.

"A" For Effort

Another problem is you may only look at the poor grades and not the reason for the deficient grades. Emphasis is placed on grades.

"If you get a C average, you can talk on the phone."

"I know he's capable of A and B work. I won't accept anything below that."

Forget about grades! Focus on the behavior that causes poor grades. Look at the child's effort rather than grades. Let's say you get your child's report card and find he has failed math. The first question to ask yourself is, "Why has he failed?" This may be answered by having a meeting with his teacher.

You may find he did poorly because he hasn't turned in his homework and hasn't completed math class work. Now that you have the reason for his poor performance, focus on improving this. Improvement in his grades will follow.

Rather than saying, "Until your grades improve" say, "Until the behavior that is contributing to your poor grades improves." If a child does poorly in a subject because he hasn't done his homework or class assignments, assume if his work habits improve, his grades will also change. Focus on the behavior(s) that contributed to the grades not on the grades.

You might say, "Each day you complete your class work and turn in your homework, you can stay up 30 minutes past your bedtime" or some other reward.

Establish a communication system with the school, and use a behavior chart to deal with the behavior. If you can get the child to turn in all his homework and complete class work on a daily basis, his grades will improve at the end of the grading period.

Focus on your child's effort and not the grades. Often this will reduce some of the pressure your child feels. If your child has average or above-average ability and you focus on improving the behavior that is producing the poor grades, an improvement in this behavior will result in an improvement in his grades.

The three general behaviors to focus on are homework, class work and participation or paying attention in class.

I tell children, "You and I could take a senior-level advanced chemistry class at the local university and may fail every test. However, we could get an A in doing homework and class work and paying attention in class." It would not be difficult to get an A in effort."

If your child gets a D or F in a class and his teacher tells you, "He's turned in all his homework. He pays attention in class and does all the seat work. He looks like he's trying." Your child has earned the D or F and this might indicate he needs a tutor.

However, if the teacher says, "He's missed 6 of 10 homework assignments, seems to be daydreaming in class and does not take notes." He hasn't earned any grade. This indicates that you need to help improve his effort and motivation.

We all tell our children, "All I want is for you to do your best. If you give it 100%, that's all that matters." Therefore, effort is much more important than grades.

CHAPTER 25

Tips to Improve Study Skills

How can you encourage your child to study and learn? What can you do to develop a positive attitude toward schoolwork or get your child to realize homework and studying are things he has to do whether he wants to or not?

Some children are born with a great deal of interest in school and self-discipline. If you have one of these children, you probably wouldn't be reading this chapter. Many kids could care less about school and view it as something to avoid. A child's school success often depends less on his level of intelligence than it does on what you do at home to help him achieve.

Life Shouldn't Revolve Around School

Your child's entire life shouldn't revolve around school and schoolwork. Does your child go to school, come home and do homework, then go to bed? He can't maintain this pace throughout his school career. If you feel your child is involved with schoolwork 24 hours a day, his motivation and willingness to become involved in schoolwork will dramatically decrease as time passes. Involvement in outside activities is important. You can possibly use this as a consequence or motivational factor. "You can go to basketball practice or karate classes only if your homework has been completed before it is time to go."

Be Positive

Avoid hassles, confrontations, power struggles and screaming matches centering around homework or school-related work. If your child sits down every night to do his homework and it's a hassle, he'll learn to avoid the situation. Try to be positive and minimize negative attention to his behavior. This may be accomplished by setting rules and consequences ahead of time. Provide structure without being a nag or constantly on the child's back.

Use His "Best" Time

Find out what time your child does his best work. Adjust his study time accordingly. Some children complete homework better right after school. Others do better if they're allowed to play first then do their homework. Some children do well studying in the morning. Try several schedules to see what fits him the best and which particular study time involves less hassle and confrontation.

Teach Him To Be Organized

Help him organize his notebooks. Have a place for him to place his homework assignments and the completed work. Help him develop a plan of study and what should be done each night.

Where To Study

Some children study better in their rooms. Others perform more effectively in the kitchen while you prepare dinner or help your other children with their homework. The place where a child studies or under what conditions he studies more effectively depends on many factors. It's different for different children.

Watch your child to decide what is best. Most children don't learn effectively if they study or do their homework in front of the TV or listening to a stereo.

Eliminate Distractions During Study Time

For some children, this involves turning off the TV and stereo, avoiding the commotion caused by younger brothers and sisters, and being in a situation free from noise, activity and commotion. A clear desk is more conducive to studying.

Work On One Assignment

Encourage your child to work on one assignment at a time. He might attack the toughest subject or the one he has the most difficulty in first. Leave the easiest subjects until later. He might study before doing written homework.

Setting Goals

Help your child set specific goals. He might use 10 to 13 minutes each night to review notes he took that day in each subject. If there's a test on Thursday, he might study a third of the material on Monday, a third on Tuesday and the remainder on Wednesday. The more specific you can make a goal, the better his study habits will be.

Don't Sit With Your Child

Avoid having to sit with your child while he does his homework. If the only way your child will work is with you sitting by him and forcing him to do it, he isn't developing responsible or independent behaviors.

Try to develop independent work habits. Have the child depend on you only for activities he doesn't understand or when he needs help studying. Don't have him depend on you to complete his homework assignment.

Don't Do His Homework

It's a big mistake to do your child's homework. Don't allow him to manipulate you so you provide more of the information and do more of the work than he does. Take time to explain how he can approach the problem. Set limits on his behavior with appropriate consequences to help him develop more self discipline and independent behavior.

No Procrastination

Encourage your child to complete projects ahead of time and not procrastinate. The use of rewards and positive consequences may be beneficial in accomplishing this.

Break Large Projects Into Smaller Ones

Teach your child how to break large projects into smaller ones. A large task might be accomplished by studying one chapter each night, or a book report might be easily attacked by doing one section every few days.

If your child has trouble with a subject, it might be best if he skips that subject for a while and moves onto another subject. The frustration and time it takes to tackle one problem may interfere with the remainder of his study time or homework.

Short Study Periods

Some children do better with homework if it's broken into periods of study divided by short breaks. Establish the best method of doing homework with your child.

General Study Tips

1. Before reading a chapter, have your child look over it and notice the headings, italicized words, summary, review questions and charts.
2. Have him read small sections. Then discuss the section or ask him questions about what he has read. Or have him verbally summarize what he has read.
3. Some children learn better if they read out loud, write their material or hear it. Use as many senses as possible in homework and study activities.
4. Teach your child to use tricks or methods to memorize things. Look for ways to associate the unknown with the known. Spelling "geography" might be seen as **George** ran **a pig** home yesterday. The difference between princi**ple** and princi**pal** is the person who is the princi**pal** of your school is a "pal. " Use devices and memory tricks to aid studying.
5. In subjects, such as math, where there is sequential learning, be sure your child knows one area before he moves on to the next. If he doesn't know the appropriate concepts by the time the class changes to other concepts, spend extra time reviewing the material.
6. Teach him not to cram for tests. Study a little bit each night.

7. Talk about current events. Encourage him to read the newspaper each day. Talk about programs, events and activities he sees on TV.

8. When working on projects or repairing things around the house, talk to the child about methods of problem solving and the approaches you use to solve the particular problem.

9. Encourage your child to read. Obtain high-interest reading material, such as magazines about skateboards, baseball, football, rock groups or other interests of your child.

10. Expose your child to different experiences. Take him to activities, visit museums and talk about things you see when visiting the ZOO or park. Relate school assignments to his interests. A particular child who is enthusiastic about baseball might write a report on the history of baseball. Another child who is interested in music or singing might do a research paper on a particular instrument, composer or singer.

11. Children have good days and bad days and sometimes good weeks and bad weeks. Don't get upset and critical of a failed test. Become concerned only if a pattern develops. If your child generally performs well, overlook mistakes, failures and weaknesses that are seen infrequently.

12. Encourage outside activities. Although school is the most important thing in your child's life, there are other things that result in development of confidence and self-esteem. Allow him to become involved in extracurricular activities, events and activities that develop self-esteem.

13. Don't set expectations too high. Look for gradual improvements. A child who is consistently making D's may find it very difficult to make an A or B to go on a hunting trip. It might be more appropriate to set the goal of C work.

14. When your child comes home from school, don't give him the third degree and ask him 400 questions about what happened at school today. Let it flow smoothly. When the child starts communicating about his day at school, stop what you're doing and give him your full attention.

15. Don't push your child to top his previous achievements. If success brings pressure, your child may find it easier to fail.

16. Don't call your child's questions stupid. Show him how to find the answer. Children learn by asking questions.
17. Encourage independence and self-discipline. You won't always be there to help, pamper or force your child into completing his assignments. You don't want to be there all the time either. Help your child set his own standards, and help him develop responsible behaviors.

CHAPTER 26

Communicating With Your Child's Teacher, Home-School Communcation Systems

For a child having behavior and/or performance problems in school, communication between the parent and teacher or administration is a necessity to deal with the problems effectively. The first step is to establish an open line of communication between you and school personnel. By doing this, you can stay informed about the problem and deal with it before it gets out of hand.

Many schools have built-in communication systems, such as report cards, progress reports, behavioral reports and incomplete homework slips. Many teachers phone parents to inform them of their child's behavior or progress. You may need to receive more frequent communication from the school. Try to establish some kind of formal communication between you and the school.

Most of the techniques I use to obtain information from the school are designed to require very little of the teacher's time each day or week. Asking a teacher to write a note or call you may involve a lot of time, especially if they have to do this for other students. But if you keep the communication system simple and have it require little of their time, the task becomes easier.

Three-part Communication System

The communication system involves three parts: you, the teacher and the child. You are responsible for designing and making the communication system, providing the materials and giving it to the child each day or week. You are also required to administer consequences for appropriate and/or inappropriate behavior.

The child is responsible for getting it to and from school and seeing that the teacher signs it.

The teacher observes the child and checks the appropriate information on the communication system. The teacher is not responsible for seeing that the child brings it to her to be signed. This is the child's responsibility.

When teachers are made responsible, children learn if they blend into the woodwork at the end of the period or day, teachers are busy with other things and forget to call them up to have the chart checked. The only excuse you take for not having the chart signed is if the teacher died! If the teacher's name isn't in the obituary column the following day, the child gets the consequence for not getting it signed.

If the child has a substitute teacher who doesn't know about the communication system, the child should ask that person to write, "I'm a substitute teacher. I don't know anything about this chart" and have that person initial it.

Be sure communication is set up so the child can't mark the chart himself or change what the teacher writes on it. Have the teacher initial the chart and make her comments in ink or by some other method so they can't be altered.

The reason for establishing good communication between you and the teacher is to be aware of and deal with school problems early, before they get out of hand. Some children respond better if progress is monitored on a daily or weekly basis rather than every 4-, 6- or 9-week period. The sooner difficulties can be identified, the easier they are to treat and the more unlikely they will get out of hand or future problems will develop.

Setting Up A Communication System

Make an appointment to meet with your child's teacher or appropriate school person. Discuss your child's behavior in great detail: how often, when, under what circumstances, in what situations and exactly what occurs. Avoid general terms.

Behavior must be analyzed to determine what corrective system will be used. After the behavior is described and discussed, you can start designing the procedure to be used. Discuss what you will use with the teacher(s). See if they will agree to observe, record or check your child's behavior.

Once this is done, at separate times you and the teacher should meet with your child to explain the system. Explain how he will earn points or how good and bad behavior will be indicated and what the consequences of his behavior will be. Explain exactly what he has to do to get good marks or indications of appropriate behavior. Avoid including too many behaviors. A child may be doing many things in the classroom, such as talking, getting out of his desk, disrupting the class, fidgeting, not doing his work.

Try to analyze the behaviors and target one. Although the child may be doing many inappropriate things in school, target one, such as not completing work. If this particular child was doing his work, he'd have less time to disrupt, talk, fidget. Try to target one or two-no more than four-behaviors to be worked on.

When starting a communication system, use it on a daily basis. After the child responds well on a daily basis, move it to every other day. Then move it to a week, 2 weeks and longer.

How frequently behavior occurs determines how to set up the chart and break up the daily or weekly period. If a child gets out of his desk 47 times a day, it's ridiculous to say, "If you stay in your desk all day, we'll give you a sticker." It might even be difficult for this child if you break the day into a morning and afternoon period.

His behavior is so severe that the odds of him successfully performing for a 3-hour block of time is impossible. You may want to break the day into 7 to 10 parts. For every period of time he remains in his desk, he is given a good mark. This is explained in detail in the discussion of the types of communication systems. For middle- and especially high-school students, a weekly system is usually more appropriate.

Individualize the system for your child to accommodate his particular area of difficulty or the behavior(s) of concern. Many schools have weekly progress reports they issue if requested by the parents. Many times I prefer not to use the school's system because it involves general comments on the child's behaviors.

I normally try to identify the child's particular problems and design the communication system based on those. Below I give some examples of various types of systems. Use these as examples. Like behavior charts, the number, type and style of communication systems is limited only by your imagination.

Communication systems can be divided into two general areas. One is when the target behavior can occur more than once a day, and the other is when the behavior occurs only once a day.

When Target Behavior Can Occur More than Once A Day

This type of communication system can be set up on a daily or weekly basis. Behaviors include staying in your seat, getting permission before you speak, completing class work, fighting, talking in class, homework, participation in class, getting along with other children and similar behaviors.

Time

Decide on a logical way to break the school day into time periods. Talk with your child's teacher and find out how many activities or subjects are normally covered in a school day.

Some teachers divide the day according to subjects (math, reading, spelling) or type of activity (story time, coloring, work sheets). Others use time to split the day into sections (8:30 to 10:30, 10:30 to lunch).

For smaller children who perform more activities in the morning, the first half of the school may be broken into five periods; after lunch may involve only two periods.

Once the division is established, construct a chart.

When using time as a way to break up the day into periods, how frequently the behavior is seen may determine how the day is broken up. A child who does no seatwork in class should not have a communication chart that involves the whole day. You don't want to tell him, "If you do all your work today, you'll get a good mark." This is too much for him to handle at one time. Break the day into several periods of time. For each period of time he completes his work, he gets a good mark. The same is true for a child who has trouble staying in his desk. If his communication chart is broken into morning and afternoon, the odds of him being successful are pretty low. It is better to break up the day into hours.

If this system works successfully, increase the time periods. If you break the day into hourly sections and the child responds well, break the day into 2- or 3-hour blocks of time. Under this system he has to be good for 2 or 3 hours to obtain the appropriate mark. Then you can have him respond appropriately for a half a day, then a whole day to get the good mark.

Once the child responds well to a daily system, move it to an every-other-day system, then to a weekly system, then to an every-other-week system.

Let's take an example of a child who continually talks in class. The first thing is to talk with the teacher to get an idea of how frequently the behavior occurs. This will help determine how the chart is divided or how frequently you want to monitor the behavior. If it's very frequent, divide the day into smaller sections of time. The less frequent the behavior, the larger the periods of time the day can be divided into.One way that we could divide the day would be based on subjects. We could construct a chart similar to the one below.

Jason's Quiet Chart

	Mon.	Tues.	Wed.	Thur.	Fri.
Math					
Science					
Spelling					
English					
Social Studies					

Tell your child he is responsible for bringing the chart to and from school and for seeing that the teacher marks it. You and the teacher explain the system to your child. "You have been talking too much in class, so we have set up a chart to help you be quiet. When you don't talk out of turn during a subject (or period of time), Mrs. Jones will put a star on that block. If you talk, you'll get an X in the block."

At the end of the day, your child brings the chart home, and you administer the consequence that was determined. Each star that your child earns during the day may represent 3 minutes past his bedtime. Or he may be working for a reward at the end of the week. The teacher keeps the chart and marks it after each period or the child keeps it and gives it to the teacher at the appropriate time. Your child is responsible for it.

When setting up this system, use positive consequences (reward) whenever possible. When punishment is used, your child will forget to get the chart marked or will lose it to avoid the negative consequence.

If your child's behavior occurs more frequently and the day needs to be divided into smaller sections, use a chart similar to the one below.

Alan's "Be Good" Chart

	Mon.	Tues.	Wed.	Thurs.	Fri.
9-9:30					
9:30-10					
10-10:30					
10:30-11					
11-11:30					
Lunch					
12:30-1					
1-1:30					
1:30-2					

If we are working with a child using a chart similar to the preceding ones and his behavior starts improving, we might want to break the day up into larger sections of time like the following two charts. In a sense the behavior is being monitored less frequently.

Jason's Quiet Chart

	Mon.	Tues.	Weds.	Thrurs.	Fri.
Early Morning					
Late Morning					
Early Afternoon					
Late Afternoon					

	Mon.	Tues.	Weds.	Thrurs.	Fri.
Morning					
Afternoon					

If the child continually does well after we start breaking the days down into larger segments of time, we may want to work toward a weekly monitoring of his behavior. This could be attempted by using a chart similar to the one below.

Jason's Quiet Chart

	Being Quiet	Teacher's Initials or Comments
Math	Good Fair Bad	
Science	Good Fair Bad	
Spelling	Good Fair Bad	
English	Good Fair Bad	

When you monitor your child's behavior less frequently (on a weekly basis), he will bring the chart to the teacher on Friday to be marked. The teacher circles Good, Fair or Poor, depending on the child's behavior during the entire week. Points can be assigned to the adjectives describing behavior.

"Good" receives 2 points, "Fair" 1 point and "Poor" nothing.

Your child must earn a certain number of points to receive some type of privilege on the weekend. To have a friend sleep over, the child might have to earn 8 points during the week. The number of points he has to earn during the week is based on how the teacher feels he performed the week before you started the weekly chart. You can meet with the teacher, describe the above chart and ask her, "Jason can earn a total of 10 points if he is quiet all week. If he had had the chart last week, how many points would he have received?" If she says "2," make the goal 3 points to receive the reward. If she says "6," make the goal 7 or 8 points.

You can also use a chart in which your child receives points. He can earn 0 to 5 points for each class. A 0 shows he had inappropriate behavior all week. A 5 means he was good all week. Three points means he had a fair week and was appropriate 3 of the 5 days. See the chart below.

Jason's Quiet Chart

	Being Quiet	Initials and Comments
Math	4	*Keep up the good work. B. Smith*
Science	5	Great Week. D.J.
Spelling	3	Doing Better. Mrs. James
English	0	**Could not keep quiet. M. Collins**

For the child who has problems outside the classroom or in unstructured settings rather than in the classroom, use a chart adapted to those circumstances. The chart below is for a child who fights or doesn't get along with other children.

Chad's Getting Along with Other's Chart

	Getting Along	Speaking Nicely	Teacher's Initials
Before School			
Recess			
Lunch Time			
Wating for the Bus			

If your child cooperates with other children, doesn't get in fights and shares, the section under getting along would be checked. If the problems with other kids involve arguing and name calling, a category such as talking nicely could be included.

The chart can also be divided according to teachers. For a child having trouble completing homework and class work, a chart reflecting these behaviors could be used on a daily or weekly basis.

	Homework	Classwork	Teacher's Initials
Mrs. Smith	Complete Incomplete	Complete Incomplete	
Mrs. Dean	Complete Incomplete	Complete Incomplete	
Mrs. Jones	Complete Incomplete	Complete Incomplete	

Many times with older children (middle-school, junior high and high-school students), you may not want to monitor the behavior on a daily basis. Using a weekly system, your child could take the chart to school on Friday and get all his teachers to initial it. Sometimes with older children you can provide the school counselor with several charts and several self-addressed, stamped envelopes. If the chart is to be mailed to you, run the chart from Thursday to Wednesday. On Wednesday, a counselor goes to the child's teachers to see how he is performing. The counselor puts it in the mail and sends it to you. By doing this, your child avoids the embarrassment of having to take it to the teacher. You can receive it by Friday so you can administer the consequences for the weekend.

Let's take an example of a child who does poorly in school. Charts should be designed to help a child who does poorly in school for reasons other than ability. These charts should have no indications of grades. You are specifically looking at your child's effort in class work and homework and his ability to pay attention in class. See the following charts.

	Homework	Classwork	Talking in Class	Attention in Class	Initials
Math	Complete Incomplete	Good Fair Poor	Good Fair Poor	Good Fair Poor	
English	Complete Incomplete	Good Fair Poor	Good Fair Poor	Good Fair Poor	
Science	Complete Incomplete	Good Fair Poor	Good Fair Poor	Good Fair Poor	
History	Complete Incomplete	Good Fair Poor	Good Fair Poor	Good Fair Poor	

Student_____   Week Ending_____

Teacher's Signature	Subject	Classwork: Working or not Working	Conduct: Good, Bad, or, Poor	Homework: Complete or Incomplete
	Biology			
	Civics			
	Geometry			
	Typing I			
	English			

For older children, tell them their job at this point in their life is to attend school and do what they're supposed to do. Everything they do on the weekend is a privilege. If they complete their job during the week, they'll have their privileges during the weekend. If they only do 20% of what they are supposed to do during the week, they only get 20% of their privileges. If they do 50%, they get 50% of their privileges.

Break the weekend into five parts (Sunday afternoon, Sunday morning, Saturday afternoon, Saturday morning, Friday after school). For the older child, this may involve weekend nights instead of mornings. The amount of work your child does during the week also determines how much phone time or driving privileges he will have next week.

Frequency

When behavior occurs more than once a day, a chart can be

set up based on the number of times a day it occurs. Let's say the target behavior is completing seatwork. You analyzed the behavior and found seven things your child has to do during the school day—he seldom completes one. You say, "I have put seven circles on this chart. For each assignment that you complete, the teacher will put a star over the circle."

"When you don't finish, you'll get an X. At the end of the day when you bring the chart home, you can trade your stars for extra play time" or whatever consequence has been determined as valuable to the child. See the chart below.

Tony's Finishing Work Chart

Mon.	Tues.	Wed.	Thurs.	Fri.
0 0	0 0	0 0	0 0	0 0
0 0	0 0	0 0	0 0	0 0
0 0	0 0	0 0	0 0	0 0
0	0	0	0	0

Another child may be disturbing the class. You analyze the behavior and find out this occurs 10 times a day. Create an appropriate chart and have it placed on the teacher's desk. Tell your child that every time there is a disturbance in class (define what you mean by "disturbance" and try to narrow it to as few a behaviors as possible), the teacher will color in one of the circles. You can then set up some type of consequence for the number of circles that weren't colored in.

Target Behavior That Can Occur Only Once A Day

Sometimes the target behavior occurs or can occur only once a day (refusing to do math). When this happens, two systems can be set up.

Several Behaviors

A target behavior may occur only once a day, but the child exhibits several different problem behaviors. Eddie rushes through his math seatwork and usually gets it wrong, talks during reading period and runs to the cafeteria for lunch. To deal with these different problems, set up a chart to reflect the several different problem behaviors.

	Mon.	Tues.	Weds.	Thurs.	Fri.
Takes time with Math					
Quiet during Recess					
Walks to Lunch					

Another child has trouble with other specific behaviors in the classroom.

	Mon.	Tues.	Weds.	Thurs.	Fri.
Has all supplies					
Stays seated during Story Time					
Completes phonics worksheet					
Cooperates during freetime					
Packs books quietly					

The same procedure described previously would be used in charts such as the ones above.

One Behavior

When there is only one target behavior a chart like the one below could be employed.

	Mon.	Tues.	Weds.	Thurs.	Fri.
Turning in Homework					

For a child having trouble concentrating in class we could set up something similar to the chart below.

	Paying Attention in Class	Comments
Spelling	Good Fair Poor	
Reading	Good Fair Poor	
Math	Good Fair Poor	
Science	Good Fair Poor	
Social Studies	Good Fair Poor	

When incomplete class work is a problem, something similar to the chart below can be used.

	Classwork	Initials or Comments
Mrs. Smith	Complete Incomplete	
Mrs. West	Complete Incomplete	
Mrs. Collins	Complete Incomplete	

Similar procedures as described previously can be used with these charts. They could be used on a weekly or daily basis.

Using Tokens

Tokens can be used instead of charts to communicate information from the school to the parent. A token can be anything the child can transport from school to home. It could be a sticker, a happy face stamped on the child's hand, a poker chip, a piece of a puzzle, a bean.

One parent was having trouble with her daughter completing her work in the classroom. The little girl wanted a new doll. The mother bought a bag of marbles and gave it to the teacher. Both the teacher and parent told the girl that every time she completed a sequence of her work, she'd get a marble to bring home. At home, the mother got a jar and put a sign on it that read "Laurie's New Doll." Laurie was told, "Each day when you come home from school, put the marbles you have earned in this jar. When it's filled, we will get your doll." Laurie got the doll in a few weeks.

Another parent used tokens to get her son to participate in class. Darren was shy, timid and didn't say anything in class. He wouldn't respond, even when asked a direct question. Darren's desire to see a professional basketball game was identified as a reward. The mother bought a puzzle (about 23 pieces) and gave the pieces to the teacher. Darren's mother told him and his teacher that each time he spoke in class, he'd be given a piece of the puzzle to bring home. When the puzzle was completed, his father would take him to the game. In about 7 school days, the puzzle was finished and Darren got to go to the basketball game.

Any type of token can be used to get a daily or weekly report on the child's progress. A consequence is identified, and the child is able to trade the tokens for the reward.

Using Established Lines Of Communication

Many times children bring things home daily from school. This may be an assignment pad, a particular notebook, folder or workbook. Sometimes children bring home materials on a weekly basis. Every Friday a stack of seatwork comes home or tests are returned every Wednesday. If your child has something that comes from school on a regular basis, it can be used as a communication system.

If your child's assignment book comes home every day, set up a system with the teacher where the day is broken into 5 parts. On the top right of the assignment, the teacher writes a number from 0 to 5 and initials it. If the target behavior was completing work, a 0 means he did nothing, a 5 all of the work, a 3 half of it. The teacher can also write good, fair or poor on something that comes home on a regular basis to indicate your child's behavior in the class setting. Different types of stickers or stamps can also be put on material coming home.

Communication Systems-Things To Remember
1. If your child has problems in school and/or has previously experienced difficulties, don't assume no news is good news. Initiate school contacts.
2. Schedule a meeting with the appropriate school person (teacher, counselor, principal). Discuss the child's problems in detail. Try to identify exactly what is happening, when and under what conditions. Analyze the behavior.
3. Try to establish how frequently behavior occurs. This is very important because it determines how frequently the behavior needs to be monitored and how the communication system is to be established. It also helps establish how much improvement the child has to show to receive the reward. Break up the day into small periods of time so your child can have some success.
4. Be sure you and the teacher have the same understanding of what behaviors are to be monitored and how the system is to be checked.
5. Don't include too many behaviors. One is best. Three or four is the maximum.
6. You and the teacher, at separate times, should explain to your child exactly what he has to do or what he has to avoid to achieve good marks.
7. Provide all the materials for the communication system and construct it. You are also responsible for administering the consequences of the behavior and for giving your child the system to bring to school.
8. Your child is responsible for getting the communication system to and from school and seeing the teacher initials and checks his chart.
9. The teacher should not assume any responsibility for the

communication system. She shouldn't ask the child for the system. All the teacher has to do is observe and check the child when he brings the communication system to her.

10. Once a daily communication system is working effectively, increase the length of time being monitored. The child who is monitored on an hourly basis may be moved to a 2-hour basis, then a half-day basis. Extend the time the behavior is monitored when it seems the child is successful. The daily communication system may be moved to biweekly, then weekly and eventually every other week.

11. Keep the system simple so it requires little of the teacher's time.

12. Use positive consequences (reward) as much as possible.

13. Look for gradual improvement. The child who isn't doing any class work is doing very well if he completes 25% of the work. Once he begins to experience success at this level, gradually increase the amount of work he has to do to receive the reward. Don't look for significant change overnight. Try to lock the child into the system by having him experience success by achieving goals. Look for movement toward the end goal. Don't try to change the behavior all at once.

14. Be sure you have a place for the teacher to initial the communication system or check it in some manner so you know for sure it's her response on the chart not your child's. Don't provide the child with an opportunity to forge the chart.

CHAPTER 27

"He Will Not Complete His Classwork"

The teacher says my child isn't doing his work in class. What am I supposed to do? I'm not in school with him."

I hear this frequently. Although you don't attend school with your children, you can do some things to help your child deal with work in the classroom setting. Before trying to change behavior, identify the possible cause of the incomplete or inadequate class work. In most cases, this refers to the child's written work. But it may also pertain to attention in class, participation in verbal discussions or activities or other behaviors indicating the child doesn't follow classroom procedure.

The child may not complete any work. Or he may rush through the work and finish it in a sloppy, impulsive way. He may put down any answer just to have something on the paper. Or it may be incorrect, even though he has put forth significant effort.

Causes

Attention Problems Or Hyperactivity

Children who are distractible, have attention problems, cannot concentrate or cannot stay still, often have difficulty completing class work. They don't finish seatwork or tests because they can't force themselves to concentrate to complete the task. They have difficulty sustaining effort. Children with these characteristics will experience difficulty in this area.

Perhaps your child is having problems with attention and/or overactivity. You have tried to improve the behavior but have experienced little success. It may be appropriate to have the child evaluated or seen by a mental health professional who specializes in child behavior. By doing this, you can get a better idea if the child can or can't control specific behavior. If he cannot sustain his attention or decrease activity level, even though he tries very hard, other steps must be taken to deal with the classroom behavior.

Perceptual-Motor Problems

Some children who have eye-hand coordination difficulties or weakness in fine-motor coordination have difficulty manipulating a pencil or copying from the board. Handwriting is extremely difficult, takes a long time and involves a significant amount of effort. Written activities are difficult, and usually the child doesn't complete the work.

Academic Problems

If a child is in seventh grade but only has the academic skills of a fourth grader, he's going to have trouble with class work. If a specific learning disability or reading problem exists, class work may often be incomplete or inadequate. Because of the difficulty this child experiences with schoolwork, he may also show a lack of motivation or a tendency to give up.

Lack Of Responsible Behaviors

Some children have not learned there are certain things you must do because you have to do them, whether you want to or not. If seatwork is presented and they're interested in the work, they usually complete it quickly and correctly. However, if given information they aren't interested in, they don't do the work or they complete it quickly just to get it done. These children lack responsibility, self-discipline and internal controls. They want to do what they want to do when they want to do it for as long as they want to do it. They usually don't complete class work because they don't want to.

Lack Of Independent Behavior

If the teacher stands over the child or works with him in a

one-on-one situation, work is usually completed. However, if independent work habits are required, the child doesn't produce. The teacher may tell the class, "I'm going to work with this reading group for a while. While I'm doing this, I want you to complete page 5 and 6 in your English workbook." In these situations, the child doesn't perform. These are usually dependent children or those who have not developed independent behaviors.

Dealing With Class work

You can do several things to help the teacher. This may result in an increase of classwork finished, complete activities or participation and attention in class.

Identify Cause Of Problem

This is the first thing to try. Talk with the child's teacher. Try to identify the exact situations and/or activities where this behavior is seen. Have the teacher tell you specifically what the child is or is not doing and how he approaches the task.

If motivation seems to be present, does she feel he can do the work and isn't trying, or does she question his ability?

Does the lack of attention or incomplete work pertain only to written work?

Does he have trouble completing certain types of tests but does well when tested in a different fashion?

Can he attend to some activities but not others? Or is his attention problem apparent in all activities?

Once you define in detail what is happening in the classroom, you may be able to figure out why the problem is occurring.

Causes of incomplete or ineffective class work are discussed in other chapters. Review the chapter or chapters that seem appropriate for your child.

Develop Other Behaviors

Many children who show attention problems, overactivity, irresponsible behavior and lack of independent skills in school show very similar behaviors in other areas of their lives. Parents usually focus only on school because it's the most important behavior. When trying to develop more responsibility in a child regarding his schoolwork, you must also develop responsibility in behaviors that occur around the home and in the neighborhood.

An irresponsible child may buck routine situations and give you trouble when it's time to take a bath, go to bed or pick up his clothes. If you can establish more cooperation and responsibility in these areas, it is easier to develop responsibility regarding school behavior.

The child who lacks independent skills and depends on you must learn independent skills at home before these skills can develop in school. Don't work only on school behavior if your child's classroom problems are similar to home problems.

Evaluate Academic Problems

Does your child have trouble because of a lack of foundation, ability problems or the possibility of a specific-learning difficulty? It might be beneficial to have him evaluated so the specific area of difficulty can be identified.

Evaluation results should provide some recommendations for dealing with the situation. The school may be too advanced for the child, or he may need tutoring. A smaller class setting may be appropriate, or he may need to repeat the grade. Some form of therapy or outside assistance may be appropriate.

Establish Home-School Communication System

Do this so you have a daily or weekly report on the child's progress in the classroom. Review the chapter on communication with the teacher. This will give you some ideas of communication systems to use.

You must have feedback from the school so you can administer consequences at home that may motivate the child to complete his work. Communication from school must be simple and involve a minimal amount of the teacher's time. It should be more frequent than interim reports or report cards.

CHAPTER 28

Taking Medications at School

Two problems are often seen when medication has to be given during the school day. The medication is not consistently taken or the child does not want to go to the office and take the medication because they may be seen as "different" and may be teased. With the increase in the diagnosis of Attention Deficit Disorders, more and more children are taking medicine in school. However, these problems are often seen regardless of what medicine or why the medicine is needed (e.g. epilepsy, heart problems).

The obvious solution to both of the above problems is if the child can take the medication before or after school. In regards to Attention Deficit Disorders, some of the newer medications (Ritalin SR, Adderall, Concerta) are longer lasting and, in some cases, can be taken before school and they last all day. If one of the above problems is a concern for your child, check with the physician to see if a medicine could be used to eliminate the school dose.

Children who take medication at school have told me that other children make fun of them when they have to go to the office and take their "crazy pills" or have been told, "you're acting weird. Did you take your medicine?" Taking medicine at school sometimes produces social problems and therefore should be done as discreetly as possible. Other children do not have to and should not know that a child is on medication. Teachers should never ask the child in front of other children "Did you take your medication?" Get with your child's principal/teacher to see what can be done to minimize the probabilities of social problems.

CHAPTER 29

"Should My Child Change Schools?"

I don't often recommend a change of schools, especially as the first step in alleviating a child's difficulty. I feel changing schools should be the last thing considered after other attempts have been made to alleviate a child's difficulties.

Often I see children who have been in 5 schools in 6 years. The parents report difficulty with each school (ineffective teaching, stupid rules, too much homework, not enough homework, too many field trips). Sometimes the child changes because he has had ineffective teachers in all the schools!

My response is, "There are 'squirrels' in every profession, and the teaching profession is no exception. Your child has been extremely unlucky because he's experienced this in all the schools he has attended. If you look at the situation a little closer, the only thing common in all of the schools your child has attended is him. Perhaps the problem is more with your child than the school setting."

Many parents are quick to find fault with the school or teaching effectiveness and defend their child or minimize their difficulty by projecting fault elsewhere. If your child has difficulty in the academic setting, look first at what is happening. Try to assess the situation objectively.

Considering A Change Of Schools

If you or your child have difficulty with a school and many attempts have been made to change the situation to no avail, a change may be appropriate. Consider a change only after attempts to deal with the problem have failed.

Dissatisfaction With School Policies, Rules, Procedures

Parents often spend 20 to 30 minutes telling me everything that is wrong with the school their child currently attends.

"The rules are stupid."

"There's no cafeteria."

"The kids don't have an opportunity to play."

"The teacher is very negative."

After hearing this, my usual question is, "If the school is so bad, why is your child attending that school?"

My children attended a school once where they had a rule that students had to wear dress shoes to school. My children are probably like yours and have four pairs of tennis shoes and one pair of dress shoes. It makes more sense to me to allow the children to wear tennis shoes to school. However, the school's rule was no tennis shoes. Either I had to try to get this rule changed or shut up and abide by the rules.

If my feeling toward the policy was extreme, I should take my children out of the school. You should not directly communicate your feelings to the child that the teacher is ineffective, the principal is crazy and most of the school rules are ridiculous. But if your feelings are so intense, the child will pick up on them through non-verbal behavior or your general attitude.

If this is the case, it is probably better to enroll your child in another school.

School Suggests It

All schools are not appropriate for all children. Some schools may be what your daughter needs but may be inappropriate for your son. If a school suggests your child not return, I hear them saying they probably feel your child won't benefit from placement in their setting-or they can't provide him with what he needs.

Whatever the reason—behavioral or academic—when this happens, have the school identify the type of setting they feel will be more appropriate. Ask for recommendations.

School Level Is Above Child's Ability

If you have a child of average intellectual capacity and he is placed in a school geared toward children significantly above average, he may experience difficulty. The same is true of a child in the low average or slower learner range in an average academic setting. If the child has to spend a lot of time on his work and is struggling to keep his head above water, then it's best to find a school more in line with his skills.

Some children can't function in large classrooms. This might be true of an overactive child or one who has attention problems. These children need a classroom with a smaller pupil-teacher ratio than the school the child currently attends. If this is the case, a change in schools is warranted.

Smaller classes are also appropriate for children with academic difficulties or those requiring special attention. In a small class, work can be individualized and presented at a rate that fits the child's ability. If the school your child attends doesn't have this classroom setting or he needs a special education setting, a change in schools will probably be beneficial.

Repeating a Grade

If your child has to repeat a grade it may be wise to change schools.

Child Has Reputation He Can't Change

Some children-because of their behavior, attitude or patterns of interaction-develop a detrimental reputation in the school. This could involve two areas, one with the adults interacting with the child and the other with his peers.

The administration and staff may see the child as disruptive, slow or having behavioral problems. Even though he makes changes in his behavior, they aren't sufficient to shake this reputation. This is seen in overactive children who have been disruptive, distracting or seen as significant behavior problems for 3 or 4 years. When placed on medication, his behavior changes dramatically. But his reputation doesn't.

The other situation occurs with the child's peers. Some

children with socialization problems have been rejected, teased or ostracized by their peers. They may have difficulty breaking into a peer group. They can't make friends and fail to develop appropriate patterns of interaction. This is especially true if the child has been in the school for several years and is in the upper elementary grades.

The child with general socialization problems may not be able to change or do anything to change his reputation with his peers. In these situations, it may be necessary for the child to change schools to get a new start and shake the reputation.

School Can't Meet Child's Needs

A child may have certain needs or behaviors that require modifications of the school's approach to the child. The child with perceptual-motor deficits may require more verbal learning experiences than written work. The child with an attention deficit may need his work periods broken up more frequently than another child with an adequate ability to concentrate.

If the school can't meet the child's needs, it's appropriate to find one that can. In some situations, it is better to fit the school around the child's needs than to try to fit the child into the school.

Refusal To Attend School

This is difficult to deal with because in most cases, the causes or reasons the child refuses to attend school have nothing to do with the school itself. This is especially true in the case of school phobias when a child shows extreme anxiety, fear, worry and uncontrolled behavior when it's time to go to school. In these situations, other modifications must be made. See the chapter that discusses refusal to attend school.

In other situations, children want to change schools because they have academic trouble. In these situations, a change of school may be appropriate because of some of the reasons listed above. Some children refuse to attend school because they don't like the school or would prefer to attend another academic setting. If this is the case, listen to the child. Consider his needs and wishes. This is especially true in older elementary-age children or high-school students.

Change In Schools Alone Usually Doesn't Help

In most situations where children have academic or behavioral problems, a change in the school setting doesn't usually alleviate the problems. Other modifications or interventions must be part of the solution.

In most of the situations discussed above, this is the case. It's the exception rather than the rule that a change in the child's school setting alone totally alleviates the problems.

CHAPTER 30

Preschool and Pre-Kindergarten

Several years ago, many children's first schooling experience was kindergarten. Before that, first grade was initially the first academic experience. Today, many parents work, and many children get their first school experience before kindergarten. A nursery or preschool experience may be necessary when a child is very young. In some cases, children who have not been in preschool are at a disadvantage when they enter kindergarten.

I don't believe it is necessary for young children to receive high-powered academic training before entering kindergarten. However, I think preschool can be beneficial because of other reasons.

One of the major things most children and adults have to do throughout life is deal with other people. Without socialization skills, certain problems develop. Being with other children provides a child an opportunity to interact with or relate to other children and develop skills to deal with other children.

Following rules, completing undesired activities and doing things you have to do because you have to is an important part in successful school performance. The pre-kindergarten setting involves rules, procedures, do's and don'ts the child must follow. Involvement in this setting helps his adjustment to an academic setting.

For dependent children, a period of separation from parents may be beneficial to help the child develop more independent behaviors. For parents who are with their children 24 hours a day, having the child in preschool for 2 or 3 days a week may give the parent a break.

Children with certain developmental delays (speech) benefit from exposure to other children. Most public-school settings have preschool special-educational programs for children identified as having a specific exceptionality. Contact your local public-school system to see if there are appropriate programs for your child.

The type of preschool that is appropriate for a child must be considered on an individual basis. Some children benefit from a more-structured environment. Others may need less structure. Generally it is better to have the child involved in preschool that is similar to the school environment where she will begin her education. If you plan to send her to a traditional, highly structured school, it is better for her to have a similar type of preschool environment.

Although many preschool environments involve academic-skill development, many are designed to help a child socialize, accept responsibility, adjust to the routines of school and develop other skills that benefit learning and a successful school experience.

Visit several preschools, and talk with administrators. Talk with other parents who have children involved in the program. The more information you have about a program, the higher the probability your choice will be appropriate for your child.

CHAPTER 31

"Is My Child Ready for Kindergarten"

Before proceeding with this chapter, I suggest reading the chapter that discusses immaturity and repeating a grade.

Many schools evaluate a child's readiness for kindergarten solely on intellectual and academic skills. However, academic maturity is only one of the five general areas to assess. In determining whether a child is ready for school, one must assess his academic maturity and his physical, social, emotional and behavioral maturity. Deficits in any area may interfere with adequate performance in a kindergarten setting.

Many well-meaning but ill-informed parents and educators push young children into school too soon. Being bright and being ready to begin formal schooling are two separate issues. When children enter school before they are develop mentally ready or mature enough to cope with it, their chances for failure dramatically increase.

Age Is An Important Factor

In determining whether a child is ready for school, assess all areas of maturity. An important factor in overall maturity is age. Children with late birthdays (significantly younger than most of the children in the class) tend to have more difficulty in school than those with early birthdays. There is a national trend to move the cutoff date for school entrance from late fall-early winter to much earlier in the fall or even late summer. Findings of research in this area are the major reason for this trend.

1. Older children in a grade tend to receive more above average grades from teachers than do younger children in the same

grade.
2. Older children are more likely to score in the above average range on standardized achievement tests.
3. Younger children in a grade are more likely to fail at least one grade.
4. Younger children in a grade are more likely to have been referred for academic or behavioral problems.
5. Younger children who were developmentally unready when they started school often have problems that last throughout their school careers.

Developmental Lags

A child's age is a significant factor in determining whether she is ready for school. But age is not the determining factor.

Many young children with late birthdays show developmental lags in many areas defined as maturity. If a child shows developmental lags in one or more areas of maturity, it may be wise to have her spend another year in pre-kindergarten than to have her enter kindergarten. At this early age, a year of physical growth often results in many positive, significant changes.

Some lags may improve with the passage of time. Others (dependency, self-discipline) may have to be worked on and don't dramatically improve with another year of growth. However, another year gives you time to develop her responsibility or independent behavior.

If your child shows some marginal immaturity and/or he has already entered kindergarten and has difficulty in the school setting, have him repeat the grade. Most children attend school for 12 or more years. If your child has academic difficulty and it continues through his early schooling, a negative attitude is certain to develop. When in doubt, have your young child repeat a grade. Consult a professional for advice. See the chapter that discusses immaturity for more information.

CHAPTER 32

"Should My Child Repeat the Grade?"

Trying to decide whether a child should repeat a grade or move to the next grade is similar to voting in a political election. You don't vote for the best choice but the lesser of the evils. In trying to make this choice, you try to assess the advantage and disadvantage of each option. You avoid the choice that involves more disadvantages.

Repeating the grade might involve some initial frustration and disappointment for the child, but after this reaction he might experience 9 months of positive attention from his school involvement. The same child moved to the next grade when he isn't ready to handle the situation may experience 9 months of frustration, failure and struggle.

Below is a list of some indications of possible school problems and reasons for considering retention. In some situations, repeating the grade is beneficial. In other cases, repeating won't help, and other things must be done. Other situations may require repeating the grade, plus additional interventions.

Indications Of School Problems

The child's life, and possibly yours, revolves around school and schoolwork. It may seem he is going to school 24 hours a day. He wakes up, goes to school, comes home, does homework and goes to bed. This cycle is repeated daily. He doesn't seem to have much time to play because of schoolwork. He is unable to become involved in extracurricular activities (baseball, scouts, dancing) because he wouldn't have time to do his schoolwork.

At breakfast or on the way to school, you may hear his spelling words or go over questions for the science test. In this situation, the child, as well as you, will probably burn out by fourth or fifth grade.

You can only run so fast, so far and for so long then you give up. Although the teacher says the child should only spend 30 to 43 minutes a night on homework, your child averages 3 to 5 hours. Most of your interaction with your child may center around school and academically related material.

There is more to life than school. If this situation exists early in your child's education, it's almost certain that he, as well as you, won't be able to maintain this intensity very long. This definitely indicates a problem.

Homework Is A Hassle

Although most children aren't thrilled about doing homework, most complete it without significant problems. If it's a total battle, screaming match or fight every night to get the child to do the homework, it may indicate school problems.

If it seems like you have to tie your child in a chair every night to get the homework completed, it's probably not a good thing to continue to do. Although you're getting the homework done, the child isn't developing independent or responsible behavior. See the chapter on Homework.

Trouble Keeping Up Or Maintaining Passing Grades

You may have to review spelling words over and over again before it sinks in. Long hours must be spent studying for a test just to make an average or low-average grade. When comparing notes with other parents, your child's study time is significantly greater than most other children.

Frequent Complaints From School Or Teacher

This may involve concerns regarding performance (he has difficulty doing the work, incomplete class work, poor test grades, inability to grasp material). Or it may involve more behavioral concerns, such as difficulty with other children, daydreaming, overactivity or discipline problems.

Physical Complaints
The child may start developing physical concerns; these may revolve around schoolwork or attending school. It may also involve a refusal to go to school in the morning. Or your child may frequently call you from school with various physical complaints and requests to come home. Complaints don't seem to have any physical basis and are primarily designed to avoid school or school-related work.

Mood Changes
Children having difficulty in school often experience a lowering of their frustration tolerance. They appear to become easily upset, agitated and frustrated. Their mood may change from very pleasant to extremely upset and fretful. The normally relaxed, happy child may become quarrelsome and cranky.

The child may seem unhappy, depressed or look like something is bothering him.

School Tires Child
The child frequently comes home from school tired or exhausted after an average day. Homework or school-related work tires him.

Summer And School Holidays Are Wonderful!
Your child's behavior and your interaction with him significantly improve during the summertime or over long holiday periods. He is a different child during these times when school and schoolwork aren't a concern. The child may not dislike school-the work is the problem. If you could find a school that only involved play, interacting with other children and pleasurable activities-not schoolwork-your child's attitude and behavior would be similar to that shown on holidays.

Why Children Are Retained

Repeating a grade is usually considered when a child is immature or has not acquired the skills necessary for promotion to the next grade level. There are several areas where children may be behind their classmates. See the chapter on immaturity for a detailed discussion of various lags in skill development.

Physical Difficulties

These revolve around lags in physical-skill development. The child is unable to perform physical activities at the level of his classmates. He may have difficulty coloring, writing, tying shoes or catching a baseball.

Academic Difficulties

This involves the acquisition of school-related information. The child may have trouble keeping up with his classmates and may be behind in his skills. This could be due to several reasons including a poor foundation, specific learning disabilities, placement in a school setting too academically advanced for the child, depressed level of intelligence and not completing required class work or assigned homework.

Social Difficulties

This is an inability to relate to other children in an appropriate manner. It may involve a lack of age-appropriate skills or the development of inappropriate kinds of interaction. The child may be 7 but relates, plays and presents himself socially as a 4-or 5-year-old.

Emotional Difficulties

These involve children who don't show the same emotional development as their peers. This may involve whining, baby talk and similar reactions.

Behavioral Difficulties

This child may show problems in attention, concentration, self-discipline, ability to sit still and responsibility.

When Will Repeating Help?

In some situations, repeating the grade alone is beneficial to a child. In other cases, it won't help significantly. Whether a child repeats a grade or moves on to the next grade, several other things must be done to improve the child's academic behavior and/or performance.

Repeating the grade by itself is generally beneficial when another year of physical development will improve the child's performance or there is a lack of foundation in academic skills. Children who are young for their grade or have late birthdays sometimes show immaturity in several areas. A child with a late birthday may be 6 months to a year younger than most children in his class. Age difference is significant in lower grades where 6 months of physical growth results in considerable changes,

For children in this category, repeating a grade or starting school a year later is very beneficial. Many times this alone will produce the desired changes. See the chapter, Is My Child Ready for Kindergarten? for details.

Achievement Deficits

Some children are intellectually capable of functioning in the present school setting but show a lag in the development of academic skills. This can be due to a poor foundation. This child will generally benefit from repeating the grade. A child may be at the end of third grade in his placement, but his academic skills are only at the end of second grade or beginning third-grade level. This academic deficit may be due to numerous factors, such as poor school attendance, not doing the required homework or seatwork, ineffective teaching, a change of schools.

If the child advances to the next grade level, he will have academic difficulties because of the discrepancy between his acquired skills and the expected skills. Repeating the grade places him at a level consummate with his abilities. Some children who have specific learning disabilities or other behavioral concerns also show this poor foundation. But in these situations, repetition alone won't help the child.

Development Lags

Some children who show lags in the development of physical skills also benefit from a year of growth and maturation. This is similar to the child with a late birthday. In other situations, lags in physical development improve with time but don't improve significantly in 1 year (perceptual-motor difficulties, auditory processing).

Immaturity

When other areas of immaturity are the cause for the child's difficulty, repetition of the grade alone will not result in significant improvement. This is usually the case with a child who has the academic skills necessary for successful performance at his grade level, but other factors contribute to his poor performance. This is also the case with a child who has a specific learning disability; repetition will not be beneficial.

Lack Of Responsibility

Let's say your child is at the end of third grade and his academic skills are at the end of third grade or above. However, he is failing school because he isn't preparing for tests, has missed a significant amount of homework, is inattentive in class and doesn't complete the required work. He receives poor grades because of a general lack of responsibility rather than inadequate skills.

Repetition of the grade alone won't benefit him. Some type of intervention must be made to help improve the areas of difficulty.

Performance Problems

Another child at the end of fifth grade shows academic skills equal to his grade placement but has extreme difficulty writing or expressing himself with a paper and pencil. Handwriting is difficult, and he is slow doing his work. He receives failing grades because he doesn't complete tests or class work. He may only finish 10 problems on the math test when he's supposed to do 20, but the 10 problems that he has finishes are correct.

This child's academic difficulties are primarily related to his performance not his ability. Asking him to repeat a grade and show knowledge through a similar fashion (handwriting) won't result in significant improvement in his performance.

Learning Disabilities

The child with a specific learning disability or lag in a skill that prevents him from learning by methods that are beneficial to most children won't significantly improve his performance by just repeating a grade.

Suppose you had difficulty seeing. I give you a book and ask you to read a particular chapter. After you finish reading the book, I give you a test on the chapter, and you fail the test. The reason you have difficulty performing is because you didn't acquire the information. Asking you to reread the chapter and giving you the test again is ridiculous because you would fail again.

Children who don't acquire information the way most children do won't significantly benefit from repeating a grade and being taught in the same way.

Rather than repeating the same procedure, a better way to deal with the problem would be to get you a pair of glasses so you could see the information on the page or provide you with the written information in verbal form. I'd put it on a tape recorder, and you could listen to it. By readjusting the methods of teaching, you'd be able to acquire the information.

Children have particular learning styles and learn through a variety of methods. If a child's learning style is different from most children, he won't acquire information if taught in a certain way. He must be taught differently. Placement in a special education class or a smaller classroom where work can be individualized or presented in a way equal to his strengths and weaknesses is more beneficial. Whether we say a fifth-grade child is in eighth grade, fifth grade or third grade isn't as important as presenting the information in a way he can learn.

Repetition of a grade for these children won't result in significant benefit. Sometimes when a child repeats the grade, he does well the second time. But the next year when he starts the new grade, he has difficulty. Repetition may be needed again. If repeating the grade is used as the solution for this child, it will take him 24 years to get out of high school!

What Are Some Solutions?

For most children with school-related problems, many things can be done. Whether a child repeats the grade or moves to the higher grade, other interventions can and must be made to improve school performance.

The child who is irresponsible, shows a lack of interest in schoolwork and has academic skills but fails will have difficulty next year if nothing is done. For this child, attempts must be made to develop a more-responsible approach to schoolwork and other areas of his life that reflect similar behaviors and attitudes.

The child who has academic skills but his performance is inadequate because of poor fine-motor coordination may need modifications in the school environment. More emphasis needs to be placed on verbal communication of information and less on paper-and-pencil tasks. The child who shows emotional, social or behavioral immaturity may benefit from becoming a year older, but other techniques must also be used to develop maturity. By doing this, schoolwork will improve. Sometimes the child with adequate academic skills who receives borderline grades because of a lack of responsibility, dependent behavior or attention deficits may need to repeat the grade. It will take some time to develop the independent or responsible behavior or work on improving his attention span. See the chapters that discuss immaturity, irresponsibility and learning problems for more information.

Repeating A Grade? —Things To Consider

1. If your child has difficulty in school, meet with the teacher, principal or counselor to find out exactly where the problems lie. Have them define exactly why the child has problems. Avoid vague concepts. Have them define exactly what they mean by "immature." Does "behind in his work" mean he is lacking in phonics skills or basic math facts? Is he doing poorly

because he doesn't turn in required homework or complete the assigned class work? Define the child's specific areas of difficulty. This must be known before any attempts to deal with difficulties can occur.

2. Find out exactly what the school has done to correct the situation and what else can be done (reading lab, peer tutoring, different consequences for inappropriate behavior, reward for appropriate behavior, giving tests orally).

3. Try to make interventions to correct the child's difficulty as early as possible in the school year. Many people wait until the last report card to deal with difficulties. This is too late and a very ineffective method of resolving the problem.

4. If the child's problem is purely academic, consider working with the child and giving him some additional instruction besides homework. Check with the teacher. She may be able to give you some activities or direction to help strengthen the child's weak areas. Consider tutoring or moving to a lower level of the same grade. Be sure the child does the necessary homework to prepare for class.

5. If the problem is behavioral, you need to identify situations in the child's total environment (home and neighborhood) where similar behavior is seen. At first, focus on changing the behavior at home and in the neighborhood rather than at school. If some changes are seen at home, but the improvement has not extended to the school situation, focus on school behavior. You may want to set up some type of home-school communication system to monitor the child's behavior.

6. If the problems are academic and behavioral, try to identify the one that seems most important. This may be difficult because it is similar to the question "What came first, the chicken or the egg?" If it seems like the child's behavioral difficulties are resulting in poor academic performance, focus on the behavioral difficulties. On the other hand, the child may seem to have behavioral difficulties because of academic deficits, and he doesn't understand the work. Attempts should be made to alleviate these weak areas and to build academic skills. At times it may be appropriate to try to obtain

improvement both behaviorally and academically.

7. If these suggestions don't result in significant improvement and repeating the grade is considered, don't take it personally or let pride or emotions influence your objectivity. When a teacher or school suggests your child repeat a grade, they are usually implying what they see in your child may not result in successful performance in the next grade at their school. The suggestion is made to minimize frustration, failure and difficulty for the child. This suggestion doesn't automatically imply you're an inadequate parent or the teacher is out to "get" your child. It is not a direct reflection of your competency as a human being. Don't try to defend the child or become defensive. Listen to what school personnel say so you can objectively evaluate and deal with the situation.

8. The next best step is to have the child evaluated to rule out a specific learning disability, behavioral or emotional problems or physical, speech, vision or hearing difficulties.

9. Implement the suggestions that result from the evaluation (tutoring, speech or language therapy, counseling, family therapy, glasses).

10. If repeating the grade doesn't seem like it will help, work on what will (develop more responsible or independent behaviors, improve homework or study skills, do things that may improve the child's attention span or decrease his level of activity).

11. Does he need a special-education class?

12. Will a less academically advanced school be more appropriate? Is a school with smaller classes the answer?

13. If the school says your child needs to repeat the grade because he won't be able to function adequately in the next grade level at the school, it may not always mean the child can't function adequately in the next grade level at another school.

14. Will work over the summer help? Sometimes when summer school is recommended for a child it is more beneficial to have him receive individual tutoring to strengthen academic weaknesses. Sometimes arrangements can be made with the school so individual tutoring takes the place of a formal summer school. The decision to repeat may be made at the

end of the summer, in some cases.

15. It's usually better to have a child repeat a grade in lower grades than in upper grades. It's often believed the earlier a child repeats the grade the more beneficial and the less detrimental it is. In the lower grades, it is sometimes better to have a child repeat. Attending summer school to pass may just mean fighting and struggling next year in the following grade.

16. For older children, summer school or a change of schools may be a better option. For older children, repetition is more of an option when and if they are changing schools.

17. If a child will repeat a grade before the end of school, don't tell him. Wait until the last report card to inform the child of the decision. I often see children who shut down completely and stop doing work in school in January when they find out that they'll repeat the grade. This is a normal reaction. If you knew you were going to be fired from your job in 9 weeks, your effort, motivation and performance would suffer. If a child knows at the end of the third reporting period he will repeat, he's not apt to want to do the required work for the remainder of school. He probably won't.

18. Explain to the child why it is necessary for him to repeat the grade. I usually discuss this in terms of a lack of foundation. I tell the child, "Suppose someone came into the office and asked us to go outside and change the carburetor on his car. Would you be able to do it?" Usually the answer is "No." I then explain, "The reason neither of us could change the carburetor isn't because we're stupid or have problems. It's because we don't have experience or foundation in changing carburetors. If we went across the street and spent a couple of weeks at Tony's Auto Repair watching him change carburetors and working on it, we'd gain more knowledge. Three weeks later the same person comes in and asks us to change the carburetor, and we could. The reason for the improvement is because we have obtained the foundation that was missing."

19. If a child repeats a grade at the same school, it's best if he has a new teacher.

20. When a child repeats a grade, it's more appropriate to have

him attend a different school.

For the child who has difficulty in school, whether he repeats the grade or not, establish an open line of communication with the school the following year. Don't assume no news is good news. The teacher might have from 30 to 130 students in his classes, and your child may be overlooked. Put an "X" on your calendar every 2 or 3 weeks to remind yourself to talk with the teacher.

CHAPTER 33

Dealing With Lack of Cooperation from School Personnel

Communicating with your child's school is a necessity if you have a child who is experiencing academic or behavioral difficulties. In some schools, communicating with the teacher, counselor or principal is no problem. All you have to do is make a phone call, write a note, etc. and you will be contacted, often on the same day. In these schools, it is easy to schedule an appointment to meet with your child's teacher.

In other situations, it is not so easy and communicating can be difficult. Phone calls are not returned, notes are not responded to and it is difficult to meet face to face with the teacher or principal.

In other situations, scheduling a time to speak with your child's principal or teacher is not difficult, but it seems that nothing is accomplished or changed after the contact. It seems like it's their way or the highway. They don't perceive the problem the same way you do. You're told "The teacher isn't doing anything wrong." "You are asking them to do something that is impossible." The teacher has many children in the class and can't provide undivided attention to your child." "What you are asking is not a school policy." "None of the teachers see any of the other students teasing your child" and so forth. The school contact does not produce any change or positive results.

In all of the above situations, you get off the phone or leave the meeting very frustrated because of the lack of communication or the fact that the school does not see your child's or your point of view. Some of the suggestions below might make this an easier task and produce positive results.

Follow The "Chain Of Command"

If you are having trouble with your child's teacher or he is having problems in the class, talk with the teacher. Don't go to principal, counselor, etc. Deal with the person or situation where the problem is seen. If you are having trouble making contact with the person or you are not satisfied with the results of the meeting, go speak to the next person (counselor, assistant principal, principal) in the chain of command.

If you had trouble making contact with the teacher, keep a record of the phone messenger you left and the notes that were sent and received no response. If you are dissatisfied with the results of your meeting, discuss this. If you feel the second meeting was not productive, meet with the next person in the chain of command and so forth.

Focus On The Child

A good way to assure that your contact with the school will be unproductive is to get into a conflict or battle with the school person. If a situation is created where one side is on the offensive and the other side is on the defensive, the meeting will not result in any positive results. If a contest or a situation to determine "who's right and who's wrong" is created, there is a good probability that the school's position will become stronger and their way of doing things will be right. In this "right and wrong contest", what you are saying will not be heard, much less considered, because the school will be too busy defending their position.

Rather than produce a contest, the focus should be placed on the child. Avoid the following:

Parent: "You are giving too much homework. It seems like there's a lot of busy work that's not necessary"

Teacher: "I'm only trying to give your child a quality education so he can get into a good high school"

Parent: "The other fifth grade teachers do not give as much homework as you give."

Teacher: "The other children will not learn as much as your child and your child will be better prepared for sixth grade."

Another unproductive meeting would be similar to the following:

Parent: "You do not have enough teachers watching the students at lunch recess. My child is being teased every day."

Principal: "We have the number of teachers on lunch duty that the school system requires us to have."

Parent: "Well it's not enough. My child says this happens every day. If you had more teachers on duty this would not happen.

Principal: "Are you sure your child is giving you an accurate picture of what's happening? Our school has zero tolerance for teasing."

The type of meetings described above usually result in the parent leaving the conference very frustrated and nothing changes. A better way to approach these situations is to have you and the school focus on the child and not get in a contest. Something similar to the following would be a better way to approach the school and start the meeting.

Parent To Teacher: I'm lost at what to do with my child's homework. Perhaps you can help. It's taking him three hours to do his homework. He gets very frustrated and it's a battle every night. He's fighting homework more and more and he's getting to a point where he is refusing to sit down and do it. Can you think of anything that can be done to help me out?"

Parent To Principal: "I'm upset about some things that are happening with my child. I'm not at school and I don't know what's happening. Maybe you can help? He comes home every day from school and says the other kids pick on him during lunch. He says he's teased a lot and has no friends. I don't know about that, but I do know that he's never invited to the birthday parties of his classmates. Although he calls the other students, no one calls him. Could you look into this for me?"

In the above situations, the parent is asking the teacher and principal for help. Both parent and teacher are looking at the child, what's best for him? what does he need?, what is happening?, etc.

It is not a contest of who's doing their job correctly or not, or who's right and who's wrong. The focus is placed on the child. Positive results are more likely to occur in these situations and an open line of communication can be established with the school.

Another situation which often produces similar problems is what I call "group meetings." In this area of the country many schools schedule meetings with parents that involve 5 or 6 school personnel and one or two parents. The child's three teachers, counselor, assistant principal and principal meet with the parent(s) to discuss the concerns. Most people would tend to get overwhelmed by this. It's six to one. Most people would tend to get defensive and a contest may occur. Don't get defensive and approach the situation as described above.

Establish A Communication System

If you ask a teacher to write you a note every day about your child's behavior or ask them to call you on Friday to give you a weekly report, this may be a time consuming task for the teacher, especially if she has 3 or 4 other parents making similar requests. In this situation the teacher may find it difficult to cooperate with your request.

All of the home-school communication systems that are we establish involve a minimal amount of teacher time, usually 30 to 60 seconds a day. The probability of cooperation is greatly increased using this type of system. See the chapter that discusses this for more information.

Change Schools

I you've tried the above and you are still not getting the cooperation, you may need to change schools. Or if the school does not provide what your child needs, another school may need to be considered. A parent tells a principal "My child has trouble writing and getting information on paper. We study for tests at home and he knows the material as well as he knows his name. When he goes to school and takes the test, he fails. He brings the test home. I asked him the questions and he tells me all the correct answers. I had him evaluated and the results indicate that he would benefit from being tested verbally." The principal responds, "It is not our policy to give oral tests. He'll have to take it written." This is not the right school for this child!

Oftentimes it is better to fit a school to the child's needs rather than to fit the child to the school or to have the school change to meet the child's needs. See the chapter that discusses this for more information.

CHAPTER 34

Extracurricular Activities

It's important for a child to develop interests and hobbies. There are several benefits from this. A child having difficulty in school needs to develop other areas of his life where he can experience positive feedback. Everyone has strengths and weaknesses.

There are many things we can do as well or better than other people. There are many things we can't do as well or things other people do better than we can.

If a child's life revolves around school and he has difficulty, it's hard for him to see other positive qualities because school is the only thing he can use to compare himself to other children . . . and this is one of his weak points.

You want your children to look at their overall positive and negative qualities and not place a great deal of emphasis on their weaknesses. A child struggling in school might think, "Johnny is making better grades than I am, but I can play baseball better than he does." Or "Mary is on the honor roll, but I'm a better dancer than she is." If the only thing the child has to compare to Mary and Johnny is school performance, feelings of inferiority and inadequacy are apt to develop.

Some children I see go to school 24 hours a day. They go to school, come home and study, take their bath and go to bed. This is repeated 4 or 5 nights a week. Parents tell me they can't get involved in any other activities because of schoolwork. Most of the time these kids have difficulty in school.

If this is the case and outside activities can't be considered, perhaps a change in schools is appropriate. Something needs to be done to allow the child to have some free time to engage in other activities. Children who start their schooling experience this may rapidly lose interest in school.

Another reason children do not become involved in outside activities is because it's an inconvenience to parents to take them to practice, meetings or activities. Realistic problems exist with working parents when they can't transport the child to activities because of their work schedule. If this is the case, get the child involved in the activity then work out some arrangement with other parents who have children in the same activity.

The hobbies, activities and interests can be a variety of things, such as, hunting, fishing, scouts, dancing, gymnastics, drama club, French club, karate, baseball, football, basketball, racing remote-control cars, drill squad, soccer, involvement with a church youth group, computer club, art classes and music. Having the child involved in these activities produces several positive results.

Interests Are Developed

One of the common elements in children who are involved with the law is a lack of interest in activities or hobbies. They live day to day. Unhappy, depressed children usually aren't involved in activities. I'm not saying that if your child isn't a cheerleader or doesn't play football that he or she will become a juvenile delinquent or depressed. I am saying many children who experience problems aren't involved in outside activities.

Children who have interests are able to set goals and work toward them. They often have things to look forward to. Many times I see children who are not involved in activities and don't do well in school. One reason is because they say life is boring and they have nothing to look forward to.

If I have a fishing trip planned on the weekend or some other enjoyable activity it seems to make my week pass faster. If the child has things to look forward to, the unpleasant parts of his life (school) tend to not look as big. Life in general is a process where goals are set and you work toward them. Sports, scouts and other activities usually involve a similar process.

Sometimes the child's interests and the activities can be used as incentives or rewards to help other areas of difficulty. A child who is extremely involved in karate and is having trouble doing his homework may be told, "You will only be able to go to karate class if you finish your homework before 6:30."

When using activities as rewards or incentives, avoid taking the child totally out of the activity because you lose the leverage. A young girl who is thoroughly involved in dancing is doing poorly in school. She isn't paying attention or completing her class work. Don't say "If your schoolwork doesn't improve, I'm taking you out of dancing."

It would be better to say, "I'm going to get a report from your teacher every day on your attention in class and completion of the work. On the days you pay attention and do your work, you can go to dancing. On the days you don't complete the work, you can't go to dancing."

Once you completely remove the child from an enjoyable activity, you lose a source of motivation.

May Help With Self-Discipline

Many activities have rules, regulations, do's and don'ts and procedures that must be followed. Outside activities help children set goals and usually involve certain behaviors that must be followed to attain the goals.

Provides Socialization Experience

The way you learn to deal with people is to be with other people. Outside activities provide opportunities for a child to interact with children his own age. This is extremely beneficial for children who lack socialization experiences or don't have many children in their neighborhood to play with.

By becoming involved at the local playground, the child comes in contact with many children who may not live in your immediate neighborhood but live close to your home. Involvement in these activities gives the child other opportunities to learn to relate to people and to develop friendships.

Builds Confidence

A person who is confident in himself knows his strengths and weaknesses. The confident person, when asked a question he doesn't know the answer to, can readily say, "I don't know." If you ask the same person to perform some kind of activity he is incapable of doing, he'll tell you.

For a person to have confidence in himself, he has to see areas in his life that are positive and successful. The child must be able to see skills he has that are better than other children.

If the only thing the child is involved with is schoolwork and he has trouble, it's extremely difficult for him to develop overall confidence.

Outside activities give the child a skill, activity or knowledge that may be unique for him. "I may not be able to get the same grades as Jeff, but I know more about karate than he does."

I'm not saying you have to get your child involved in 37 different activities. Some children go to soccer practice on Tuesday and Thursday, a scout meeting on Friday and take music lessons on Monday and Wednesday. Saturday and Sunday usually involve games or scouting activities. A lot of times these children tell me, "I wish I had some free time just to play."

Involve the child in outside activities but not to an extent his entire life is structured around them. Kids need time just to be kids and to play.

Some parents have their children involved in sports or music because they want them involved in it. The child could care less. The other day a child told me he didn't like taking piano lessons. When I asked him why he was taking them, he said, "My mother said I have to take it because I have a talent in music."

Don't live your life through your child's activities. Don't pressure him to continue in things in which he has no interest.

Give the child an opportunity to experience the sport or activity. Then listen to what he says after he has been involved in it for a period of time.

Here's the general procedure I normally use for children who are hesitant to become involved in any activities. Let's say you have a young girl who likes to dance and constantly dances around the house and loves music. She expresses an interest in going to dancing school. When the time comes to register, she doesn't want to participate.

Many times a child is hesitant to get involved because of the newness of the situation, she doesn't know what to expect or she may lack a little confidence in this area. Identify an incentive (sleeping out), and tell the child, "You've been wanting to go spend a weekend at your aunt's house. Go to dancing for five times. At the end of the fifth time, I'll ask you if you want to continue taking lessons. If you still want to be involved, you can continue dancing. If you want to quit, that's OK. You can quit. Regardless of your decision, if you go to dancing five times, you can spend the weekend at your aunt's house."

Dealing with situations like this allows you to avoid two mistakes—not getting the child involved in something she will enjoy or forcing her to continue participating in something that isn't a positive experience.

CHAPTER 35

Summer School, Tutoring and Extra Work

Most children view summer school, extra studying and tutoring like adults view income tax, house payments and utility bills. It isn't something you look forward to. It is something you dread and want to avoid. However, some children need additional services or are required to attend summer school. "Extra" schoolwork is a necessary evil that sometimes has to be dealt with.

Summer School

Summer school is usually a result of the child not performing during the 9 months of the regular school year. It is considered because the school suggests or requires it. Or you feel additional work in a particular subject is necessary. Summer school is considered, recommended or required in three general situations.

To Pass A Subject Or Earn Credits

The fifth-grade student fails reading and must attend summer school to advance to the sixth grade. The high-school freshman fails English and must attend summer school because he needs four credits in English to graduate from high school. This is probably the major benefit of summer school.

Perhaps your elementary-school child is struggling in school and is barely passing. Summer school is a frequent activity for the child. It might be wise to get an evaluation to determine the reason for the child's difficulty in school. For the child who has to attend summer school frequently, consider something different. It may be more appropriate to have him repeat a grade. Or a change of schools may be necessary. See the appropriate chapters in this section for additional information.

To Strengthen Academic Skills

Summer school may be required or recommended for the child who barely passes or fails a particular subject to help develop weak academic skills. Summer school is designed to strengthen the child's foundation and to strengthen academic weakness.

When this is the reason for summer-school attendance, we try to substitute tutoring for the formal classroom summer school setting. In general, individual or very small group tutoring strengthen skills better and faster than traditional summer school.

Some schools allow you to substitute a certain amount of individual tutoring in place of summer school. This individual or small-group work is seen by the school as equivalent to the formal summer-school setting.

Consequence Of Not Performing In School

In this situation, summer school is usually seen as punishment for not performing during the regular school year. This usually occurs when a child has the academic skills necessary for adequate achievement in school but doesn't perform. This is usually the case of the irresponsible child who does not do what he is supposed to do (homework, class work, studying for a test) and performs poorly. It's almost as if summer school is designed to get the child's attention, make him realize the wrong he has done during the school year and change his attitude toward school for the next year.

Big, severe or harsh punishments don't work well with some children. For some, going to summer school won't offset the fact they got away with not doing homework 483 times, paid attention in class 30% of the time and only completed 40% of the class work. This one big punishment won't change some children's attitudes.

If this is the primary reason for summer school, it won't be beneficial. It's better to do many small things during the school year as a consequence for his poor performance than to do one big thing at the end of the school year. Monitor the child's school performance on a weekly basis. His privileges for each weekend can be based on his performance. If he completed the required schoolwork and did what he was supposed to do during the week, he earns privileges for the weekend

Another situation is the child who is told if he doesn't perform in school during the regular school year and has to go to summer school he won't be able to go with the family on summer vacation. This also is a big punishment that occurs over a long period of time. With some children, this is a very ineffective method to change school behavior.

If summer vacation or any big reward is used, it's better to break the performance period into small segments. After Easter, monitor the child's weekly school performance. He can earn points for completing work or doing what he's supposed to. If he receives a certain number of points by the time summer occurs, he can go on the summer vacation. If he doesn't receive the points, he won't go.

Tutoring

Tutoring is usually recommended or considered for the child who demonstrates academic weaknesses. The primary purpose of tutoring is to develop academic skills and strengthen the child's foundation. Tutoring can occur during the school year, over summer vacation or as a substitute for summer school. This attempt at dealing with academic weaknesses can be done individually or in small groups. Tutoring can be beneficial in several situations.

To Strengthen Academic Weaknesses

The fifth-grade child may be reading on a third-grade level. He has difficulty with fifth-grade work. In this situation, tutoring is designed to build the child's reading skills. This particular type of tutoring usually involves working with the child at his current level. The tutor works with the child in reading on a third-grade

316 The Parent's Guide To Solving School Problems

level. This type of tutoring doesn't involve any work with the child's current subjects, homework or class work. It is primarily designed to strengthen weak skills and usually continues until the child's skills have significantly developed or he is on grade level.

To Clarify Information Or Give Child Better Understanding Of Material

Your child has just started learning about fractions, and you have difficulty helping him with the work and getting him to understand the concepts. A brief amount of tutoring may be beneficial. For the high-school student having trouble in chemistry or geometry, working with a teacher in this area may clarify some of the concepts and allow him to understand the material.

This type of tutoring is usually brief, infrequent and designed to get the child over a difficult period of time or a stumbling block he encounters in a certain subject.

To Help Child With Homework

If you work, have difficulty doing homework with your child or don't understand the material enough to help the child with his homework, a tutor may be employed to do this. This type of tutoring involves a person helping the child with his homework, studying for a test or helping him prepare for the next day of school.

Some after-school programs provide this service. For this type of tutoring, it may not be necessary to have a teacher work with the child. A high-school or college student could perform these services.

To Help Child With Responsibility

Some children do poorly in school because they are not doing what they are supposed to do (not turning in homework, studying for tests, reading assigned material). This child does not have an academic problem. He needs help with responsibility. I call the type of tutor child needs a "lead tutor" because this child needs help "get the lead out." This tutor sees that the child is doing what he's supposed to do. Often times we will use a child in a higher grade at the same school to tutor. This way the tutor can find out exactly what the child has for homework. As in the situation above, a teacher is not needed here. A student could provide these services.

Extra Work And Required Summer Work

Some schools assign work to be completed over the summer. Parents sometimes want their children to do extra work during the school year and/or practice their math facts, reading, etc. over the summer time. Kids love this! This often produces problems, especially for children who are not to thrilled about doing schoolwork, because they view the summer as a time when school should be forgotten.

Rather than fighting and battling your child to read the books he's been assigned by the school, you could set up something similar to the following. "We are going to the movie Saturday and, if you have chapters one, two and three read in your book, you can come with us. If not, you will stay home with the baby sitter." For the child who has to write a book report during the summer, the activity could be broken up into several sections (reading a certain number of chapters, preparing an outline, writing the rough draft of the report, writing the final report). A consequence or incentive could be set for each section that is completed. "Your friends can come sleep over when you have half of the book read." "We can go rent the video game you wanted when the outline is finished" and so forth.

When we want a child to do extra work, especially in the summer, we set up a "time bank account." Let's say we want a child to practice his math facts during the summer. We could require the child to do this for a minimal amount of time (5 minutes) each day. We would tell the child "We are going to practice your math facts for 5 minutes each day. I made up a bank account and will put the amount of time you practice each day in the bank account. You have to practice for 5 minutes, but if you want to practice longer we will put the time in the bank account. The time in the bank account will be your time to do whatever you want to do. Go to the movie, fishing or baseball game." If the child wants to go to a movie, he'll have to have 2 or 3 hours in the bank account. Often under these conditions, the child brings the flash cards to his mom and says, "Let's practice." He wants to work on his math, not because he likes math, but because he wants to go to the zoo. This extra work during the summer becomes less of a negative experience and more of a positive one.

Things To Consider

1. Summer school and/or tutoring alone don't usually develop responsibility, self-discipline or motivation. If you have a child who has performance problems at school-not because of his ability-but because of other factors, these services alone will not be beneficial. Try to develop an overall level of responsibility or self-discipline. That involves working on behavior in the home and in the neighborhood that is similar to those that were interfering with the child's school performance. Try to change the habit and develop a responsible child in many areas of his life.
2. Tutoring is more likely to build academic skills and strengthen weaknesses than is summer school.
3. Summer school is most beneficial when it occurs infrequently and is used to allow the child to pass to the next grade or to earn credits toward graduation.
4. If you have a child who frequently has to attend summer school or receive tutoring, it is wise to have an evaluation to determine what the problems are and how to solve them. A child in this situation may need to repeat the grade or change schools.
5. The smaller the pupil-teacher ratio, class size or tutoring group, the more beneficial it is.
6. If tutoring is recommended to strengthen academic skills, be sure you get a qualified person who specializes in the area in which your child has difficulty. Get a reading specialist to tutor your child in reading.
7. If the tutoring doesn't seem to benefit the child, ask questions.

Are we working on the right problem? What else should be done? What can I do to help at home? Is the problem correctly identified?

8. If the child sees a tutor once or twice a week, be sure you get material and suggestions from the tutor so you can work on similar areas at home during the rest of the week.

9. If the tutor says the child is improving or shows results that indicate it, but the child's performance in school has not significantly improved, start asking questions. Maybe the child doesn't need tutoring as much as he needs motivation or responsibility. Has the problem been correctly identified? What else needs to be done? How can you get this improvement to occur in school so the child's performance will improve?

10. If you give your child extra work, try to keep it positive and set it up so he wants to do it rather than something he wants to avoid. Don't "overdose" your child with extra school work. I saw a second grader whose mother required him to do 1 hour of extra study every school night, 2 hours on the weekend and 2 every day during the summer. By fifth grade, this child is going to be "burned out" and is not going to want to do school related activities.

CHAPTER 36

Intelligence

Some parents have an inaccurate idea of what intelligence is. As a result, they set excessive expectations for school performance. If their child is unable to meet the expectations, he receives unnecessary negative attention.

What Is Intelligence?

There is a great deal of disagreement among professionals about what constitutes "intelligence." For our purposes, intelligence is a child's capability, his potential, how smart he is and his ability to learn.

Intelligence is inherited. A child is born with a certain level of intelligence. For all practical purposes, it does not change throughout his life. The child's capacity to learn is inherited primarily from his parents and grandparents.

It's possible for a child to inherit characteristics from any generation of his family tree. An example pertaining to height serves to make several points. My mother is 4' 10" and my father is 5' 5". I was unlikely to be tall. I am about 5' 5", this was set at birth. When I was born, I had a certain genetic capacity for height. No matter what I did or how hard I tried, I wouldn't grow taller than 5' 5". If I had been sick, had an accident or didn't eat properly, I might not have reached this height.

Intelligence is determined the same way. It is fixed at birth. No individual can get smarter with time. But his capacity might be decreased if something interfered with his development.

Measuring Intelligence

Intelligence is measured by various tests. A child is given a test that has been given to thousands of children his age in years and months. His score is compared to the scores of the other children to determine a relative level of intelligence. Individual tests, given on a one-on-one basis, yield more accurate results than tests given in a group.

Intelligence is often described in terms of an Intelligence Quotient (IQ). This is simply a child's mental age (as determined by a test) divided by his chronological age, multiplied by 100.

Some problems were encountered with this method of determining IQ. Most modem tests use a deviation IQ. This obtains IQ by statistical comparison. Each child's test performance is compared with scores earned by children in his or her own age group.

The actual IQ number is not very important. What should be considered is the range of a child's intelligence. The distribution and ranges of intelligence are shown in this graph.

An average range of intelligence includes about 50% of the children in the United States. On each side of the average range, there are various levels of intelligence. About 25% of the children are above average, and about 25% of children are below average in their ability.

One way of viewing intelligence is to think of each child as being born with a certain-size bucket. Children falling in the superior range of intelligence have very large buckets. Children in the mentally disabled range of intelligence have small buckets. Most children fall within the average range and have average-size buckets.

Intelligence is what a child is capable of learning. Achievement tests measure what a child has learned. If a child is entering fifth grade and is of average intelligence, we would expect him to be at a beginning fifth grade level on an achievement test. If he's above average, we would expect his achievement level to be above a fifth grade level. The child below average in his intelligence would be expected to have his reading, math, etc. levels as measured by an achievement test to be below average. Grades are a result of combination of the child's intelligence and what he has learned plus the child's interest in what he is doing, motivation and effort. That is why school performance does not always reflect the child's intelligence ability. See the chapter that discusses The Bright Underachiever.

Expectations For Performance

Regardless of your child's range of intelligence, your primary concern should be, "Is he doing his best? Is he working up to his capacity?"

Some parents don't look at it this way. They want, expect and demand above-average work, even though the majority of children have only average ability. Look at 100 children in school, and you'll find 50 with average intelligence, 25 above average and 25 below average.

Let's say you have no idea of your child's range of ability. If you assume he is average, the chances are 7-1/2 out of 10 you have not overestimated his ability. However, if you assume he is above average, the chances drop to 2-1/2 out of 10 that you have not overestimated his ability. If you were betting, you'd have a better chance to win if you guessed average. But most parents expect above-average school performance from their children and don't accept C-level work.

What happens if you expect more from your child than he is capable of giving? He is certain to fail. If he isn't capable of attaining the expectations set for him, whatever he does will become a negative experience. We all tend to stay away from things that are difficult or negative for us. If high expectations make schoolwork negative, the child will avoid duties and tasks related to school.

You have a much better chance of being correct if you assume your child has an average intellect. If you assume a child is average when he is above average, he will eventually perform on his actual (above-average) level. Schoolwork involves success, praise and accomplishment. He will engage in things that involve positive attention. See the chapter that discusses grades.

On the other hand, if you expect above-average work and the child is average, he will perform on a below-average level because schoolwork involves failure, punishment and frustration.

CHAPTER 37

CHILDREN WITH HIGH LEVELS OF INTELLIGENCE

Most parents would like to have their children exhibit a high level of intelligence, but sometimes high cognitive ability produces problems or concerns. Children I am referring to in this section primarily include those with IQs in the range of 120 and above. I'll discuss some general areas of concerns parents have and the most frequent problems that I see these children encountering.

How Different Are These Children?

Being above average in any skill, ability or characteristic makes a child unique and different. A child's level of intelligence is usually measured by an IQ (intelligence quotient) test. Scores from this test are usually based on a norm of 100. Children who score lower than 90 are considered below average. Those who score above 109 are considered above average. See the chapter on Intelligence for a more-detailed discussion.

Most people who report intelligence scores to parents usually provide a range rather than a specific IQ score. Intelligence is supposed to remain stable and usually does, but there may be some variation in specific scores attained because of motivational factors, how the child was tested and standard error of measurement in tests. Below is a frequency of certain intelligence levels seen in the general population.

IQ Score	Classification	Approximate Incidence in Population
160	Very Superior	1 out of 10,000
155	Very Superior	3 out of 10,000
150	Very Superior	9 out of 10,000
145	Very Superior	4 out of 1,000
140	Very Superior	7 out of 1,000
135	Superior	2 out of 100
130	Superior	3 out of 100
125	Superior	6 out of 100
120	Superior	11 out of 100
115	High Average	18 out of 100
110	High Average	27 out of 100

Most public-school systems have special education classes for children with high levels of intelligence. These are usually called gifted classes. Criteria for program eligibility differs from state to state. Contact your local public-school system for additional information. You may also want to review the chapter on Special Education.

Characteristics Of Gifted Children

Below are characteristics based on research compiled by Dr. J. Renzulli.

Learning Characteristics

1. Unusually advanced vocabulary for age or grade level.
2. Quick mastery and recall of factual information.
3. Wants to know what makes things or people "tick."
4. Usually "sees more" or "gets more" out of a story, film or other activity than others.
5. Reads a great deal on his own. Usually prefers adult-level books. Doesn't avoid difficult materials.
6. Reasons things out for himself.

Motivational Characteristics

1. Becomes absorbed and involved in certain topics or problems.
2. Easily bored with routine tasks.
3. Needs little external motivation to follow through in work that initially excites him.
4. Strives toward perfection. Self-critical. Not easily satisfied with his own speed or products.
5. Prefers to work independently. Requires little direction from teachers.
6. Interested in many "adult problems," such as religion, politics, sex, race.
7. Stubborn in his beliefs.
8. Concerned with right and wrong, good and bad.

Creativity Characteristics

1. Often offers unusual ("way-out"), unique, clever responses.
2. Uninhibited in expressing opinions.
3. High risk taker. Speculative.
4. Often concerned with adapting, improving and modifying institutions, objects and systems.
5. Displays a keen sense of humor.
6. Shows emotional sensitivity.
7. Sensitive to beauty.
8. Nonconforming. Accepts disorder. Isn't interested in details. Individualistic. Doesn't fear being different.
9. Unwilling to accept authoritarian pronouncements without critical examination.

Leadership Characteristics
1. Carries responsibility well. Self-disciplined.
2. Self-confident with children his own age, as well as adults.
3. Can express himself well.
4. Adapts readily to new situations.
5. Sociable.
6. Generally directs the activity in which he is involved.

Gifted Personality

There are many characteristics of the bright or gifted child. Most school systems and parents view the concept of "gifted" primarily as it relates to ability. Most school systems evaluate a child in terms of intellectual and achievement skills to determine if he or she is gifted and eligible for special educational services. Most criteria is based on a child having a certain level of intelligence and/or an achievement level (math, reading) above his actual grade placement. Many parents tell me, "He has a high level of intelligence, but he isn't working to his potential."

Some children may be bright or gifted in terms of ability but do not have what I call a "gifted personality." This relates to the school situation and the child's performance. Many children who are classified as bright or gifted have the intellectual abilities but have an "average personality."

A child with a "gifted personality" can be characterized as self-disciplined, responsible, interested in school and learning and involved in his studies. He usually shows a high interest in school and school-related work.

Some children with the same intellectual skills don't show these personality characteristics. They have more of an average personality. They can take or leave school or could care less about homework, class projects and studying. These children don't like school and would rather be playing than doing schoolwork. School is not fun. It is boring and viewed as an unpleasant activity and something to avoid. They don't spend a lot of time reading or in school-related activities. They usually do just enough to get by. See the chapter on The Bright Underachiever.

Management Problems

Some bright children do not produce any management problems and are generally cooperative and easy to discipline. Others are just the opposite. Dealing with them daily can be quite difficult. It seems you have to always run fast to stay one step ahead of them.

Stubborn, Strong-Willed Personality Characteristics

Some gifted children are independent, nonconforming, resistant to authority, stubborn and display other similar personality characteristics that produce some management problems. They buck the system. They want to do what they want to do when they want to do it and for as long as they want to do it. Getting them to cooperate with routine activities (doing homework, taking a bath, coming in from playing, cleaning their room) can be quite difficult if they don't want to do it. Review the chapter relating to these personality characteristics for more information on managing this type of child.

Manipulation

Most children are good con artists and manipulators. Add increased levels of intelligence to this ability, and you may have a very skilled manipulator. Many times bright children are smarter than their parents. They can figure out ways to get what they want and can be more in control of you than you are of them.

Avoid Power Struggles And Confrontations

Bright children may find themselves in conflicts with those who place limits on their behaviors or who try to direct them into certain activities.

Stay away from power struggles and confrontations. Deal with the behavior in a calm, matter-of-fact fashion. Set rules and consequences for behavior. Spell them out ahead of time and enforce them consistently.

Because of their intelligence, these children are very skilled in asking questions that you can't answer logically. "Why do I have to make my bed every morning if I'm going to sleep in it at night and mess it up?" If you try to reason why certain things must be done, these children may out-talk and out-reason you. With some requests, there are no logical reasons why they must be done other than you said they must be done.

Suppose you have a child who asks many questions about why he has to take a bath or why he needs to do homework at a certain time. You find yourself talking in circles. For every reason you give the child, he has 37 reasons why he shouldn't do it or why he doesn't need to. Minimize these discussions. Tell him he has to do it because you say he has to. You're the adult, and he's the child. End of discussion!

Review the chapters under the section Methods and Techniques for additional behavior-management techniques.

School Problems

Many gifted children enter school and don't have any problems. They do what they're supposed to do, receive good grades and cooperate with school-related work. These self-disciplined children are interested in school. They have a "gifted personality" to go along with their high intellectual abilities. If you have one of these children, you probably aren't reading this section. It seems like you could lock these kids in a closet, and they would still learn. School placement is not of great concern. These children do well in average or above-average school settings or in a closet.

Other bright children experience problems in school. Parents often wonder why a child has so much trouble in school if he is so intelligent. I'll discuss several situations I have seen and explain how they relate to problems with this type of child.

Average Personality

As mentioned above, some children with gifted intellectual abilities do not have what I call a "gifted personality." They have more of an "average personality" and are not into schoolwork, studying, homework. They receive grades in the C-to-B range. Parents feel if the child would try harder, he or she would maximize his or her potential. If this is the situation, it may be best to accept this performance to help create a positive situation and maintain the child's motivation regarding schoolwork. If a great deal of negative attention, punishment or restrictions are placed on the child because he is not a straight-A student, school may become negative. His motivation to achieve will decline. Even though he has the ability, emphasize effort and doing what he is supposed to do rather than grades. If he has the ability and does what he's supposed to do, grades will automatically follow.

Irresponsibility

These children have stubborn, strong-willed personality characteristics and want to do what they want to do. If they're interested in something, they give 1,000% effort, energy, motivation, attention. But if they aren't interested, they'll do it half-way or not at all. They may not do homework or refuse to study for tests because of a lack of responsibility or self-discipline. They have academic problems. A child in this category often shows irresponsibility in school and in many areas of his life. In dealing with this type of problem in the gifted child, work on developing responsible behavior in school-related activities and in behaviors in the home and neighborhood. See the chapter that discusses responsibility.

Schoolwork Too Easy Or Doesn't Challenge The Child

When a bright child has problems in school, they generally fall into two types.

The first involves the child who completes his work fast; the work may seem too easy. Although he may have 20 minutes to complete his math problems, he finishes them in 3 minutes. Then he talks, fidgets, gets up and walks around, aggravates others or disrupts the class. This child is doing his work correctly, but it takes him less time than the other children. Behavior problems are apparent when he has free time with nothing to do. The other kids are still working on the assignment. This child may need to be given additional work, advanced work or moved to a higher-level class.

The second situation occurs where the bright child refuses to do work in school and shuts down his performance. Many bright kids having trouble in school say the work is too easy and they're bored. The child knows the work and refuses to do it because it's boring, routine and repetitious. It's like asking you to write your telephone number 100 times so you remember it. Your answer would be, "I already know it, and I'm not going to write it 100 times." This situation usually occurs in a child who has gifted ability, a "gifted personality" and is generally responsible in many other areas of his life. He cooperates with cleaning his room, taking a bath, getting ready for church. However, he shuts down in school and shows irresponsibility and a lack of self-discipline there. If the child is responsible in many areas of his life, but shuts down in school, the work may be too easy or not challenging.

If the child finishes his work quickly then creates problems or refuses to do the work and the school cannot give him higher-level work or move him to an advanced class, it may be best to change schools. If the child shows many other irresponsible-type behaviors, a change in the amount or level of work or a move to a new school will probably not alleviate the problems.

The child I am describing is not doing the work because he does not want to do it or is not interested in it. He'd rather be doing anything but schoolwork-like playing or having a good time. This child shows a lack of self-discipline or responsibility in many areas of his life. Change schools only if you are very sure work is the problem and difficulties in school are the major difficulties you have with your child.

Study Habits Not Developed

In lower grades, material and information are presented frequently. There is a lot of review. If your child is bright, does some of the work and pays attention some of the time, his grades will be fine. Not studying and partial involvement in schoolwork doesn't work too effectively in the middle grades.

Some children's lack of effort catches up with them around the middle grades or in high school. They are unable to maintain high grades with this approach to schoolwork.

In the middle grades, more work is presented. There are many teachers and things aren't repeated as frequently. The child who did well in the lower grades starts receiving poor test scores. A's drop to Cs, or he begins to fail.

Many times every year I see bright children whose grades have significantly declined when they entered fifth, sixth or seventh grade. In talking to the child and the parents, the only thing that appears to have changed is the decrease in performance. The child still approaches school the way he did in the first four grades. Many of these children tell me, "I'm doing the same thing I did in third grade, but now it's too hard. I can't keep up and maintain the grades the way I used to." These children have not developed any study habits or have never done what they were supposed to do. In the lower grades, their level of intelligence was enough to carry them, but this doesn't work in the upper grades.

It is extremely important to help your child develop study skills and habits. If this situation occurs with your child, try to establish some kind of home-school communication system to monitor his effort in his class work, homework, studying. If you can get your child doing what he is supposed to do in his school-related work, his grades will improve significantly.

Socialization Problems

Although many bright children socialize extremely well and have many friends, some have trouble relating to their age mates. This seems to occur in two general situations.

Lack Of Age-Related Social Skills

Many bright children are better at solitary play and activities than average children. They can amuse themselves much better, create things, have a good imagination. This child is likely to be very happy in his room playing, reading or building things. He is not apt to aggravate you to have somebody come over to play.

Children with high intelligence levels may get more adult attention or fit into adult conversations more easily than the average child. If you were in a room with a few adults talking and your typical 5-year-old came in the room, you'd say, "Hi. How are you doing? What's happening? See you later. Go ahead outside and play." The bright child may come in and start talking about dinosaurs. Or she sits down and relates to adults much better than another child. She tends to "fit in" with adults better. A bright child may spend more time with adults because she can relate to them more effectively.

An intelligent child may not play and interact with children his own age enough to develop age-appropriate skills. When this happens, socialization skills don't develop. When a bright child is placed with his age mates, he may feel uncomfortable, not know how to relate to them, or relate to them in an adult or inappropriate fashion.

Interaction with peers may be difficult and the child retreats back to solitary play or adult interaction. It's important for gifted children to develop social skills and be with children their own age. Be sure the bright child gets the proper amount of socialization with children his age.

Different Interests

Many bright children show different interests than most other children. They may not have a common activity that warrants interaction and the development of friendships. The young gifted child may be interested in dinosaurs, reading, computers or board games. While most other kids his age are into athletic activities or riding bikes, skateboards and cartoons, the bright child may be more concerned about computers, experiments, music and art.

Although it's important to try to develop interests similar to most children, try to get the child involved with other children of similar interests. If the child is interested in computers or art, involve him in a class or summer activity where he can meet other children with similar interests. Some public-school settings have summer-activity programs for gifted students. Many colleges have summer or after-school programs that may be appropriate.

There's more to life than school and schoolwork. A major part of our lives is dealing with other people. It's extremely important for a gifted child to receive opportunities to develop friendships and age appropriate socialization skills. See the chapter that discusses making friends.

Gifted Associations

Most states have associations for gifted children. If you live in a large city, there may be a chapter there. These associations provide valuable information for parents of children with high levels of intelligence. They may be able to provide information on many activities, camps and programs. For more information, write to:

National Association for Gifted Children
4175 Lovell Road, Suite 140
Circle Pines, MN 55014
(612) 784-3475

CHAPTER 38

The Bright Underacheiver

Before reading this chapter, I suggest you read the chapters on Intelligence and Children with High Levels of Intelligence.

Frequently parents bring their children to me because they are bright but "not working up to their potential." Many of these are middle and high school age children. They say "The teacher say he's capable of all A's and he's making B's, C's and D's. Usually this statement makes me crazy because this is inaccurate for some children. The correct statement should be "He has the ability to make all A's" with some qualifications.

Your performance at work and your child's performance (grades) in school are based on five factors:

1.   Ability
2.   Health
3.   Interest
4.   Motivation
5.   How well you like what you're doing.

Some children possess all of these factors. These are the "gifted children with gifted personalities." These are the children who make straight A's. Other children only have two of the five factors. They have the ability and are healthy. However, they are not self-disciplined. They do not like to do school work and would rather be doing a thousand other things than homework or studying. A good grade for them is 70% because they didn't fail or do not have to go to summer school. These are the "gifted children with average personalities". They do not perform up to their ability because they only posses 40% of the factonecessary for "A" performance in school.

The gifted child with the gifted personality has 15 minutes of homework. He'll do 30 minutes of homework and then go look at TV or get on the computer. The gifted child with an average personality may spend three and a half hours trying to get out of 15 minutes of homework. Although both of the children have the ability to be "straight A students", they do not perform (grades) the same. The average child may receive grades in the C to B range or lower. These children usually do not achieve according to their intelligence. They are not motivated or interested in schoolwork. They do not do what they are supposed to be doing (homework, study) and put forth minimal effort.

When looking at your child's abilities and actual capacity as they relate to his school performance, other factors have to be considered, especially personality characteristics. Just because a child is bright and has a high intellectual capacity does not necessarily mean he will or should perform exceptionally well in school. For children who are bright but do not have a "gifted personality," it may be wise to try to maintain their motivation, develop responsible behaviors, see that they do what they are supposed to do and accept less-than-perfect work in order to make school a positive experience.

If a great deal of negative attention is placed on their inability to perform to their potential and they frequently hear "You could do better," school becomes negative and motivation declines. The child's performance may be below his intellectual capacity and fall below average. Many gifted kids with "average personalities" learn enough to keep their heads above water. They don't let school interfere with their play, fun or other activities with a higher priority!

With these children you do not place emphasis on grades. Emphasize effort, participation and doing what you are supposed to do. I'll use an example to show what often happens. A child with the ability to make straight A's wants an expensive bike. His parents tell him at the beginning of the report card period "If you make the B honor roll the next report card, we'll buy you the bike you want." The self-disciplined, gifted child with the gifted personality would make the A honor roll! The child with the average personality looks a this situation and thinks "You know how much effort I'll have to put forth to do that. It's too much work. The bike's not worth it." This actually decreases this child's motivation toward school and he receives C's and D's.

A better way to do this for this child would be to talk to his teacher(s) and find out the reason(s) he is receiving the low grades. The teacher explains that he is not turning in all his homework, does not complete his class work and often does not bring the necessary supplies to class. We place emphasis on this. We focus on his effort, responsibility and doing what he's supposed to be doing. Not his grades. The parent tells the child "I'm going to check with your teacher every Friday. If she indicates that you did all your homework, completed your class work and were prepared for class we'll put a check on the calendar on that Friday. If not we'll put an X on that day. At the end of the nine weeks period, if you have seven checks, we'll buy you the bike you wanted." This type of child looks at this at a more attainable goal and the likelihood that he will perform is much grater. I'll get with these children and tell them "What your parents are asking is easy. You could be stupid and get a new bike. All their asking you to do is do the homework, etc." The bright child who does what he is supposed to do will get good grades.

Another reason to emphasize responsibility and doing what you are supposed to do rather than grades is to develop study habits. Many of these children, especially in the elementary school years, can put forth a very minimal amount of effort, pay attention in class and get very good grades. However, this method or lack of study often catches up with them when they get to a point in school when they have to study. For some children this happens in middle school and the grades decline. Others show this when starting high school. While others can "wing it" until they get to college and then have major grade problems. A "B" or "A" grade for this type of child who put forth minimal effort and only turned in half of the homework is not a good grade because he is not developing responsibility and study habits and is not doing what he's supposed to be doing.

Another reason to emphasize effort instead of grades is to keep school positive and something the child wants to do rather than avoid. Most of these children are not motivated when it comes to school. If you told them, "You don't have to go to school anymore," they would stay home. They are going to school and doing school related work because we are "making" them do it. Late in high school or the early part of college, many of these children realize the value of education. Now they are going to school for "me" not because their parents are forcing them to go. They then realize that with a good education they can get a nice car, better job, etc. Now they are motivated. Many children who have hear the majority of their school life "You're not working to your potential" "You should be doing better" or "You are capable of better grades" never get that far because school becomes a negative experience which you avoid.

You and I avoid activities, events, and people etc. that produce negative attention. So do children. Emphasizing effort rather than grades increases the probabilities that these children will view school as positive and will reach late high school and/or college.

In addition to the chapters mentioned above, I suggest that you review the chapters that discuss grades and responsibility for more information in this area.

CHAPTER 39

Children Who Need a Smaller Classroom Setting

Most schools average about 30 children in a class. Some children can handle this setting fine. Others need a smaller setting because of academic and/or behavioral difficulties. A smaller pupil-teacher ratio enables a child to receive more individual attention. Work can be presented at a level commensurate with his ability. Frustration and failure can be minimized. In some cases, it's better to try to fit the school to the child's needs rather than trying to fit the child to the school.

Academic Concerns

Children who have problems with schoolwork may not be able to handle the academic expectations in a large classroom. This may involve a poor foundation (the child is in sixth grade but reading on a second-grade level). A depressed level of intelligence or developmental lags (learning disability, perceptual motor deficits, auditory-processing problems) may also cause problems. The child can't keep up with the other children in the large classroom.

Behavioral Concerns

The child may display "bad" behavior, such as disrupting the classroom, acting out, difficulty with authority. Or it may involve other behaviors that interfere with the child's performance (attention deficits, overactivity, lack of responsibility, independent behavior and self-discipline). In a large classroom, the child can't receive the individual attention that may be necessary for him to function.

Some children need a special-education class or a specialized school. Most can function in a regular school if classes have a small pupil-teacher ratio. In some areas, a school with 10 to 20 children in a class may be difficult to find. In areas where there are many schools, this academic setting is usually available.

Determining If A School Can Help Your Child

To determine if a school can help your child, look at a couple of things. First, contact a mental-health professional, educational specialist or someone who is familiar with the schools in your area. Have them try to identify the needs of your child and generate a list of possible schools.

Once schools have been identified, the second step is to visit each school and talk with the principal or counselor. Describe the needs of the child and the approach that is needed to maximize the probability of success. School personnel must make a decision as to whether they feel they can provide the necessary services.

For children I work with, I have the parents contact the school to see if there is an opening in a specific grade. If there is, I contact the school and describe what I feel the child needs and get some type of feedback from the administration. Then the parents and I try to make a decision regarding the appropriateness of the school.

Ask the school to give you the names of parents who have children with similar difficulties. Contact them for feedback about their perceptions of the school and the help received.

Grade Placement Is Important

In a smaller school setting, grade placement of the child often determines if the school can help. You may have a third grader who is academically behind. When considering the child, the school may say their third-grade class is advanced. If he was in fourth grade, they could help him because several children in that grade receive special help and have a poor foundation.

You may have to look at the child's grade in the school rather than the overall school.

CHAPTER 40

Special Education

Most parents have the wrong idea about special education. They equate special education with low intelligence. If someone says, "My child is receiving special educational services in his school," most listeners think the child is limited in their intelligence.

I tell parents, "I think your child will benefit from a resource room or special-education class."

They often respond, "I thought you just said he was average intelligence. Why does he need special education?"

To view special education as only providing services to children of low levels of intelligence is like saying, "The only type of car anyone needs is a compact car." Special education provides a wide range of services for children who have physical, behavioral or academic problems or who will benefit from a smaller, more individualized learning environment. Although children with low levels of intelligence are included, they represent only a small portion of the children served. The belief most people hold regarding special education is very inaccurate.

Special education classes are designed to meet the educational needs of many students who have difficulty with or do not benefit from a regular classroom setting. These students will not learn by the same methods used to teach the majority of the student population.

There are two types of special education classes: self-contained classes and resource rooms. In a self-contained special education class, the child usually remains in the same classroom and receives specialized services the entire day.

A resource room provides children with part-time services in special areas. The child attends regular classes for part of the day. The other part, he receives individual attention in his weak subjects in a special-education class. Resource rooms are more common in public schools. They are used to avoid labeling and to keep the child in as many regular classes as he can handle.

"Mainstreaming" is a term used to mean a child receiving special educational services is placed into the mainstream and is attending regular classes with minimal assistance. "Inclusion" refers to a child receiving special educational services placed in a regular class with considerable help. Often when this child is included in a regular class a teacher or aid comes with him and provides the help he needs. Although most educators would say that they would want children out of special education and in regular classes, there is controversy centering around inclusion. Some educators think it is great. While others are strongly opposed to it and feel that it is detrimental to the children involved.

Special education classes offer two advantages: First, they place the child in a classroom with a smaller pupil-teacher ratio than regular classes. With fewer students, the teacher can give more individual attention to each child. Work can be presented in a manner and at a rate commensurate with the child's strengths and weaknesses. The special education teacher can use the child's abilities to teach and train him in weak areas.

Secondly, special education classes make learning and school a pleasant, positive experience to keep the child motivated. Many children who require special education have had months, if not years, of failure, frustration and negative attention in school.

These children can't compete in a regular classroom. Because their weaknesses have been continually emphasized, they turn off to school and show a lack of interest in academic work. They may avoid sitting down with a book or doing anything that resembles schoolwork.

Special education classes are designed to present work to ensure success and achievement. Learning becomes a positive experience. Combined with teacher emphasis on the child's accomplishments and strong points, it maintains a child's interest and motivation in academic endeavors.

There are many types of special education classes or resource rooms. The terms classifications different differ from state to state, but roughly include the same children.

Types of Classes

Gifted And Talented

These classes are for children with significantly above average levels of intelligence. Work designed for average students may be below their level. Some regular classes are boring for these children. The special education classes individualize the work for the child and present it at a stimulating level.

Learning Disabled

This type of special-education class is designed for students who are average or above average intelligence who are prevented from learning in a regular class setting. See the chapter that discusses learning disabilities for a more detailed discussion.

These children can learn but have difficulty learning by methods used in a regular classroom. They must be taught in a specialized way. The teacher in the special education class or resource room presents work in a manner that will help learning. Children with learning disabilities just need to be taught differently to learn.

Emotional Or Adjustment Difficulties

This special education service is for children who have the ability to learn, but emotional and behavior problems interfere with their ability to perform in a regular classroom setting. A small class that focuses on behavioral and emotional difficulties is necessary to give the child an opportunity to learn.

Educationally Handicapped Or Slow Learner

These classes are designed for children who fall within the gray area between average and mild mental retardation. See the chapter on Intelligence. Slow learner means exactly what it says.

These children can learn, but at a pace slower than the child of average intelligence. You're an average student, and I am a slow learner. The teacher gives us 10 math problems and 13 minutes to complete them. You finish all 10, but I complete only 6. Give me another 10 minutes, and I'll finish all of them.

Special education classes for slow learners are designed to present work at a rate that fits their learning style.

Physical Problems

A variety of special education services are available for children with physical difficulties that would interfere with their ability to perform in a regular class setting. These may include children who are handicapped, visual or hearing impaired or children with speech difficulties. These classes are designed to meet the physical needs of the child and provide the necessary therapy and learning materials designed to compensate for the child's physical impairment.

Mental Disability

This special education service is for children whose level of intelligence falls below the slow learner range of intelligence. Classes for the mildly mentally disabled are designed for children who can learn, but only to a certain level. Classes for the moderately mentally disabled are designed to teach children personal self-sufficiency and daily living skills necessary for living in society.

Multiple Handicapped

There are special education classes designed to provide services for children who suffer a combination of several of the difficulties described above.

How Big Is The Problem?

It is conservatively estimated that 10% of all students have difficulty in school. Some children experience monumental difficulties if they don't receive assistance.

Special Education Not Always Helpful

In the 1960s and early 70s, special education was seen as a solution for all problems of children experiencing difficulties in school. As a result, many children were placed in special educational settings. In the late 1970s and early 1980s, research data indicated special education was not beneficial for all children with academic problems. In fact, a large group of children received little, if any, benefit from special-class placement.

Trends

The trend of the 80's and 90's was away from special educational as the first step in solving a child's academic difficulties. Placement in a special class, for some children, is now seen as the last step to take after other attempts have failed. The emphasis is to try other things to keep the child in regular classes or to avoid labeling and unnecessary placement.

If a child has learning or behavioral problems, modifications may be made in the classroom or teaching methods. Other things may be tried before a child is considered a candidate for special educational placement.

Each state has different procedures and guidelines to determine eligibility for special-educational services. Your local school system has information regarding the services available and criteria for eligibility.

504 Program

Each state has a criteria in order to qualify to receive special educational services. For example, in Louisiana in order to be classified as Learning Disabled a child has to have an academic strength and an academic weakness that are at a certain level when compared to the average. Sometimes children who are having trouble in school do not qualify for help because they do not meet the criteria.

Throughout the United States this was happening. These children were "falling trough cracks", not getting help and continued to do poorly in school. A number of the national child related organizations (e.g. National Association For Children With

Attention Deficit Disorder) brought these concerns to the government. When the Americans With Disabilities Act was revised, Section 504 was included to address these concerns.

I will not go into details about this because you can get all the information you want about this from your local public school system and I discuss this program in another chapter. Briefly the regulations say that children who show characteristics of an Attention Deficit Disorder, dyslexia, dysgraphia, etc. and have trouble in the regular classroom are entitled to receive accommodations and modifications in the regular classroom. This could include a variety of things (e.g. extra time on tests, timed tests, oral testing, note taking assistance, reduction in amount of homework). In Louisiana, each school has a coordinator of the 504 program. Although these are not special educational services, this program is usually housed in the Special Educational Department. You could get more information by contacting your local public school system and reviewing the chapter on the 504 program.

CHAPTER 41

Trouble Following Directions, Auditory Processing Problems

When you're looking for services for your child, be sure to locate someone who has experience and is a specialist in the area of need. I wanted to include this chapter in the revised book, but this area is not consistent with my training. So I asked Dr. Annell McGee, a speech and language pathologist, to provide assistance. Most of this chapter was prepared by Dr, McGee.

Auditory processing can be defined as what the brain does with what the ear hears. A normal ear hears sound and can reflexively respond to it without the sound meaning anything to the person hearing it. For one sound to be distinguished from another, to be remembered and to be understood, the brain must process it. When an auditory-processing problem exists, there is some interruption in the flow of information to the part of the brain that interprets the particular sounds.

There are many sounds in our environment. We attach meaning to them due to past experience. Some of the most important sounds we hear are speech sounds.

Speech

Speech has meaning to you based on past experience and learning. When you listen to someone speaking a foreign language, you are aware he is talking. But the words mean nothing if you haven't learned that particular language.

Speech and language are intimately interrelated, but a

distinction should be made between them. Language is made up of words and combinations of words that are spoken and listened to. Speech is the vehicle or mechanism that carries or expresses the language. This chapter focuses on the speech and language that is listened to and understood. This is the aspect of speech and language that is affected in auditory-processing problems.

Auditory Processing

Auditory-processing is usually thought of in terms of specific abilities that involve attention, discrimination, sequencing, association and memory. These abilities must be adequately developed before a child can understand language in the classroom. Development of these skills occurs almost automatically if the child has a pair of normally hearing ears, a normally developed brain and exposure to a normally stimulating environment.

Attention

Attention involves paying attention to what is being taught in the classroom. It also involves figure-ground. This is the ability to select and attend to the most important message from a background of extraneous sights and sounds.

Discrimination

This is the ability of the various senses to recognize differences in things that are similar. Auditory discrimination refers to the ability to hear the fine differences in sounds that are almost the same. The child may be able to distinguish between the sounds of "f" and the quiet "th," as may be heard in the words "fie" and "thigh" or between the short "e" and "i" vowels, such as in "pet" and "pit."

Sequencing

This process requires the child to hold information in a particular order, such as being able to remember the names of the days of the week in the order they occur.

Association

Association refers to the ability to "make connections" between and among things. It involves categorizing things that have common characteristics and being able to learn something new by "connecting it up" with something already learned. Associations can be very simple and concrete. Or they can be very complex and abstract. There is also a continuous range from very simple-concrete to very complex abstract, within which any concept may fall.

Memory

There are two important aspects of memory.

Auditory short-term memory involves the ability to listen to, remember and immediately respond to a message. It is closely related to auditory sequencing because auditory signals are usually expected to be remembered in a particular order. The sequential aspects of auditory signals are very "fleeting."

Auditory long-term memory involves the ability to "store" information and retrieve it from "storage" when needed. Beyond these skills, the child must learn to understand and use vocabulary and grammar appropriate for his age and grade level.

Vocabulary

Vocabulary refers to the words and their meanings that we use to express our thoughts, ideas, feelings or whatever else we have to say.

Grammar

Grammar is the organized way in which we put words together into phrases, sentences, paragraphs and dialogue that can be understood by others. Language is very complex. A thorough explanation of its varied aspects is beyond the scope of this chapter.

Causes Of Problems

Auditory-processing problems may result from one or a combination of several causes. Often the cause of the problem can't be clearly detected. In these cases, there is a developmental lag or a delay in the development of these skills. Even when causes are known, the result is a developmental delay because skills don't develop automatically at the age levels they should. In some cases, there is a history of infant prematurity, illnesses of the mother during pregnancy, jaundice at birth or an early childhood disease, heart condition or other medical problem.

These and other similar causes may result in a very subtle form of brain injury that is difficult, if not impossible, to detect in the usual pediatric-neurological examination.

Environmental deprivation or variation may also cause auditory-processing problems. If the child is not exposed to normal preschool opportunities and experiences, his auditory-processing skills may not develop correctly. If a child is raised in a culture whose native language is different from the language of the classroom, he may have difficulty learning the differences in the sounds of the classroom language.

Ear Infections

Perhaps the major cause of auditory-processing problems is a history of early childhood middle-ear infections. These infections rarely result in permanent damage to the peripheral hearing mechanism-the middle and inner ear where listening begins. But they cause mild to moderate hearing losses. When periods of hearing loss occur, the infant's and young child's brain doesn't receive the information from its environment that it needs for auditory-processing to develop normally.

The auditory-processing problems discussed here are not associated with major problems, such as significant and permanent hearing loss, brain damage or mental retardation. These children have difficulty processing auditory information. But they are not included in this discussion.

Effects On Learning

Auditory-processing problems can affect learning in many ways. To learn, a child must first be able to remain reasonably still and pay attention. Next, he must be able to pick out the important messages from the noisy background of sounds that occur in a classroom. If he can't select important sounds, he can't begin to learn at the level he should for his age.

Academic skills that appear to be most affected by poor auditory-processing abilities are language arts-phonics, reading, spelling and English.

The inability to follow directions and comprehend classroom instructions may also result from an auditory-processing problem. In this case, all aspects of academic learning could be affected. In addition, not all language-arts subjects may be affected.

Word-Attack Skills

The child must be able to make sound-symbol associations-know what sound the written letter makes. Then he can "sound out" letters when reading a new word he doesn't recognize. This is called "word-attack" skill. Children with auditory-processing problems may have difficulty developing this skill.

Sound Blending

The ability to blend sounds into words depends on discrimination synthesis, which is a form of sequencing and association. In sound blending, the child must know the sounds of the letters and be able to say them in sequential order as he reads them. His brain must make the association so those word parts can be blended into a whole, meaningful word.

Many children are able to blend word parts into whole words when the word parts are spoken by another person, such as a teacher or other adult. However, the same child may not be able to blend the parts into wholes when "sounding out" the letters by himself. The ability to make sound-symbol associations and the use of sound-blending skills are essential for learning how to read.

Reading

Some children learn to read through the visual system. Others are more auditory learners. Reading involves both auditory and visual skills. The learning of language through the auditory system is essential to learning how to read. Children with auditory-processing problems have difficulty learning that skill.

The degree to which problems in auditory-processing affect the ability to learn to read depends on how well the student can use his strengths in the visual system to compensate for his auditory weaknesses.

Spelling

The ability to learn to spell depends on auditory discrimination, sound-symbol association, sequencing and memory. The child must be able to hear or discriminate the spelling word as it is said by the teacher. If the teacher says "cat" and the child thinks the teacher said, "cap," he will make a spelling error.

Not all words are spelled as they sound. The child must be able to perform a quick sequential task which is the opposite of blending. He must be able to break down the word into parts and write the individual letters in the word he hears. He must be able to get the letters in the correct sequential order. When he is studying the spelling words, he must be able to make a visual and auditory mental picture of each word. He has to be able to store it in his long-term memory bank and retrieve it when taking the spelling test or writing his compositions.

English

Learning the vocabulary and grammatical structures taught in English depends on all of the auditory-processing skills. These skills are basic to the understanding and use of all aspects of language.

Characteristics Of Problems

Most auditory-processing problems go undetected until the child enters school. Skills should develop automatically from the time a child is born and exposed to his environment. They should continue to mature up to a certain point as he gets older. They aren't usually fully developed when the child enters school, but their development should be adequate for the child's age level.

Development of auditory-processing skills is not usually put "to the test" until a child begins to be taught academic skills. Normal academic-skills learning depends on the normal development of auditory-processing skills. The child with an auditory-processing problem may begin to lag behind other students even as early as kindergarten.

Some words of caution-Not all children with learning problems have auditory-processing problems. But don't rule out these problems in cases of academic failure. Not all children who lag slightly behind their fellow students have an auditory-processing problem. There is variation in the development and maturation of these skills and all skills required to learn.

Delays Or Difficulties In Speech

If a child's speech doesn't develop as it should, the lag may be due to an auditory-processing problem. An example is the child who has difficulty pronouncing his words or saying letter sounds correctly. His speech is difficult to understand.

Abnormal Voice Quality

A voice that is too loud or too soft, one that is harsh or unpleasant to listen to or one that sounds like it's coming through the child's nose may signify upper-respiratory problems, allergies or even structural abnormalities associated with middle-ear infections. Infections could be the cause of an auditory-processing problem.

Difficulty Expressing Thoughts

A child may not express himself well in words or complete sentences. He may have this problem because he can't process language through his auditory system.

Inability To Attend To Or Tell Difference Between Auditory Signals

Some preschool children seem not to hear, do not attend to auditory signals or can't tell the difference between signals such as telephone and doorbell rings. They may be exhibiting early signs of an auditory-processing problem. The inability to distinguish between pleasant and unpleasant vocal tones or to respond to sounds by turning to the object or person who is making the sound may be signs of problems.

Difficulty Following Simple Commands

A preschool child who has difficulty learning rhythm games, such as "patty cake," is unable to follow simple commands, can't listen to simple stories, can't repeat a certain number of digits, words or sentences of certain lengths may have an auditory-processing problem.

The child of 2-1/2 to 3 should be able to follow simple, two-level commands. By 4 to 5, he should be able to follow more complicated directions involving 2 to 3 actions; the 2- to 2-1/2-year-old should be able to listen to a simple story for 3 to 10 minutes. By 2-1/2, he should listen for 20 minutes.

The ability to repeat numbers from short-term memory varies from two at age 2 to 2-1/2, to three at age 2-1/2 to 3. Repeating four numbers is appropriate for 4 to 4-1/2 and five digits at 6 to 7 years,

The 2- to 2-1/2-year-old should be able to repeat six- to eight-syllable sentences. A 3-1/2-to-4-year-old should be able to repeat 12-syllable sentences.

School-age children may not have learned how to tell left from right or how to do serial activities, such as saying the alphabet, days of the week or months of the year. Some can't report personal information, such as birth date, age, address and phone number. They may have difficulty learning to tell time or following instructions that involve space and/or time directions.

Academic Difficulties

Parents of school-age children may not have seen any difference in their child's behavior before he enters school. Consider the possibility of an auditory-processing problem if your child begins to have difficulty in the classroom. This is particularly true with following directions and/or language arts subjects, such as phonics, reading and spelling.

Behavioral Difficulties

In extreme cases, a child with an auditory-processing problem may be a behavior problem in the classroom and/or at home. His acting-out behavior may be due to his inability to control his behavior or the frustration he experiences because of his academic failure. Or the child may be very subdued or depressed because of his failure. He may have difficulty paying attention in class and doing homework. He may be "all over the place" with gross body movements or fidgetiness and hand movements. He "can't sit still." He has to handle everything in front of him.

Self-Cuing And Work Habits

Children who show auditory-processing problems may use self-cuing behaviors, such as verbally repeating or finger writing the statement or question. These behaviors are compensatory. They are not bad in themselves but may tend to slow the student down so he can't keep up with the normal pace of the classroom. Other behaviors interfere with his ability to keep up. Responses may be delayed, he may self-correct his errors or he may need to have instructions repeated.

What To Do?

Hearing Examination

Have the child's auditory sensitivity checked to see if the peripheral hearing mechanisms (middle and inner ear) are normal.

Have a child with a hearing problem, whether permanent or temporary, examined by an otologist (a physician who specializes in diseases and disorders of the ear). A temporary hearing loss can be treated and usually cured. This type of hearing loss may cause an auditory-processing problem.

Psycho-Educational Evaluation

If some other type of learning problem, such as a learning disability, mental disability or emotional disturbance, is suspected, have the child tested by a psychologist. The child's educational performance and progress in the classroom should be reported by the teacher. Rule out any possible physical problems, such as gross-motor or fine-motor problems or visual problems. It may be necessary for an educational specialist to test the child or work with him to determine his learning style.

Speech And Language Evaluation

The professional who most commonly evaluates and provides remedial services to children with auditory-processing problems is the speech and language pathologist. If a problem is suspected, have the child seen by a qualified specialist who can evaluate the problem. He or she will explain the evaluation results to you and make appropriate recommendations for dealing with the problem.

School And Home Interventions

When an auditory-processing problem is detected, the child usually needs remedial services as soon as possible. Some classroom interventions and/or parent assistance may be all that is necessary if the problem is mild and hasn't affected the child's educational performance and progress significantly.

In the classroom, put the child in a setting that is as distraction-free and noise-free as possible. He should be seated where he can see the teacher at all times and be encouraged to move in his seat to see any student who is directly involved in a lesson. He should be encouraged to "use his eyes to help him listen."

The teacher should speak clearly to him at all times and give him directions that are broken down into fewer steps. She should allow and encourage him to ask to have directions and instructions repeated if he doesn't think he understands. She should seek advice from the school speech and language pathologist for specific activities that will help the child. You can also contact a speech and language pathologist for specific suggestions and activities to practice with your child.

At home, eliminate noise and other distractions when talking to your child. Be sure he pays attention. Position yourself close to him. Use simple language. Provide a general atmosphere of structure and order in the home.

Some children with auditory-processing problems function

better in a smaller classroom where there is a lower pupil teacher ratio. Some may need to be taught in a special education classroom.

An auditory-processing problem may be part of a more complex problem called learning disability. A child with a learning disability may require special education. The learning disabled child's eligibility for special education in a public school program depends on criteria for placement established by the school system. For more information regarding auditory-processing and other types of speech and language problems contact:

Annell McGee received her Ph.D. in speech and language pathology from the University of Denver, where she specialized in studying neurologically based communication disorders and disorders of the auditory nervous system. She began her career as a speech-language pathologist 35 years ago, working with neurologically impaired preschool cerebral-palsied children.

Dr. McGee has diagnosed and treated thousands of children and adults with neurologically based communication disorders many of who exhibited an auditory-processing problem. She has also taught courses in language and language based learning disabilities to graduate students at Louisiana State University and Tulane University Medical Centers. She is currently in private practice in Metairie, Louisiana and recently retired from public school system in Jefferson Parish, Louisiana.

CHAPTER 42

Learning Disabilities and Other Learning Problems

Many studies have been done on reasons children have difficulty learning. The more comprehensive the study, the greater the number of causes that have been found. Although this chapter focuses on learning disabilities, I have presented general areas of learning difficulties. Some areas overlap or may interact with one another to produce problems.

Causes Of Learning Difficulties

Intelligence
About half of all children in the United States have average intelligence. About 25% are above average, and 25% are below average. Some learning problems result from a depressed level of intelligence. A child's abilities may be in the slow-learner range of intelligence, and he has difficulty competing in an average school setting. Children whose intellectual abilities fall below average often have difficulty competing academically.

Child Is In The Wrong School
A child is having a significant amount of academic trouble in school. He is failing, has to spend a tremendous amount of time on homework and study in order to be prepared for the next school day or has trouble "keeping up." We evaluate the child and find no evidence of a learning disability or problem. He has average intelligence and his achievement level in reading, math, etc. is consistent with his intelligence and also average. However, he is

in an "above average school" that is geared to children with above average intelligence and skills. This school expects their third graders to be functioning one or two grade levels above their grade placement. The average child in this setting looks like he has a learning problem. He has a problem in this setting, but it is not one that pertains to learning. He's 6ft tall and trying to compete with 7ft basketball players. If the child is placed in an average school environment that expects average performance, the problems go away.

Physical (Includes Neurological)

Sometimes physical problems or disabilities interfere in learning. These may be obvious, such as in a child with cerebral palsy who has motor problems and has difficulty writing. Or they can involve problems with vision or hearing. Health related problems can also interfere with a child's ability to acquire information in the academic setting.

Genetic

A person who has reading problems is more apt to have a child with reading problems. Skills are often inherited. Learning difficulties can also be inherited.

Developmental Lags

Thousands of skills and abilities develop in children. Skills don't develop at the same rate. You might have a 5-year-old who can ride a bike like his 8-year-old brother, but he can't color like a 3-year-old. If there is a lag in a skill a child needs for school (memory, hand-eye coordination, ability to follow directions, attention span), he may experience difficulty. This is discussed in more detail later.

Emotional

Children who experience emotional problems sometimes have difficulty in school. These problems can be a result of environmental conditions (divorce, death of a parent, separation) or they can center around the child's emotionality (depression, anxiety, worry).

Environmental

This can include lack of physical care of a child (malnutrition), a lack of language experience or exposure to educational materials and cultural deprivation.

Education

Inappropriate or ineffective teaching may contribute to a child's learning problems. Difficulties may arise when children change schools and move to a school that is at a higher level than the previous one.

Behavioral

This usually centers around behavioral problems, such as irresponsibility, lack of independent behavior and disinterest in school.

Biochemical

Recently chemical structure of foods, artificial ingredients in foods, drugs, nutrition and their effects on the human body have been studied. Although research is limited and results suggest only a slight connection between drugs and learning problems, some professionals believe there is a connection between these areas.

Learning Disability

Many children who experience learning problems are given the catch-all label of learning disability as the cause of difficulties. Many professionals do not agree on what learning disability means, so it's easy to see why most parents don't know what the term means. Most professionals feel for a child to be classified as learning disabled he must have average or above average intelligence or have the potential to function at this level. A child may have average intelligence or superior intelligence but is unable to read.

The above definition of a learning disability is the one that is most accepted. Each state school system with criteria that makes a child eligible for special education. Their criteria for classification of a learning disability may differ from the above. For example, in Louisiana, in order to be classified as having a learning disability, a mental disability has to be ruled out and the child must show a discrepancy in his achievement level. He has to have an academic strength and weakness that is at a certain level when compared to the average child.

The term learning disability covers a wide range of learning disorders. It usually relates to lags in the development of skills or abilities necessary for learning. This learning problem may occur in several areas.

Learning disabilities are more common in boys than girls and cover a wide range of learning problems. Sometimes they affect reading, handwriting, memory, mathematics or other learning processes. A child may be able to spell cat, but when he sees it written, he can't read it. He can't remember how to pronounce the c or can't blend sounds together.

Many skills and abilities (memory, coordination, language) develop in children. These skills do not develop at the same rate. Your 7 year old can hit a baseball like a 10 year old, but he can't color like a 3 year old. Your 5 year old may have an excellent concept of math, but his phonics skills are poor.

All children have strengths and weaknesses in developmental skills, and they do not grow at the same rate. If your child has lags in gross motor coordination and cannot hit a baseball or shoot a basketball, it isn't a big deal. However, if he has lags in auditory memory or similar processing skills, he may not be able to follow verbal directions. He will probably have trouble in school-this is a problem. Lags in development of skills needed to acquire academic abilities prevent the child from learning by methods that are successful with most children. In another situation, the child is acquiring or learning the material the same way as the other students. However, he can't produce the material like the other children. For example, a child may read a short story and be able to orally give you a summary of the story or give you the correct answers to questions about the story. However, if asked to write them he was trouble.

Let's assume an 8 year old needs 5 basic skills to read. (The actual number of skills needed to read may be 20, 30 or 100.) The child who can read has all the skills developed at the same level.

A learning disabled child shows uneven development of the skills necessary to read. This child can perform some parts of the reading process excellently, but he has difficulty in other areas. When it becomes necessary to use all the skills together, he can't read. Although some skills are adequate, others may be 4 years below where it should be.

You can observe this child and see he can learn in many other areas and is not stupid (he can take his bike apart or put together complicated models). He may be classified as lazy or not caring about school. In addition, his performance at school is often inconsistent. One day he gets an A, the next day an F.

This may lead you to feel he isn't trying.

But when the inconsistent performance is more closely analyzed, it is directly related to the skill being used. Schoolwork done on Monday required certain skills, and the child did well. On Tuesday, the work was similar but required another type of skill. The child did poorly. When this is considered, his inconsistent performance is more understandable. He may have difficulties grasping some concepts (phonics, blending sounds) but does extremely well in other areas (math).

Signs Of Learning Disabilities

The signs or symptoms of learning problems related to developmental lags are many and complicated. They usually occur in clusters. I discuss the most frequently occurring, common areas below.

Visual Processing Or Visual Perceptual-Motor Problems

Children have difficulty perceiving things visually. Their eyesight is usually excellent, but they may have trouble in visual discrimination, copying from the board or a book, reverse letters or numbers, confuse b and d or p and q, read "on" for "no" or "saw" for "was." See the chapter that discusses perceptual motor problems.

Auditory-Processing Or Auditory Perceptual Problems

The child has nothing wrong with his hearing but has trouble processing or making sense out of information he hears. The child may have trouble discriminating between two words of similar but not identical sound such as "book" and "brook."

Lags in language development may be present.

When a word is broken down into its phonic elements, the child may have difficulty putting parts together to form a word he knows. He may have trouble remembering what is read to him, but he remembers what he reads or vice versa. He may have difficulty remembering a series of directions or numbers. See the chapter on Following Directions & Auditory-Processing Problems for more information.

Memory Problems

He may remember things he sees but not what he hears or vice versa. He may show excellent memory at times and very poor skills in this area at other times. He may be able to remember things that happened months or years ago (long-term memory) but can't remember what he studied last night or what he ate for lunch (short-term memory).

Coordination Problems

This could be in gross and/or fine motor coordination. He may have trouble riding a bike, throwing a ball, copying from the board, poor handwriting and using eating utensils. These problems as related to school performance are discussed in the chapter that includes perceptual motor problems.

Problems Forming Concepts And Abstracting

The child may have trouble applying information or problem-solving skills that he learns. It is as if he has to relearn the entire process. He has trouble making generalizations or inferences. He may not "catch on" to jokes most of his age mates enjoy. He has trouble in math and can't understand the rules of some games.

Overactivity, Attention Deficit And Impulsivity

Some children with deficits in attention, impulse control and concentration problems may have difficulty in acquiring information or in performance. See the chapter on Attention-Deficit Disorders.

Labels For Learning Problems

Although classifications help identify or label the problem they don't provide specific information needed for dealing with or developing educational plans. Recent trends emphasize terms, labels and classifications that relate to the cause of the difficulty. One stresses perceptual-motor functioning, and the other stresses language functioning.

Aphasia-Without the capacity to interpret and express language.

Alexia-Without the capacity to read or interpret letters or words.

Acalculia-Without the capacity to understand and interpret numbers and engage in problem solving dealing with numbers.

Apraxia-Without the capacity to make movement.

Agraphia-Without the capacity to make fine-motor movements, especially writing.

Dyslexia-Disturbed function in the process of reading or interpreting letters or words.

Dyscalculia-Disturbed function in the process of understanding and interpreting numbers.

Dyspraxia-Disturbed function in the process of making fine-motor movements, such as writing or drawing.

Dysgraphia-Disturbed function in the process of making a fine-motor movement, such as writing and drawing.

Hyperlexia-The ability to read fluently, but not to understand what is read.

Why Does My Child Have A Learning Disability?

When I'm asked this question, my response usually is, "I do not know." It's difficult to determine why a particular child has a learning disability. Through interviews and collecting background data, the best a professional can do is make an educated guess about the cause of the learning disability. There are several theories that explain the origin of the type of learning disability.

Brain Damage Or Brain Injury

Damage to the brain can occur before birth, at birth or after birth. This damage or injury is identified as a destruction of nerve tissue. Inadequate prenatal care, inadequate nutrition on the mother's part, use of drugs by the mother and other similar factors may influence healthy development of the fetus. When this occurs, there is a probability of inadequate development. Complications at birth may also result in brain damage. Childhood illnesses (high fever) or accidents can result in brain damage.

Developmental Lags

This is slowed growth and slowed process of physiological development. Certain skills do not mature as they should. The child develops more slowly than his peers in some areas.

Genetic Factors

Learning disabilities can be inherited. Most of our children's traits and characteristics are inherited from us and our parents. Just as the parent who is a talented artist is more likely to have a child who is artistically inclined, the parent who has or had reading difficulties is more apt to have a child with similar problems.

There also is the possibility of chance variation in genetics. Two tall people are more likely to have a child who is tall, but sometimes two tall people have a short child. Through chance variation, it may be possible that families that do not have histories of learning difficulties may have a child who shows these problems.

Dealing With The Problem

It's very difficult to determine the cause of the learning

problem. But the cause is not as important as the treatment. No matter what the cause, methods to deal with the problem are very similar.

There are various methods to help children with learning disabilities who experience academic problems. Attempts to deal with the problem result in significant improvement, slight improvement or no improvement.

Let's go back to the example I used earlier about the child who can't hit a baseball. Your child can't hit a baseball with a bat when it is pitched to him. You could tell the child, "Every day after work when I come home from work, we're going to practice baseball." Every afternoon after work you practice throwing to him so he can learn to hit the ball.

For some children, a short period of practice results in significant improvement. Others, even with a very long amount of practice, show only slight improvement. Some children, after a short or long period of practice, show almost no improvement.

Children whose skills will improve show it over a relatively short period of time-a month or so. For the child who doesn't show any major improvement over the same period of time, two other conditions may occur. You may need to put the ball and bat in the closet and wait a few months until some physical maturation occurs. With time and some practice, this child can begin to hit the ball. For another child, time and practice will not enable him to hit a baseball. A very similar process occurs when attempts are made to deal with learning problems.

Dealing With Developmental Lags

There are three ways to deal with children with developmental lags or learning disabilities.

Strengthen Skills Needed For Learning

If a child has a reading problem, sometimes it's recommended that emphasis not be placed on reading skills but on the development of the abilities the child needs to read. Rather than working on reading, the child may be involved in language therapy to help strengthen auditory memory or processing skills. This is similar to a child experiencing perceptual-motor difficulties.

Rather than directly working on academics (tutoring), attempts are made to strengthen the child's weak skills. See the chapters that discuss auditory processing problems and perceptual motor deficit. Treatment usually involves having the child in therapy with a developmental optometrist, occupational therapist or speech-and-language therapist.

Strengthen Academic Skills

This is tutoring. If a child has problems in reading, get him a tutor to help develop his reading skills. If English or math is a weak area, have someone work directly with the child to strengthen these skills.

Fit School To The Child

The child who has learning difficulties may need individual consideration in the classroom. The child who has visual perceptual-motor difficulties and trouble writing may need to do his tests verbally.

A child who has trouble following verbal directions given in a series may need to receive them one at a time. The child with the learning disability needs work presented at a level, rate and in a manner that recognizes his strengths and weaknesses.

Many times these children need a smaller classroom or a school environment with a small pupil-teacher ratio. In a smaller setting, work can be individualized. Some schools can and are willing to do this; others are not. If the school is unable to work around the child's difficulty, find another school.

Special education is an attempt to place the child in a smaller classroom setting so he can receive more individual attention. See the chapters that discuss these concerns.

Learning Disabilities-Things To Consider

Learning Styles

All children have learning styles. Children have strengths and weaknesses. Some learn better if they utilize one skill more than another. If a child is a visual learner, he acquires information better if he sees it than if he hears it. He won't benefit from lectures or similar methods of presenting information. It is better to provide him with visual aids to capitalize on his learning style.

Try to identify your child's strengths, weaknesses and particular learning style. Try to place him in a school environment that can work around and with his individual strengths and weaknesses.

Continuous Assessment

If your child is in therapy (perceptual-motor training or language therapy) or a particular learning program is designed to strengthen skills necessary for learning, there must be continuous assessment. This determines whether treatment results in improvement. If treatment will benefit the child, you should see some results.

Some children do not significantly improve skills through training. Only time helps. Some children have been in this training for 2 years and have improved. But they didn't improve because of the training. Improvement occurred because of physical development.

Fad Treatments

Be cautious of fad treatments. Many programs are expensive and make claims of success that are not supported by scientific research.

Ask professionals in your area and your child's pediatrician about particular programs. Gather as much information as possible. Be very hesitant about programs that do a lot of advertising, require up-front money and guarantee success.

Tutoring

For a child who has academic problems, try tutoring. If your child has trouble reading, have him tutored. Try to find someone who specializes in your child's area of difficulty. Individual tutoring is best. The smaller the group of students being tutored, the better.

Individualized Instruction

The most effective method of dealing with a child with a learning disability is to get him in a school or classroom setting where some individualization of instruction and consideration can be given to him. This may involve special education. It could also involve a school with a small pupil-teacher ratio.

Keep School Positive

Some children's learning problems get better with time and physical growth. The reason they had problems in third grade might not exist when they are in eight grade. It appears that the problem gets better on its own. It is as if they "outgrow" the difficulties. Deficit area(s) remain in some children through their life, but children with average or above average intelligence are often able to compensate for the weaknesses. They learn to work around the problem.

If school remains positive for these children, they will not view it as something to avoid when it comes time for high school and college. Children who view their school experience as positive will want to continue their education. In recent years the number of high schools and colleges that have programs for children that have learning disabilities has significantly increase. Therefore, it is much easier now for the child who wants to continue his education to do so.

Putting It All Together

All children have strengths and weaknesses. Many children show the characteristics of a learning disabled child. Many research studies tested children having trouble in school and children not having trouble in school in basic skill areas (perceptual motor skills, language skills, memory skills). Without the child's report card grades or achievement level, it was often difficult to identify the children who had problems and those who did not.

If your child shows some of the characteristics mentioned above, it doesn't mean he has a learning disability. All of us compensate for our weak points. Some children are able to do it much better than others. Some do not have problems in school, even though they have some weaknesses in the skills necessary for learning. The major criteria is if he's doing poorly in school. See the chapter on Support Groups And Organizations for places to get more information on various aspects of learning problems.

CHAPTER 43

Visual Processing And Writing Problems, Dysgraphia, Perceptual Motor Deficits

Some children experience fine-motor and/or gross motor coordination problems. Deficits in fine motor coordination are also called perceptual motor or visual motor problems. These fine motor skill deficits interfere with school performance, especially reading and writing, more than gross motor weaknesses. For this reason, I've devoted the majority of this chapter to perceptual motor deficits.

Academic Problems

Perceptual motor or visual motor skills pertain to visually processing information. What the brain does with what the eyes see. In regards to school, it generally relates to two areas.

1. Reading: Some children learn to read primarily through the visual system (eyes). Others are more auditory learners (ears). However, reading involves both auditory and visual skills. In some children weaknesses in visual processing effects reading. What the eyes see is different from what the brain tells the child to say. The problem in processing the visual information. A "b" may be read as a "d". Words may be read backwards, "was" for "saw". What we call "nuclear" may be "unclear" to the child with visual processing problems. Words come out wrong, "basgetti and meat balls," or in the wrong order, "please up hurry." See the chapters that discuss reading and auditory processing problems for more information in this area.

2. Writing. While it seems as if everyone has heard of dyslexia (inability to read). Dysgraphia (difficulty with writing) seems to occur frequently in children with perceptual motor or visual motor deficits. This pertains to how well the child's eyes and hands work together, how well he can reproduce with his hands what he sees or how well he can transfer information in his brain to his hands and write it down on a piece of paper.

3. Math. Sometimes these deficits effect performance in math. It is not so much the math skill, but the writing difficulties. These children's handwriting is poor and they tend to be disorganized and sloppy when writing. This often leads to careless or "stupid" mistakes. When adding they add "2" instead of "3" because their "2" looks like a "3". They don't line up the columns correctly when doing multiplication or division and the problems is wrong. When doing a number of problems on a page, one problem "runs into" or overlaps the space of another problem. There's addition and subtraction on a test and the first problem is addition so they add all the problems on a test. They write "91" instead of "19" and the answer is wrong.

This chapter will focus on writing problems.

Gross-motor coordination refers to skills and abilities we normally think about when we discuss coordination (riding a bike, jumping a rope, playing sports). When a child has problems in this area, he is usually described as poorly coordinated, having "two left feet" or clumsy. While this deficit alone usually doesn't interfere with the child's ability to perform in the academic setting, it often produces social problems, especially for boys. These children have difficulty with sports and are usually picked last when sides are formed for a game. They are usually seen as poor athletes, cannot ride a bike as fast as the other children, come in last in races and are often criticized. Problems in this area sometimes produce socialization difficulties or negative attention from the child's peers.

Fine Motor Problems

Children who have perceptual motor or visual motor deficits have trouble with paper and pencil tasks. School work involves a significant amount of handwriting, especially as the child approaches middle school. So it is easy to see how this child is likely to have academic problems.

As youngsters, children with visual motor problems often stay away from paper and pencil tasks. They don't like to color, draw, cut and paste or practice their ABCs. Handwriting is a difficult task, and it requires a great deal of energy and effort for them. Penmanship is poor and work is sloppy and disorganized. These children often reverse or invert letters and numbers. Sometimes they write words or their names backward.

Writing, for these children, requires a great deal of energy and effort so they tire easily. Their penmanship may start out beautiful but at the end of the page it looks like "chicken scratch." It takes them a long time to complete written tasks. What might take your average third grader 15 minutes to write may take this child 3 to 5 times long to complete the same written task. Therefore, they may have trouble completing seat work and complain that they do not have enough time to copy information from the board. Homework often takes hours. When an answer requires ten words, they write three because writing is difficult.

You study with your child for a social studies test for several hours and he knows it perfectly. He goes to school and takes the test and gets 60%. He brings the test home. You tell him "You knew all of this" and you ask him all the questions he missed and he gives you all the correct answers. In another situation the teacher says "We went over the material all week in class." He participated and knew all the information, but he failed the test. Another child is asked, "What did you do during the summer vacation?" He tells you everything he did in great detail and it took 30 minutes. You then tell him to write you a paragraph about what he did over the summer. You'll get seven sentences of three words each. From this information, you do not know if the child went to Florida of had heart surgery because it doesn't make any sense!

They have trouble transferring information from one place to another. The child can copy a word from a book next to his paper and misspell it. The definition he just copied from the dictionary has three words left out of it.

If he has to fill in his answers on a "bubble" or "scantron" answer sheet, he may lose his place, skip questions or put the answer in the wrong place. These children usually have trouble with "essay test" and may have trouble on other types of tests (matching, fill in the blanks when a word bank is present).

You sixth grader writes a report and when you look at it, it looks like a first or second grader wrote it. Not only is the penmanship terrible, but there are no periods or commas and none of the sentences begin with a capital letters. It looks like he never had a course in grammar or the mechanics of writing.

These children also have difficulty in spelling. Not only do they reverse letters, "fsih" for "fish", they can spell the word orally but have trouble getting it correctly when they write it. You can ask this child to spell a word and he will orally spell it correctly ten out of ten times. However, nine out of ten times it is incorrect when he writes it. A child who was slow in writing told me "When I take a spelling test, the teacher goes too fast. I'm trying to spell a word, remember the one she said last and listening to the one she is calling out now." Obviously, this child had trouble making a good grade on a spelling test.

They have trouble copying from the board because they lose their place, leave out letters, words or whole phrases. It often is a monumental task for you to read what the child has written for his homework assignment. Sometimes they confuse letters, "d's" are written as "b's" and "w's" are "m's."

This is an appropriate time to make a couple of important points. First, the majority of kindergarten children reverse letters and numbers or write them backward. If this is seen in kindergarten, don't be concerned. About 50% of beginning first graders show reversals, but this should be phasing out toward the end of first grade. Only about 10% of beginning second graders have problems in this area. If the characteristics of perceptual motor deficits are seen at this grade level, there is a strong

374 *The Parent's Guide To Solving School Problems*

probability the child has a problem.

Second, the child with perceptual motor problems doesn't necessarily have eye trouble or poor vision. He could have 20/20 vision and still have difficulty. The trouble is not in his eyes or his hands, but in processing what his eyes see. He sees something, then his brain processes the information and tells his hand what to do. The problem lies in translating or transferring the information from his eyes to his hands or from his brain to his hands when writing. Although these children usually don't have vision problems, it's good to get a vision exam.

Perceptual motor deficits seen in some children often result from a developmental deviation or lag. In the chapter on learning disabilities, I explained what was meant by a developmental lag or deviation. You may want to review this. Perceptual motor deficits from developmental lags or deviations mean the child's handeye coordination is slow in developing. He may be 7 years old but shows the visual motor development of a 5 year old. He may be in second or third grade, but has the perceptual motor skills of a kindergarten child. The problems that are common in children in kindergarten are seen in this child in second or third grade and now are a problem. Sometimes the lag in the skills are a result of a developmental deviation lag and will get better or diminish as the child gets older. In other situations, they will not improve.

In some children, perceptual motor deficits are related to brain or organic damage. For example, children who have had some type of head injury, had poor prenatal care, and high fever or those with a relatively low level of intellectual functioning. Another group of children are just weak in this area. For example, you can practice with some children for days and weeks and they will still have trouble hitting a baseball because this is a weak skill. The same is true for some children with writing or paper and pencil skills.

What Causes Dysgraphia?

A few people with dysgraphia lack only the fine motor coordination to produce legible handwriting, but some may have a physical tremor that interferes with writing. In most cases, however, several brain systems interact to produce dysgraphia. Some experts believe that dysgraphia involves a dysfunction in the interaction between the two main brain systems that allows a person to translate mental into written language (phoneme to grapheme translation, i.e., mental sound to symbol, and lexicon to grapheme translation, i.e. mental to written word). Other studies have shown that split attention, memory load, and familiarity of graphic material affect writing ability. Typically, a person with illegible handwriting has a combination of fine motor difficulty, inability to re-visualize letters, and inability to remember the motor patterns of letter forms.

What Are The Different Types Of Dysgraphia?

While dysgraphia may be broadly classified as follows, there are many individual variations that affect both treatment and prognosis:

1. In *dyslexic dysgraphia*, spontaneously written text is illegible, especially when the text is complex. Oral spelling is poor, but drawing and copying of written text are relatively normal. Finger-tapping speed (a measure of fine motor speed) is normal.

2. In *motor dysgraphia*, both spontaneously written and copied text may be illegible, oral spelling is normal, and drawing is usually problematic. Finger-tapping speed is abnormal.

Hand-eye coordination difficulties don't improve with age in these children, as do those in children with lags resulting from a developmental deviation. These children may show some improvement but generally their visual motor deficits remain, and they don't show significant improvement with practice. Parents of these children may have to accept the child's difficulties and attempt to work around them.

Perceptual-Motor Training

For some children, perceptual motor training or therapy is recommended. To better understand the effects of this training and how to assess its effectiveness, let's take an example. We have two 5 year olds. We put each on a two wheeled bike.

One rides the bike very well. The other can't ride the bike. For the boy who can't ride, we'd say the skills he needs to ride the bike are not developing as fast as the other child's skills. There is a lag in development. There is a lag in the development of the skill or it is weak skill. There are three general ways to remediate or try to improve these bike riding skills, as well as writing skills.

The first approach would practice riding the bike with the child every afternoon when you come home from work. In regards to writing, this could involve practice with penmanship, to improve the child's speed in writing, in holding the pencil correctly, in forming the letters in the correct manner, etc. If you have been practicing with this child for a couple of months and there has not been significant improvement, you need to put the bike in the garage and approach this from a different direction. If the writing skills have not improved, something else needs to be done.

The second approach would be to try to improve the skills needed to ride the bike or write. We do not deal directly with the deficit area, but try to improve the skills needed for the activity. By doing this, the weaknesses indirectly improved. For the child who can't ride the bike, this would involve strengthening the muscles in his legs, teaching him balance, etc. For the child who has trouble writing, this would involve perceptual motor training or therapy.

Research does not extensively support the fact that improvement in perceptual-motor skills by therapy results in improvement in academic skills or generalizes to the school setting. Many physicians and scientists don't look favorably on this method to improve school performance. It is recommended that money be spent for tutoring in academic skills. However, it can be something that is tried in an attempt to see if the skill will improve, especially if the therapist or agency is reputable. This therapy is usually done by occupational therapists, but some developmental optometrists or physical therapists provide these services. You may want to check with your child's pediatrician or the occupational therapy department at hospital or medical center near you for additional information.

You would want to avoid an agency or individual who approaches the situation in this way. You bring your child in for an evaluation and after the evaluation you are told. "We will see the child twice a week for the next eight months" In eight months the child's skills may be better, but maybe because he's eight months older and not as a result of the treatment. It is difficult, if not impossible, to tell from an initial evaluation if this skill can be improved and how long it will take. The same is true for tutoring. A tutor or agency cannot say, "It will take 36 hours of tutoring to remediate your child's reading problem" after an initial evaluation. Most reputable places use an "extended evaluation," As described below, to determine if these skills can be improved.

Children enrolled in the better perceptual motor training programs usually go for ½ hour to 1 hour a day, 1 or 2 times a week. They engage in activities to build perceptual motor skills. Usually parents are also given activities to do with the child at home. Most reputable trainers or therapists work with the children for several weeks (4 to 6) then make an assessment. If improvement is occurring, they will keep working with the child. If not, they will discontinue the therapy. This brings us to the third way to deal with this problem.

If both of the above techniques are tried and the child still can't ride the bike or is having trouble writing, we need to put the bike in the attic and wait for some physical growth to occur. Time, not practice, is the important factor. Some children's skills improve with time. Others do not.

At our center, we suggest activities to help improve these skills. Generally, parents can try to gear the child's play toward games and activities that strengthen these skills. Toys that require hand-eye coordination skills can be bought. A store that has educational supplies for teachers usually has many games and activities to enhance perceptual motor abilities. The list below gives you some general ideas of things you can do with children who have visual motor problems.

Fine-Motor Activities

1. Tracing, coloring, cutting, pasting
2. Dot-to-dot, puzzles, finger-painting
3. Building models, lacing boards, weaving games, clay
4. Jacks, pick-up sticks, puppets
5. Building blocks, Lincoln Logs, Tinker Toys, Erector sets, Lego's
6. Buttoning, unbuttoning, tying, zipping
7. Video and computer games

If a child has poor penmanship, it's better to have him practice paper and pencil tasks he enjoys (coloring, tracing) than to have him practice his penmanship excessively. While most children who show perceptual motor deficits don't necessarily have grossmotor coordination problems, practice in this area seems to improve fine motor skills. Below are some activities that are beneficial for children experiencing gross motor and/or fine motor coordination difficulties.

Gross-Motor Activities

It's important for you to understand a child with motor impairment appears clumsy and awkward. He may also appear disoriented. This is usually because he hasn't developed left-right perception. He must learn to move his body in an organized way. To accomplish this, try the following activities. Activities included in this list are done easily and require no specialized materials. You shouldn't have difficulty doing these with your child.

Walking Activities

Have the child walk in various ways (forward, backward, sideways). The child can also imitate various animals (elephant, duck, crab).

Crawling Activities

The child can crawl in various ways (move like a snake, worm, soldier).

Walking Hockey

Have the child move an object across the floor with his feet to a goal. Use points, and play with teams.

Obstacle Course

Arrange an obstacle course using chairs, tables, boxes. Have the child move through the course in different ways.

Balance Beam

Put a 2x4 board on the floor. Have the child move on it in different directions.

Exercises

Any exercise is good. Jumping Jacks, hopping, bending are all good.

Other Activities

Try dodge ball, leapfrog, Simon says, hokey pokey, bike riding, roller skating, skateboarding, hopscotch.

Ball Games

Engage in throwing, catching and kicking activities. This does not necessarily include organized sports. Don't force a child with motor problems into participation in organized sports until he wants to participate. This list was prepared by Mallary Collins, M.Ed.

While waiting to see if these skills can be improved with training or physical growth, these children will usually have trouble in school if nothing else is done. Modifications, accommodations and interventions need to be made in order to reduce the child's frustration and to keep school positive.

School Interventions

Whether or not a child receives perceptual motor training, major improvement in his school performance will result primarily from a teacher or school system willing to give the child some individual consideration and work around his deficits. Some children with perceptual motor problems have learning disabilities that significantly interfere with their ability to learn. They have difficulty learning material. They don't learn from the methods that work with most children. Information doesn't get in, and they may require special education or specialized instruction.

Most children with perceptual motor deficits do not have trouble learning. Their major problem is writing. They have difficulty with handwriting activities. Ask them to write the answer to a question, such as, "What is lightning?" and they'll give you 4 words. Ask them to answer verbally, and they'll give you 4 minutes worth!

Much work in elementary grades involves paper and pencil tasks. This child's performance is frequently inadequate. Handwriting is difficult, penmanship is poor, he may not finish his seatwork. Children with this difficulty need less emphasis on written skills and more emphasis on verbal abilities.

You'd never think of putting a child with sight problems in the back of a classroom or expect him to see the board from there if he had difficulty. You'd put him in the front of the room to minimize his difficulties in seeing. You would modify the environment to accommodate his deficits. Many modifications can occur in the classroom and with homework to help a child with perceptual motor deficits. I have enclosed some below. More detailed information can be found in the chapter on the Individuals with Disabilities Education Act and 504 Program.

Minimize Handwriting

The general approach is to minimize the handwriting or perceptual motor skills and maximize using verbal skills. In most cases, this can be done in an average size classroom. It may have to be done in a classroom with a smaller pupil teacher ratio. With fewer students, a teacher has more time to give each child some special consideration. The child with perceptual motor difficulty may have difficulties copying material, be slow in handwriting tasks and show poor penmanship.

Many children reverse numbers and letters and may add $10+31=$ instead of $10+13=$, spell cat cta or dog as bog. Instead of marking the math problem or spelling word wrong when it's obvious the child has reversed some part of it, the teacher could ask him how to spell the word orally. Or watch him do the math problem.

Give him credit if the problem is correct but he reversed the numbers. Or use some other method to see whether the child knows the correct information or the correct method.

Penmanship is usually poor. Sometimes it's easier for them to print than to write in cursive (longhand). Don't compare the child's penmanship to others, but to his own previous efforts. If the child is trying his best, he should be graded accordingly.

The child may write slowly and may require extra time to do seatwork. He may need to be graded on what he has completed. A teacher gives the class 10 questions, and students have to write the answers. The child with perceptual motor difficulties only finishes 6, although he tried hard, didn't fool around and put forth 100% effort. He should be graded on the 6 completed and not receive a failing grade. Or he could be given extra time to complete the task.

A reading teacher gives the class 10 vocabulary words to find in the dictionary, write the definitions and make a sentence using each word. The main purpose of the assignment is for the child to learn how to use the dictionary, learn word meanings and how to use the words appropriately. Copying the definition and writing in a notebook have nothing to do with the learning experience. The exercise may take 1-1/2 hours for a child with perceptual motor deficits. Minimize the writing or have someone else write the information that the child dictates.

Writing spelling words 10 times each is designed to help the child learn the words. With cooperative parents, the teacher could eliminate the writing and ask you to be sure the child knows the words.

Copying math problems out of the text book or from the board or copying an entire sentence from an English book (to select the correct verb) will take him a long time. Someone else could copy the math problems or the child could write the correct verb instead of the entire sentence. Parents may be able to purchase textbooks or workbooks so the child can underline words or use other techniques to minimize writing.

Copying from the board and taking notes may also present difficulties. Using a photocopy machine to copy another student's notes may eliminate the problem. These children usually do poorly on some tests. Essay tests and matching questions are particularly difficult for them to complete. Some test questions could be given and answered orally.

Manipulative Children

If your child is a con artist or does minimum amount of work to keep his head out of water, be careful when using the above techniques. Some children may use their problem as a crutch. It is difficult for teachers to use the above techniques if the child fools around 80% of the time and only works 20%. Try to have the child put forth effort 100% of the time to assess if the trouble is with perceptual motor skills or motivation, irresponsibility or lack of independent behavior. Use positive consequences and methods described in other sections of the book.

Review the chapter on Learning Disabilities and Other Learning Problems for information related to this.

CHAPTER 44

Reading Problems, Dyslexia

There is a wealth of information available to parents on reading problems and dyslexia so I have only provided an overview in this chapter. The International Dyslexia Association (IDA) has numerous books, pamphlets, fact sheets, etc. Some are free and others can be purchased. The interested reader should contact them. See the chapter on Support Groups And Organizations for the address and phone number of the IDA. Most of the information in this chapter came from this organization.

What Is Dyslexia?

Dyslexia is often referred to as a language based learning disability. It is the most common form of learning disability. Approximately 15% of the population have a learning disability and The National Institutes of Health report that 60% to 80% of those with learning disabilities have problems with reading and language skills. Individuals with dyslexia usually have difficulty with either receptive oral language skills, expressive oral language skills, reading, spelling, or written expression.

Dyslexia varies in degrees of severity. The prognosis depends on the severity of the disability, specific patterns of strengths and weaknesses with the individual, and the appropriateness of the intervention. It is **not** a result of lack of motivation, environmental opportunities, low intelligence, or other limiting conditions. It is a condition which is neurologically based and often appears in families. Individuals with dyslexia respond successfully to timely and appropriate intervention.

What Causes Dyslexia?

The exact causes of dyslexia are still not completely clear, but anatomical and brain imagery studies show differences in the way the brain of a dyslexic person develops and functions. Moreover, people with dyslexia have been found to have problems with discriminating sounds within a word, a key factor in their reading difficulties. Dyslexia is not due to either lack of intelligence or a desire to learn; with appropriate teaching methods dyslexics can learn successfully.

How Widespread Is Dyslexia?

Current studies suggest that at least 15-17% of the population is dyslexic. Dyslexia occurs in people of all backgrounds and intellectual levels. There is strong evidence that dyslexia runs in families; dyslexic parents are far more likely to have children who have dyslexia. Some people are identified as dyslexic early in their lives, but for others their dyslexia goes unidentified until they get older. People who are very bright can be dyslexic. They are often gifted in areas that do not require strong language skills, such as art, computer science, design, drama, electronics, math, mechanics, music, physics, sales, and sports.

What Are The Effects Of Dyslexia?

The impact that dyslexia has is different from each person and depends on the severity of the condition and the approaches of the remediation. The most common effects are problems with reading, spelling, and writing. Some dyslexics do not have much difficulty with early reading and spelling tasks but do experience great problems when more complex language skills are required, such as grammar, understanding textbook material, and writing.

People with dyslexia can also have problems with spoken language. They may find if difficult to express themselves clearly, of to fully comprehend what other mean when they speak. Such language problems are often difficult to recognize, but they can lead to major problems in school, in the work place, and in relating to other people. The effects of dyslexia reach well beyond the classroom.

Dyslexia can also affect a person's self-image. Students with dyslexia often end up feeling "dumb" and less capable than they actually are. After experiencing a great deal of stress due to academic problems, a student may become discouraged about continuing in school.

What Are The Signs Of Dyslexia?

The problems displayed by individuals with dyslexia involve difficulties in acquiring and using language reading and writing letters in the wrong order is just one manifestation of dyslexia and does not occur in all cases. Other problems experienced by dyslexics include:

- Learning to speak
- Organizing written and spoken language
- Learning letters and their sounds
- Memorizing number facts
- Spelling
- Reading
- Learning a foreign language
- Correctly doing math operations

Not all students who have difficulties with these skills are dyslexic. Formal testing is the only way to confirm a diagnosis of suspected dyslexia.

How Is Dyslexia Treated?

Dyslexia is a life-long condition. With proper help people with dyslexia can learn to read and/or write well. Early identification and treatment is the key to helping dyslexics achieve in school and in life. Most people with dyslexia need help from a teacher, tutor, or therapist specially trained in using a multisensory, structured language approach. It is important for these individuals to be taught by a method that involves several senses (hearing, seeing, touching) at the same time. Many individuals with dyslexia need one-on-one help so that they can move forward at their own pace. For students with dyslexia, it is helpful if their outside academic therapists work closely with classroom teachers.

Schools can implement academic modifications to help dyslexic students succeed. For example, a student with dyslexia can be given extra time to complete tasks, or help with taking notes, and/or appropriate work assignments. Teachers can give taped test or allow dyslexic students to use alternative means of assessment. Students can benefit from listening to books-on-tape and from writing on computers.

How Is Dyslexia Diagnosed?

A formal evaluation is needed to discover if a person is dyslexic. The evaluation assesses intellectual ability, information processing, psycho-linguistic processing, and academic skills. It is used to determine whether or not a student is reading at the expected level, and takes into account the individual's family background and overall school performance. The testing can be conducted by trained school or outside specialists.

Why Is An Evaluation Important?

If you suspect dyslexia, it is important to have an evaluation to better understand the problem. Test results determine eligibility for special education services in various states, and they also determine eligibility for programs in colleges and universities. They provide a basis for making educational recommendations and determine the baseline from which remediation programs will be evaluated.

At What Age Should An Individual Be Tested For Dyslexia?

Individuals may be tested for dyslexia at any age. Test which are selected will vary according to the age of the individual. Young children may be tested for phonological processing, receptive and expressive language abilities, and the ability to make sound/ symbol associations. When problems are found in these areas remediation can begin immediately. A diagnosis of dyslexia need not be made in order to offer early intervention in reading instruction.

Who Is Qualified To Make The Diagnosis Of Dyslexia?

Professionals who possess expertise in several disciplines are best qualified to make a diagnosis of dyslexia. The testing may be done by a single individual or by a team of specialists. A knowledge and background in psychology, reading, language and education is necessary. The tester must have knowledge of how individuals learn to read and why some people have trouble learning to read, and must also understand how to measure appropriate reading interventions is necessary to make recommendations.

What Test Is Used To Identify Dyslexia?

There is no one single test which can be used to test for dyslexia. A battery of tests must be administered. Tests should be chosen on the basis of their measurement properties and their potential address referral issues. Various tests may be used but the components of a good assessment should remain constant. Tests which measure expressive oral language, expressive written language, receptive oral language, receptive written language, intellectual functioning, cognitive processing, and educational achievement must be administered.

What Should An Evaluation Include?

The expert evaluator will conduct a comprehensive assessment to determine whether the person's learning problems may be related to other disorders. Attention Deficit Hyperactivity Disorder (ADHD), affective disorders (anxiety, depression), central auditory processing dysfunction, pervasive developmental disorder, and physical or sensory impairments are among the other causes of learning problems that a competent evaluator will consider in making the diagnosis of dyslexia.

The following elements should be included in an assessment for dyslexia:
   1) A developmental, medical, behavioral, academic and family history,

2) A measure of general intellectual functioning,

3) Information on cognitive processing (language, memory, auditory processing, visual processing, visual motor integration, reasoning abilities, and executive functioning),

4) Test of specific oral language skills related to reading and writing success to include tests of phonological processing,

5) Educational tests to determine level of functioning in basic skill areas of reading, spelling, written language, and math-testing in reading/writing should include the following measures:
- single word decoding of both real and nonsense words,
- oral and silent reading in context (evaluate rate, fluency, comprehension and accuracy),
- reading comprehension,
- dictated spelling test,
- written expression: sentence writing as well as story or essay writing,
- handwriting,

6) A classroom observation or interviews with teacher(s), and a review of the remediation programs which have been tried.

What Happens After The Evaluation?

Discuss the test results with the individual who did the testing. You should receive a written report consisting of both the test scores as well as an explanation of the results of the testing. Administered tests should be specified. The strengths and weaknesses of the individual should be explained and specific recommendations should be made.

In the case of school aged students, a team meeting should take place when the evaluation is completed. This meeting should indicate the student's teachers, parents, and individuals who did the testing. When there is a reading problem, the report should suggest recommendations for specific intervention techniques. This instruction should be provided by skilled teachers, specifically trained in structured language, multisensory programs.

How Long Does Testing Takes?

An average test battery will take approximately two to four hours. Sometimes it will be necessary to conduct the testing in more than on session, particularly in the case of a young child whose attention span is very short. The extent of the evaluation is based on clinical judgment or the evaluator.

See the chapter on the Individuals with Disabilities Education Act for more information on what can be done to help the child with reading problems.

CHAPTER 45

Spelling Problems

How Common Are Spelling Difficulties?

Almost all people with developmental reading or language disabilities have great difficulty spelling. In the new definition of dyslexia, people with the condition known as dyslexia are noted to have "conspicuous" problems with spelling and writing. People can also have specific spelling disabilities-that is, they can be poor spellers, even though they are pretty good readers. These problems are very common, although no one has done an accurate estimate of the prevalence to date.

What Causes People To Be Poor Spellers?

Spelling problems, like reading problems, originate with language learning weaknesses. Spelling disability does not reflect a general "visual memory" problem but a more specific problem with awareness of and memory for language structure, including the letters in words. People who are poor spellers typically have trouble analyzing the sounds, syllables, and meaningful parts of words in both spoken language and written language. In addition, they often have trouble learning other types of symbolic codes such as math facts and math operation signs.

In the early grades, weaknesses in speech sound awareness (phoneme awareness) predict and are closely associated with poor spelling. In the later grades, difficulty understanding spelling rules, word structure and letter patterns are the hallmarks. The "visual memory" problems of poor spellers are specific to memory for letters and words, so a better term for poor spelling is *orthographic memory problem.* A person may be a very poor speller but a very good artist, navigator, or mechanic; those professions require a different kind of *visual memory.*

How Do Children Learn To Spell? Is Invented Spelling Good Or Bad?

Spelling develops in a more or less predictable sequence. Children begin by writing strings of letters and symbols that do not represent the sounds in words. Next, they begin to write a few the sounds in words that are easily detected; then, get better at "inventing" spelling by sound, using the letters they have learned. This stage, called phonetic spelling or temporary spelling, usually occurs in kindergarten or early first grade, before children learn to spell words correctly. At this crucial early stage, inventing spellings by sounds is an effective way of discovering the separate sounds that make up words. However, invented spellings should never replace the organized instruction that should begin about the middle of first grade.

Dyslexic students have difficulty going through the stages of spelling development. Phonetic spelling (spelling by sounds rather than by the correct letters) is a desirable but brief stage of early spelling development. If a student has good phoneme awareness, that is, can segment all the sounds in a simple word, the student is much more likely to remember the "true" letters and letter combinations in the word. Whole word, or "sight" word learning, is also bolstered by good phoneme awareness.

Is Our English Spelling System Predictable Or Unpredictable?

English is a pattern-based writing system that uses an alphabet to represent speech sounds. The English system of using letters for sounds is more complex than some languages such as Spanish but is nevertheless a predictable, learnable system. The English spelling system is complex because the spelling patterns come from Old English (Anglo-Saxon), from Latin and Greek, and from other modern languages. It is also complex because the regular patterns occur at several levels: the level of individuals sounds, such as how we spell the sound /K/; the level of syllables, such as how we spell the syllables in the word *ta-ble*; and the level of meaningful parts (morphemes), such as how we spell the pieces of *ac-com-mo-date*.

English is predictable overall, but several "layers" of language organization must be learned by those who would spell it well.

What Methods Of Instruction Are Most Effective?

A well designed program for students who do not learn easily will emphasize the sounds in the words, the letter combinations that usually spell those sounds, the spelling of six basic syllable types, and how the spelling rules of English work. Such a program would teach spelling patterns in a structured sequential way. At the more advanced levels, spelling instruction should focus on the meaningful parts of words: the prefixes, roots, suffixes, and grammatical endings that are often spelled consistently. Multisensory techniques, those that join listening, saying, looking, and writing in various combinations, and that consciously engage the student in feeling how the word is spoken and how it is written, are most successful. If word lists are used they should emphasize the regular spellings for sounds and sound patterns. Special memorization techniques are necessary for the odd words that must be learned as wholes.

In summary, effective spelling instructions should emphasize these principles:

- knowledge of sounds, letter-sound association, patterns, syllables, and meaningful parts;
- multisensory practice;
- systematic, cumulative study of patterns;
- memorizing a few "sight" words at a time;
- writing those words correctly many times;
- using the words in personal writing.

Review the chapters on Learning Disabilities And Other Learning Problems and the one entitled Individuals With Disabilities Education Act for information related to this.

CHAPTER 46

Math Problems, Dyscalculia

In comparison to disorders of language, reading and writing, math difficulty, dyscalculia, has received minimal attention. Perhaps because they do not occur as frequently and/or we are more concerned about a child's reading, writing and speaking ability.

In fact some experts feel that true dyscalculia, trouble with calculating, a neurologically based disability, is rare. They feel that problems with math are more related to language based learning problems. These students can execute problems in a "recipe style", i.e. step by step. They are able to remember formulas, but may not understand why the formula makes sense. They prefer to do paper and pencil tasks and are attentive to the details, but do not see the big picture. Then, there are those that see the big picture and have insight into the pattern of math, but are poor at computation and have problems with remembering step-by-step procedures. They also understand math concepts and like to solve problems mentally and quickly, but have difficulty verbalizing and explaining their answers. These students often have language based learning problems that interfere with their performance in math.

Math involves recognizing numbers and symbols, memorizing facts such as the multiplication table, aligning numbers and understanding abstract concepts like place value and fractions. Problems with attention, impulsive control and visual processing may also contribute to math difficulties. Inadequate teaching or a poor foundation in basic math facts will also produce problems. I have presented below some general reasons for difficulties in this area.

Causes And Cures

Genetic

A person who is a good athletic is more likely to have a child with good athletic skills than a person who is not. A parent with math problems is more apt to have a child with difficulty in math. Skills are often inherited. Learning difficulties can also be inherited.

Poor Foundation Or Weak Basic Concepts

Children who have "gaps" in their math skills may show problems in this area. This probably accounts for more cases of problems in arithmetic than any other single factor. Children who are the victims of poor teaching or inadequate parental help or involvement with homework or studying can frequently be identified by their relatively good performance with math concepts that are acquired incidentally (e.g. size relationships or value of coins), as compared to skills that are usually as a result of specific instruction or practice (e.g. "carrying" in addition and subtraction). Children who are frequently absent from school or who are not consistent with completing homework may also show this pattern. Tutoring, receiving basic facts and practice will usually remediate this problem.

Higher Cognitive Weaknesses Or Difficulties With Abstract Thinking

Before reading this section, I suggest you review the chapter on intelligence. Look at the graph on page _____ that shows the distribution and ranges of intelligence (i.e. Mentally Disabled, Borderline, Low Average Range, Superior, Very Superior) and draw a line through the middle of the Average range. Children on the left side of the line, the lower ranges, are more apt to be concrete thinkers. The children to the right of the line, upper ranges, have better abstract thinking ability. The child's ability to abstract usually improves as the intelligence increases. A child in the High Average range of intelligence has much better ability to abstract than a child in the Low Average Range, and so forth.

A concrete thinker has trouble abstracting, making inferences, drawing connections between things he cannot see or touch. "How is a table and chair alike or similar?" The concrete answer is that they both are brown, made of wood or have four legs. The abstract answer would be they are furniture. You cannot see or touch furniture. It is a concept. Concrete thinkers miss the "punch line" of subtle jokes and have trouble understanding some math concepts. They learn information A and information B. Ask them questions that relate to A or B and they will be able to give the correct answer. However, if you ask them a question where they have to use the information from A and B and apply it to C they have trouble. These children have trouble conceptualizing and understanding things that require abstract thinking or higher cognitive skills.

Concepts like place value and fractions, the relationship between units of measurement or between numerals and objects that they represent, algebra, geometry, etc. require these skills. Consequently these areas of math will be difficult for the concrete thinker. For example you are helping your 7th grader with pre-algebra homework. You explain how to work the problems, etc. and he seems to get it. You give him a hundred problems and he gets all of them right. The next night you sit down to do the same type of homework and it is like he's never seen it before. He's completely lost. Doesn't know where to start. You have to teach it to him all over again. This is probably because he memorized what to do and could mechanically get the right answer but didn't "understand" what he was doing. So he "forgot" it the next day because it did not make sense. It would be like me telling you my home phone number and ask you to walk to the phone and call my house. Three hours later I ask you "what's my home phone number?" and you forget. Not because you have a bad memory, but because the information made no sense to you. It was a series of numbers with no meaning. This is why nine weeks exams are so difficult for these children. They have to relearn or memorize everything because they did not understand it in the first place. They usually have trouble with this type of test because it contains too much information to retain in a mechanical fashion. The child with good abstract thinking ability who understood the concept only has to review for the nine weeks exam to refresh his understanding/memory.

Students who have trouble with higher order cognition and abstracting thinking can benefit from a less abstract approach to math. Concepts such as fractions, proofs and equations can be taught with manipulatives. Materials that can be visualized and handled to illustrate quantitative relationships, place value, basic math operations could be used. These students would benefit from practical mathematics applications. Measuring, making change, balancing a check book, cooking, calculating the relative speeds of moving objects or other real life situations are likely to have a greater meaning to students frustrated by the abstract elements of math.

Writing Difficulties

Review the chapter that discusses perceptual motor deficits and dysgraphia to get a better understanding of problems in this area. Children that have problems with paper and pencil tasks sometimes have trouble in math. They then tend to be disorganized and sloppy in their work. They may write "19" when they meant to write "91". They may make many careless errors because of poor alignment of numbers in a column or illegible number formation. These students can benefit from the use of a good mechanical pencil, using graph paper to write the numbers in the squares, the use of columns on lined paper, a strong emphasis on deliberate slowness, the use of a calculator and an emphasis on monitoring their work. The chapter mentioned above and the one on Individuals with Disabilities Education Act has more ideas on how to help the child with writing problems.

Attention Deficits And Impulse Control Problems

Children with attention deficits may be too impulsive and

inattentive to detail to attend to correct operational signs. They may add when they should subtract or multiply when they should add. Some children with attention deficits may also have trouble retaining the components of a problem while solving it. They get distracted and this interferes with their memory. They "forget" what they are doing. Focus on detail is another skill needed to be successful in math and children with attention deficits are at a disadvantage.

Methods and planning need to be stressed in children with attention deficits. Their approach must become less impulsive, they need to slow down and become more aware of details. They need to be taught to closely look at the problems and cue or highlight operational signs before beginning. They could draw a highlighted line across the page where addition stops and subtraction starts. Encourage them to devise a plan for solving a problem and talk about it before beginning. Encourage children who work quickly to take more time. Preferential seating in the classroom where distraction is minimal would be helpful.

See the chapter on Attention Deficit Disorders for more information.

Language Disability

As mentioned children with language based learning difficulties may experience problems in math. Review the chapters on Auditory Processing Problems and Dyslexia for more information. These children may have problems with the language of math and the concepts associated with it. These include concepts such as before, after, between, one more than or one less than. Math terms such as numerator and denominator, prime numbers and prime factors, and carrying and borrowing may produce problems. Difficulties may also occur around the concept of place value and the function of zero. Solving word problems may be especially challenging because of difficulty with decoding, comprehension, sequencing and understanding math concepts.

These children will benefit from drill on math vocabulary. They need visual models and repetition of verbal explanations. They will benefit from computer software, with its predominantly visual mode of presentation. They are apt to need special help in solving word problems.

Attitude, Anxiety And Confidence Problems

Some children do not like math for whatever reason, become anxious when it is time to do math and/or lack confidence in their ability. Careful observation on the part of the teacher or parent may provide the first indication that this is the cause of the problem.

If problems exist in one of these areas, attempts should be made to modify this. See the chapters on confidence, responsibility and tutoring for more information.

Related information on understanding and dealing with math difficulties can be found in the chapters on Learning Disabilities and Other Learning Problems and the Individuals with Disabilities Education Act.

CHAPTER 47

Individuals with Disabilities Education Act, Section 504

As mentioned above, the educational systems in all states have criteria to determine if a child is eligible to receive special educational services. For example, in Louisiana, a child has to have an academic strength and an academic weakness that is at a certain level when compared to the average child in order to be classified as Learning Disabled.

In many states children where having academic difficulties and doing poorly in school, but when evaluated were not found to meet the state's criteria for eligibility and were denied services. They were being classified as "No Exceptionality," remained in regular class with no extra help and continued to do poorly. Because of this, many of the national associations for children with learning difficulties (e.g. The International Dyslexia Association, The Association for children with Attention Deficit Disorders) brought this to the attention of federal government in an attempt to get some help.

As a result, the Individuals with Disabilities Education Act (IDEA) Section 504 of the Rehabilitation Act of 1973, and the Americans with Disabilities Act (ADA) was established.

These acts defined the rights of students with learning difficulties/disabilities. These students are legally entitled to special services in the regular class setting to help them overcome and accommodate their learning problems. Such services include educational programs designed to meet the needs of these students. These Acts also protect people with learning disabilities against unfair and illegal discrimination.

While these programs are supposed to exist in all schools in the United States, they exist in varying degrees. Very briefly in order to comply with these Acts a school must accommodate or provide a modification for the child with a learning problem that they do not provide for the other students in that grade. For example, a child has significant writing problems (slow in completing written work, trouble taking notes, difficulty with written tests) and requires modifications. One school may only accommodate this child by giving him extra time on the nine weeks exams. That's four times a year this child will receive help! Another school will provide extra time on all tests, do oral testing, reduce the amount of written work, give note taking assistance, etc. The former school has a "paper program" in order to meet compliance with the regulations, the latter school has a "real program" to help the child.

As with many education acts or laws they define what needs to be done but they do not define the quantity or quality of the services. This is defined by the school or local school system. It is like a big tiger with no teeth or claws. If your child's school is one that provides minimal services, I would suggest, if possible, to look for another school that has a "real program" rather than to fight the system. For the child who needs accommodations and modifications, it is usually better to find a school that "fits" your child rather than to try to change the school to "fit" your child.

I have gathered a list of accommodations and modifications that possibly could be done. Keep in mind, that the amount and quality of the services are usually defined by the school. It should also be noted that when accommodations are made they should be subtle. That is, between the child, parent and teacher and not knowledge of the whole class. Just recently a child with severe writing problems told me that his teacher said he did not have to copy the notes from the board. She would give him a copy of the notes. She told him just to sit and listen. That was great, however, she gave him a copy of the notes in front of the class. This promoted the other students saying "Why do I have to copy the notes and Alan doesn't?" Eventually the other students started teasing him. What started our to be a positive move for this 11 year old ended up as a negative experience. Advise the teacher to make the accommodations and modifications in ways that will not be obvious to the other students.

Modifications And Accommodations

Modifications and accommodations can be made in number of areas. I have put together some that are used in this area.

Physical Arrangements Of Room

The seating arrangement can be planned in such a way that the student has close proximity to the focal point of the instructional area. Often it is helpful for the student to be placed close to the area where the majority of direct instruction takes place. This placement may mean sitting near the teacher's desk or near the board or near an activity center. He could also be placed in an area of the room that would avoid distracting stimuli (air conditioner, window, high traffic area). Increasing the distance between the desks may also be helpful.

Lesson Presentation

Making sure directions are understood. The teacher could paraphrase both written and verbal information. Condensing verbal or written information. Condensing verbal or written information in such a way that it is complete, but is shorter and/ or uses alternate vocabulary in order to make the ideas and information easier to comprehend. The purpose of this technique is to take into account the auditory processing difficulties of the student. The teacher could also have the student repeat the instructions to be sure they are understood.

Teaching Through Multi-Sensor Modes

Instructions, practice activities, and directions could be given by using more than one modality. Using methods to instruct, guide practice, or give directions which are multi-sensory: that is, the instruction, directions, or practice activities physically involve the student and require that multiple modalities (auditory, visual, kinesthetic, tactile) are used simultaneously or in rapid succession. Direct instruction techniques that engage the student's hearing, vision, and tactile senses help assure that the student's strongest learning pathway is tapped. Tape records with headphones, chalk boards, small writing boards, plenty of visual aids—such as pictures, slides, and video as well as three dimensional manipulative and real-life examples—help increase the multi-sensory aspects of teaching and learning.

Allowing Students To Tape Record Lessons

Allowing students to record classroom instruction, lecture notes, and/or directions. As with any use of the tape recorder for learning, guidelines for use should be established, and special training should be given so that the technical aspects of using the tape recorder do not hinder the student's access to the information captured on tape. The teacher may wish to control the tape recording of many activities in order to use the tapes with multiple students and in more than one class. This accommodation is especially important for some class events, such as giving directions. While, sometimes the student needs to have directions repeated or paraphrased in different words, other times it is helpful for the student to hear the exact same wording for instructions more than one time. This strategy enables the student to begin to cue in to the consistent direction-giving style of the teacher.

Providing A Written Outline Or Copies Of Teacher's Notes And Plans

Allowing students to have copies of the teacher's lecture notes and class plans to ease writing requirements and to assure that information for home study is accurate, sequentially, ordered, and well organized. Although it is not always possible, if the notes are given to the student ahead of time, he may be able to follow the classroom instruction more readily.

Providing A Peer Notetaker

Having a classmate take notes, preferably on carbonless duplicating paper. Care should be taken to make sure that the peer assistant wants to perform this volunteer job and is an excellent and thorough note taker who follows a consistent pattern for taking notes, accurate spelling, and writing legibly. Sometimes if is preferably for the student to continue to practice taking notes and have a peer note taker whose notes serve as a model. This modification must be instituted with self-esteem issues in mind and should not be used as a substitute for teaching note taking skills except with students who have severe dyslexia or dysgraphia.

Providing Peer Tutoring
Other students who excel in the student's weak area could provide assistance.

Getting Assistance From An Amanuensis
Having someone other than the student record notes, daily assignments, class work, homework, and/or test answers or transcribe essays and reports. This modification may be made for short periods of time, for selected courses, or for selected activities within a course.

Using Cooperative Learning
Learning by being part of a small group in which students pool ideas, trade information, and make group decisions. This modification is considered a modification only if the cooperative learning situation is not part of the whole class instructional methodology or is in someway different. It should be noted that cooperative learning methodology may be very good or very bad methodology for students depending on the characteristics of individuals within the group and the group dynamics. Passive students whose skills are minimal may be left out of the learning situation or become too dependent on stronger group members. More aggressive or socially inept students may not be ready for the complex social interaction required for successful cooperative learning.

Having A Peer Assistant
Having a classmate serve as a facilitator for the student.

Although this modification is frequently used for students when there is little curricular and staff support within the school system, a strong word of caution should be given. It is usually unwise to believe that peers without training will have the knowledge, skills, and empathy to help students appropriately.

Breaking Longer Presentations Into Shorter segments

A one-hour presentation could be broken up into four 15 minute sessions.

Assignments/Worksheets

Allowing students extra but specified time in which to complete a full assignment (i.e. over the weekend). Giving extra time to complete tasks: Extra time could also be given to complete class work.

Allowing To Tape Record Assignments/Homework

Using a tape recorder to record answers to homework questions or problems. This accommodation is especially useful in content courses such as the social studies and sciences. Careful guidelines should be given as to the format and organization of the taped assignment. For instance, tapes should be carefully labeled. The student should begin each new assignment with the usual "heading" of name, date, and subject. Each assignment section should be orally titled including page number, and every question or problem should be orally numbered. If the teacher normally requires the questions be written as part of the homework, parent may read the questions into the recorder.

Allowing Typewritten Or Computer Printed Assignments

Utilizing various computer applications or typewriting to do homework assignments. The intent of this accommodation is to alleviate handwriting, composition, spelling, and time problems. Some assignments—such as, essays and reports—are obvious candidates for computer completion. Other assignments—such as, math and grammar—are less obvious but may be equally helpful for the student.

Reducing Or Altering Assignment (In Class)

Requiring less academic output of the student, usually on work which involves extensive copying and paper-and-pencil tasks or lengthy reading passages. It may be that fewer questions or problems are answered or that shorter written compositions are allowed or that reading amount is reduced. This modification, in many cases, gives face-saving validity to the reality that the student does not work so quickly. Consequently, the amount of work output is smaller. Reducing the amount of work may, in some cases, ease the constant pressure to produce work quickly rather than accurately, completely rather than correctly, and sloppily rather than neatly.

Reducing Or Altering Assignments (homework)

The same as above except that the specific practice problems, reading, and written work must be more carefully planned to make sure that all new learning is adequately practiced. Often the assistance and monitoring by parent are required to enable this modification to work well.

Giving Frequent Short Quizzes And Avoiding Long Tests

Having short quizzes for a student so that less information is asked on the test. One way to make sure all the information is covered is to give more frequent tests.

Giving More Frequent Opportunity For Review

Giving the student frequent (preferably daily) opportunities and ways to review the most recently presented skills and information and frequent (weekly) opportunities to review the cumulative information and skills presented in the course. There are a number of ways to create multi-sensory learning opportunities. The teacher, teacher aid, peer helper, or the student may create an audio or video tape of the most important information for easy review, and/or they may create a review "deck" on index cards. The review cards should whenever possible contain pictures that can serve as visual mental cues as well as written words. The tape or review decks may be organized according to units or may be cumulative throughout the semester and might even serve the needs of more than one student. When this accommodation is utilized, teachers should plan and provide for routine times for review, which become everyday habits for the student.

Giving Opportunity For Increased Response Time

Allowing the student who has slower processing skills the opportunity to think of and give a more complete answer that reflects his actual knowledge. The student may be given the questions well in advance so that his rehearsed response can be made more quickly.

Not Grading Handwriting

For students who have difficulty in writing, the teacher should not compare him to other students, but compare and grade him according to himself and his effort.

Test Taking

Having Larger Print For Assignments Or Tests

Having students read, do assignments, or take tests on pages that have been photocopied and enlarged by 30% to 100% or that have been originally created with larger size print. The benefits of this accommodation can be that reading and paper and pencil tasks are easier.

Giving Special Study Sheets For Tests

Creating review sheets that outline in logical, sequential manner the most useful or salient information. These review sheets should be given to the students as early as possible, should follow the questioning format (though not exact questions) that the test will have, or might use multiple questioning formats for the same information. Once created they might be used numerous times.

Giving Extended Or Untimed Tests

Providing a place and time for students to take tests without the pressure of time. This accommodation may mean dividing the test into multiple parts so that students may take the first portion of the test before school and additional portions during class and after school. If this accommodation is necessary in every class, shorter tests for some classes should be considered.

Allowing Oral/Taped Testing And Answering

Giving tests that have been previously read into a recorder. The student reads along with the test and then writes answers on the test form, or records answers on another tape, or tells an amanuensis who writes the student's answers. The amanuensis may be a teacher, an aide, a volunteer, or a peer helper. As with other accommodations which utilize tapes, procedural formats should be taught and followed.

Using Alternate Format For Test (Multiple Choice Or Essay)

Changing the format of the test either partially or completely to tap the actual knowledge of the student more effectively. For some students this modification means giving a subjective test-such as, an essay or oral essay test-rather than an objective one, such as a multiple choice. For other students, this modification means giving multiple choice rather than essay test. For still others, the objective format is fine; but matching questions are better than fill-in-the blank, and true-false questions are better than short answer. At this time, there is no clear-cut, universal trend as to which testing format is best for students. Individuals needs should be studied and taken into account. The key in alternate format testing is to find the best way to access what the student knows.

Providing An Alternate Method For Test (Open Book Or Take Home Test)

Same as the above except in this case the format of the test may be the same as the format for the other students. Ask the student to keep track of the time spent working on a take home test. If the time demand is so great that other subjects suffer, another method for testing should be considered.

Modifying Test

Changing or adding to certain parts or questions of a test to best tap the actual subject knowledge of the student. For instance, a lengthy matching test with 20 or more matching choices might be divided into two sections of 10 each; a labeling question might have a wordbank for the student; a question requiring graphing might have three graphs, one of which is the correct answer. This way the student can show that he does know the information asked, though he is not yet able to plot the graph. This modification should be based only on specific modification needs of the student. The needs may be determined by analyzing the previous tests.

Shortening Test

Changing the test for a student so that less information is asked on the test. One way to make sure that all information is covered is to give more frequent tests that cover less material.

Reading

Although many students want to be able to read well, that task is often overwhelming. They have trouble with many important aspects of reading. Their reading rate can be characteristically halting or slow. Some are prone to numerous kinds of reading errors: such as, reversals, omissions, substitutions, and transposals of letters and words. They have problems "tracking": that is, as their eyes move across the page, they lose their place because they skip up or down to the wrong line or back to the same line instead of moving smoothly from left to right. They have difficulty using punctuation as a guide and difficulty reading with appropriate intonation. To overcome these problems, some students need special training in reading. Some may never become good readers.

The following strategies may help students cope with reading tasks in the regular classroom setting.

Subvocalization

Moving the lips inaudibly or quietly while reading. It has been called "reading out loud inside your head." This multi-sensory technique helps the student "feel" and "hear" the words he is seeing on the page.

Use of index card, pencil, highlighter and/or window card for keeping place
Using any instrument to help alleviate tracking difficulties. Which item is most useful is a decision for the student and may change over time. An index card placed under or over the line or reading is especially helpful in the lower grades, but may be needed throughout school. The eraser end of a pencil or a highlighter scanned across the page while reading not only helps with tracking, but also creates tactile reinforcement for the student. The student with severe tracking problems may find a "window card" helpful. A small section the size of a word or group of words is cut out of the center of an index card. The student places the card on the segment of words being read. This strategy masks out the other words and prevents mistracking.

Cursive Trace-over
Tracing the cursive shape of a letter over the printed letter as a cue to the sounds within the word. This strategy often helps the student recognize reversals. For example, the cursive letter *b* swings up and loops back to the left while the letter *d* curves up, over, and back very differently from the *b*. The same idea works for other easily confused letters: *t* and *f*, *m* and *n*, etc. Again this strategy is a multi-sensory one that involves the tactile sense with the visual sense.

Name the letter
Naming the letters of a word as a cue to the word. The student should name letters when words are misread. Naming letters helps the student associate the name with sounds and helps eliminate reversals.

High frequency word/phrase practice
Isolating some high frequency words or phrases for special practice. Some words or word pairs tend to give the student special

trouble. Shorter, more abstract, easily reserved words-such as, *a* and *the*; *of* and *to*; *when*, *where*, and *then*-are easily incorrectly substituted in the student's reading. The student is especially prone to misreading prepositions. Some reading theorists believe that misreading or skipping the smaller words is relatively unimportant. For the dyslexic misreading words-such as, *on* and *no*, *of* and *to*, *when* and *then*-is devastating to comprehension.

Highlighted and/or marked texts

Marking textbooks in such a way that the most important information is clearly indicated so the student knows what ideas should receive the most attention. This strategy does not help with reading per se; it helps reduce the amount of reading, thus saving time.

Colored film overlays

Placing a colored film (usually blue, yellow, rose, or gray) over the page to reduce the contrast of the black letters on a white page. While this controversial practice has not been proven to help, many students report that the "words move the page" or that they become "fatigued" from looking at the page of words. If this problem exists and if the student feels that the color helps, then overlays should be an option.

Altered lighting conditions

Changing the lighting (usually reducing it) to reduce the contrast: Another controversial strategy, but worth investigating for individual students.

Books on tape

Listening to textbooks that have been recorded verbatim. If the student is able to follow along in the text, this activity becomes another multi-sensory technique. This often recommended strategy requires careful planning and special training to work successfully. The student should be given a format and procedure for using the tapes. Caution the student to focus on the information and to stop often, at least at every section of text, to review the information and ideas mentally. A strong word of caution, the "readers" on the tape must be good readers who use appropriate rate, intonation, and inflection. They must provide verbal clues as to the location of the reading within the text; otherwise, the student will become hopelessly lost in avalanche of words. Oral reading rate is approximately 150 to 185 words per minute. The student's optimum listening comprehension rate should be considered. For some students 150 to 185 words per minute is fine; for others, it is to slow; for some, it is too fast.

Paraphrased or annotated version of books on tape
Listening to textbook tapes that have been paraphrased. The same conditions as above apply. Some books may be taped using both verbatim and annotated style. As long as the student is told on the tape which style is being used, this strategy can be a good way to model paraphrasing techniques for the student.

Lower reading level text of same topic
Having the student read texts on the same topics that are easier to read. Be very cautious with this strategy. Depending on the reading ability and age of the student, this technique can be either good or bad. In some ways, it is similar to paraphrasing of text and may encourage the student to read more; but there is a strong chance it will discourage the bright student whose knowledgeable and ability to learn are far above his reading level.

Synopsis text
Using a condensed, information packed version of a text that gives a great deal of information in just a few words. Synopsis texts are often used in upper level areas of science or business. If available, these jam-packed texts reduce the amount of reading while maximizing the information. This strategy is best used with the high school age student who learns easily but still struggles with reading rate.

Spelling
Spelling is often viewed as a very difficult part of the dyslexic

student's academic life. Long after other aspects of written language have begun to progress, the dyslexic student still has great difficulty spelling correctly. Some are able, with inordinate effort, to hold the visual memory of a list of words just long enough to pass a test; but composition spelling usually remains erratic. The problems stem from poor auditory memory for sounds and/ or poor visual memory for letters.

The dyslexic student is frequently unaware that he has misspelled a word. This problem makes teaching spelling, accommodating, and modifying more difficult because the student does not think to circle the word or use the quick chart when he has no idea he is spelling the word incorrectly.

The trend toward eliminating spelling-list tests and allowing "invented" spellings to encourage writing is initially helpful for the dyslexic student. From the perspective of spelling, he is indistinguishable from other students who are also spelling creatively. However, with the dyslexic student, the non-traditional spellings are likely to continue indefinitely. Ultimately the dyslexic student will need accommodations, modifications, and special strategies; he should be taught the basic spelling rules.

Subvocalization

Moving the lips quietly or, in some cases, inaudibly to rehearse a word before spelling it out loud or before writing it. This multi-sensory strategy helps the student "hear" in his own voice the word he is about to spell. This accommodation should be monitored carefully, since the student often omits, reverses, or transposes sounds and syllables when he repeats or say words. Teachers should initially listen to make sure the student is able to say the spelling word accurately. If the student is unable to say the word, it is sometimes helpful to use a small hand mirror and have the child echo your pronunciation while watching their own mouth in the mirror. If this practice is not sufficient for accurate pronunciation, a speech/language evaluation should be considered.

Spelling check option

Checking, circling, or putting *sp* above the words when

writing. This face-saving strategy encourages the student to express ideas in writing without fear of embarrassment. This technique encourages better vocabulary in writing assignments, better word awareness and editing, and gives the teacher important information about the dyslexic student's spelling problems. The circled words can then become the focus of future spelling lessons or form the basis for the personal spelling quick chart discussed below.

Scratchpad practice page
    Using a scratchpad to make certain the word is correct before writing it on the homework, test, or composition. This common adult strategy is often overlooked for students. Again the scratchpads can be kept so the teacher can analyze them for future lesson planning.

Spell checks partner
    Pairing with a classmate to check other's work for spelling errors. As with other cooperative learning or peer situations, care must be taken to see that this activity is a positive experience and that both students are learning from the activity.

Frequent word spelling quick chart
    Creating and using a list of spelling words known to give student problems. Frequently these words are homonyms that cause problems of usage—such as *there, their, they're*—or are words that are noted spelling "demons," such as *misspelled*. Many such lists are available in books. However, be sure to personalize the list you create for the student so that it is age/grade appropriate. Guidelines for when the quick chart may be used should be established.

Personal spelling demons quick chart
    Creating and referring to a personal, ongoing list of words that give the student persistent spelling problems. The chart can be created from the circled words of their compositions, the scratchpad words, or from the teacher's observation. It is best to

make the list special in some way. For instance, the list might be written on colored paper, or might have a special design, or might be typed on the computer. When the page is complete, it might be laminated and another one started. Students should be encouraged to cross out words that no longer give them difficulty.

Spelling rules and generalizations chart
     Using a quick chart that lists the major spelling generalization and rules.

Writing - Handwriting

Dysgraphia is a severe handwriting problems associated with dyslexia. Like dyslexia, dysgraphia is not something the student is able to change or control by "trying harder" or "caring more." This disability is sometimes difficult to understand, since the student who cannot legibly write his own name may be able to draw the most intricate creative picture, play the piano, or type well. The handwriting of the dysgraphic student is characterized as erratic, misshaped, and cramped. The act of writing is often laborious and time consuming: the student has no energy to attend to what is being written or to how the words are spelled. He seems not to remember how the letters are formed. Even when he does remember the letter forms, his poor spelling may encourage poor handwriting. For instance, if the student does not know whether a word is spelled with an *a* or a *u*, he may write the letter in such a way that the teacher cannot recognize the letter. The "spell checking option" in computers helps to alleviate this problem.

The increased availability of computers will provide the dysgraphic student with a tool that will assist him in his school work. Until that time, careful teaching, patience, and empathy are needed.

Slant form
     Using a parallel-lined page underneath the writing paper to serve as a guide to help the writer keep the backs of letters straight and parallel. Often the straight lines (or down-strokes) of a

dysgraphic student's handwriting are erratic and not parallel. Making the down strokes straight and parallel will increase handwriting legibility. Have the student place a piece of paper over the slant page and write, making sure the down strokes of the letters are parallel to (not necessarily on) the lines of the slant form. A student may prefer a different slant: an individual form may be created for his particular style.

Personal letter forms chart

Practicing with or referring to a chart as a reminder of the letter forms. A letter chart may be designed for the student who may be experiencing difficulty forming specific letters. The chart may contain the whole alphabet including lower and upper case letters, if beneficial. Troublesome letters in cursive writing include *e*, *i* and *t*; *a* and *u*; *a* and *o*; *b* and *k*; *g* and *j*: in manuscript, *b* and *d*; *p* and *q*; m and n are sometimes troublesome. Primary grade classrooms typically have the alphabet displayed on the wall. However, a dysgraphic student needs a closer model. A chart may be reduced in size for personal use by the student.

Change in writing form

Allowing the student to use the writing style that is the quickest and most legible style for him. This accommodation may mean switching from one style to another.

Writing - Copying

Copying is rarely taught as part of the language arts curriculum. However, because of its complex nature, copying is often a difficult task for the dyslexic or dysgraphic student. The language skills of reading, letter formation (handwriting), and spelling, as well as attention and memory are required for accurate copying. For a student who can not read, who has difficulty forming letters, and who cannot spell, the simplest copy activity becomes extremely difficult, confusing, and meaningless. In addition, the student is prone to make the same types of errors in copying that he makes in reading, including reversals, substitutions, and omissions.

Computers may assist the student in routine copying activities. However, some academic copywork is essential. In addition, the ability to copy is a lifetime skill that cannot be entirely ignored or avoided. It is important to determine which academic copying activities are essential for the student and plan the activities accordingly; teach copying skills to students as carefully as you teach any other language arts skills; and make accommodations and modifications for copying activities, whenever needed.

Common copying activities

a. *Final drafts of papers* can be an important copying activity but may require more time for the student. The teacher might consider giving extra time or allowing only a portion of the final draft to be hand copied. In many cases, however, it is more realistic to allow papers to be typed and to use other activities for copywork practice.

b. *Prose or poetry passages for handwriting practice* may be an important copying activity. The same notes as above apply. This activity may be preferable, since passages are generally shorter.

c. *Homework questions from a textbook* are rarely a good copying activity. The large amount of time spent copying from the text is better spent learning the concepts of the textbook.

d. *Copying and writing errors in mathematics* may include failure to keep numbers in columns or failure to separate the numbered list from the mathematical problem. These difficulties may lead a teacher to believe that the student is having trouble in math when such is not the case. The teacher may consider keeping a master set of the textbook problems copied for the student or may consider providing enlarged print copies.

e. *Letters or notes to parents from the school* may be an appropriate copy activity if the letter is short and is read to the student. However, the teacher should provide a "model" for copying.

Writing - Composition

Some students may have difficulty expressing themselves

orally. Many have good and creative oral expression. Therefore, it is sometimes difficult to understand why a student may have difficulty expressing himself in writing. Often, a student's written composition does not reflect the depth or range of his ideas. Much of the composition problem is related to the physical aspects of written language. If critical mental attention is devoted to the forming of letters and the spelling of words, then less attention is devoted to the forming of letters and the spelling of words, then less attention is available for composing. If the student's writing rate is slow, then the creative and complex ideas are lost amidst the laborious task of writing them down. Other composition problems stem from organizational and sequencing difficulties. The student may have difficulty in separating superordinate from subordinate ideas and in putting the ideas into a logical order.

The two key strategies for the teacher in helping the student with classroom composition skills are to encourage and nurture the flow of ideas through accommodation that allow the ideas to be "captured" before being written, and to provide models for practice.

Taping/transcribing

Using a tape recorder to "capture" the ideas before they are lost: The student should be encouraged to make this accommodation a routine activity. A character in the movie "Night Shift" used just such a technique to hold onto his bright (funny) ideas. He even named his recorder Charlie. This example may encourage a student to use a tape recorder for writing. As with other tape recording accommodations and modifications, care should be taken to teach the student formats and techniques for recording. Transcribing and editing from the tape may be performed by the student, a peer, a parent, or a teacher's aide, depending on the assignment, the needs of the student, and the availability of volunteer assistance.

Prototype models of compositions

Using a variety of model compositions as examples for the student. A student may practice "writing" by changing the topic, but shadowing the framework of the composition. This activity may be performed orally with a full class or individually with the student until the process is learned. Patterns for organization such as "box" paragraphs and composition "pictures" are also helpful guides.

Study Skills For The Content Areas

The following suggestions are primarily for content courses: such as, science or social studies.

Textbook approach

Using a specific procedural approach to learn from a textbook. The oldest and most widely used is Francis P. Robinson's S Q 3R technique (which stands for Survey, Question, Read, Recite, Review) from Effective Study (1970). Students should be carefully taught to use the method and should be given numerous opportunities to use it in class.

Marking a textbook

Using a specific system of marks or highlighting to organize the information in a text for immediate understanding, for tactile reinforcement (the pencil eraser may be used when the textbook cannot be permanently marked), and for later review. Although not all students can or should mark in every textbook, some students need this accommodation on a consistent basis. Some study skills books give detailed directions for this task. General guidelines are given here. Students should

- circle unknown words;
- underline keywords and phrases with a single or double line;
- box vocabulary words and underline the corresponding definition;
- bracket information that is important but too long to underline;
- number superordinate, ordinate, and subordinate information Roman numerals and Arabic numerals should be circled and used to designate the relationship of ideas;

- number (do not letter) all ideas multiple points, lists, etc.;
- star key ideas; and
- question-mark information that is unclear.

Vocabulary deck

Using a personal and on-going word deck for vocabulary building. This activity may be conducted with written words and definitions or with pictures where appropriate. The cards may be color coded by subject (i.e. blue for science, green for social studies, etc.)

Organizational Techniques

Many students have problems with organization such as difficulty remembering what to do for homework, holding on to assignments once completed, and filing papers for future reference. Some also have difficulty using time efficiently. These students need special assistance with organizational skills. The key component for the success of organizational skills instruction is to have a detailed system and to be consistent in its use.

Assignment page

Writing homework assignments on a special page designed to help the student, teacher, and parents monitor the student's academic work. There are three kinds-a day-at-a-glance, a week-at-a-glance, and a month-at-a-glance-of assignment keeping systems that seem to work best. The key is to choose the one that is best for the student. The week-at-a-glance has the most advantages. It allows space enough to write complete assignments (unlike the month system) and still lets the student get an overall picture of the flow of assignments (unlike the daily system).

System of organization

Using a centralized system (usually a 1" to 2" binder) for maintaining all school paperwork. This activity prevents the student from becoming fragmented. The specifics of the system can be varied depending on the teacher's wishes; however, there should be only one system. If the student has multiple teachers, there will need to be coordination to provide consistency.

Study time monitoring
    Keeping a written record of study activities and study time. This activity helps both the student and teacher keep track of how much time is spent on each academic task. Though the process does not need to be an on-going activity, periodic monitoring will assist the teacher in determining which accommodation and modifications may be helpful for the student.

Suggestions For The Classroom Teacher
    The intelligent student who has unusual difficulty with written language skills often performs well in areas of verbal or experiential learning. Whenever possible, the curriculum and school work requirements need to be adapted to his unique learning abilities. The following suggestions will help the student learn more successfully.

1. LOWER THE STRESS LEVEL OF THE STUDENT
    a. Do not require the student to read aloud unless he wants to read aloud.

2. ORAL PARTICIPATION
    b. STRESS Substitute oral reports for written reports.
    c. Accept work dictated by the student and written by the parent or amanuensis.
    d. Provide tapes of content area textbooks.

3. MAKE DIRECTIONS BRIEF AND SIMPLE
    e. Give only one step at a time.
    f. Ask the student to repeat directions to assure he understands.
    g. Encourage the student to ask questions; treat each question patiently.

4. TEACH THE STUDENT HOW TO ORGANIZE ASSIGNMENTS
    h. Break assignment into small steps.

     i. Allow the student more time to think.

     j. Help the student schedule long-term assignments.

1. FIND A WAY FOR THE STUDENT TO USE HIS SPECIAL ABILITIES
     a. Participating in the performing arts.
     b. Building three-dimensional models or projects.
     c. Demonstrating and/or discussing hobbies.

2. PROVIDE MEMORY AIDS
     a. Post visual reminders or examples.
     b. Provide matrix charts.
     c. Allow the student to tape record lectures and test reviews.

3. GRADE ABILITIES, NOT DISABILITIES
     a. Grade oral performance more than written performance.
     b. Give credit for effort and time spent.
     c. Test the student orally whenever possible.

4. REQUEST PARENT'S COOPERATION AND HELP
     a. Encourage parents to read the student's homework to him.
     b. Designate a regularly scheduled time and place.
     c. Teach the student how to keep up with homework.
     d. Make parents aware of the need for structure in the student's daily life.
     e. Encourage parents to provide opportunities for the student to discover and develop his unique talents.
     f. Help parents develop a positive attitude and understanding of their child's worth.

CHAPTER 48

Forty Ways to Help Your Learning Disabled Child with Schoolwork at Home

Learning is a full time job for a child and learning takes place both inside and outside of the classroom. It is important that parents and teachers work together so that the child has every opportunity possible to grow in skills, stature and spirit. For most parents, helping a child with homework is very much like a married couple hanging wallpaper or putting up curtain rods. They agree on the goal, but each person has very specific, if not different opinions on how that goal should be accomplished. If the student has learning problems, and the parent(s) may have similar problems, the parent-becoming-teacher has a very difficult job. The student is already a challenge to teach in school by dedicated, well-trained professionals. What then can parents do to help their child at home?

1. Teachers have to remember that homework is only to be used as a reinforcement for already learned material. Homework is practice work and should NEVER involve new things to be learned.

2. If a child and parent cannot accomplish a homework task, the parent should write a note to that effect along with a notation of the amount of time spent and send it along with the unfinished assignment back to the teacher. Find out AHEAD OF TIME if the teacher is willing to accept a "quick" phone call in the evening if there is a question. It is very helpful if there is an agreement as

to "the maximum time" spent on a subject. A quiet kitchen timer set to the agreed-upon time is helpful.

3. Since school is often very frustrating to an LD child, the time immediately after school is usually not the time for homework. Each family needs to establish a set time in the evening when homework can be accomplished and yet it will not interfere with other members activities. Right after supper might be a good choice for most. See the chapter regarding this for more information.

4. Structure is a universal need and the LD student needs more than anyone. A consistent place for study is very important. It should be away from distraction such as the TV. One good place that has been used for over hundreds of years is the dining room table. If the LD student is left to study in isolation, then no monitoring can be done.

5. It is a tradition in most homes that the responsibility for education is the mother's responsibility. Since most LD students are male, it is suggested that whenever possible, both parents alternate homework shifts. The father's influence and participation, as well as interest, is very important factor in determining educational success. Students do better when dad is actively involved. Many teachers blame over-mothering, but they forget that it is a compensation for under-fathering.

6. LD children may have one or two parents who also have a learning problem that only becomes obvious when dealing with school work. Parents should pool their talents and decide who should help whom and in which subjects. It is very helpful if a child knows that mom or dad or Uncle Charlie had a problem learning too. It's not to be used as an excuse, but it is to be used as the reason to work hard. It also helps if a student is involved in meetings with the school so that he understands his responsibilities in the learning process. If a student is a part of the planning, chances are greater that he/she will be successful.

7. Adults, like their children, enjoy time to relax and to do other things after a busy or tiring day. Homework time is a good time for adult activity than CAN be interrupted to answer questions. Knitting, reading the paper, balancing the checkbook, all can be interrupted. Getting homework done needs to be a commitment made by all members of the family.

8. If your child has to write an assignment, have him dictate it to you. Then the student can copy it later.

9. Use graph paper for arithmetic assignments if a student has trouble keeping columns straight. If graph paper is not available, turn lined paper sideways and that will help keep the columns straight.

10. Purchase only wide-lined paper. Teach the student to write on every other line, or invest in the new light blue and white notebook paper printed by Norcom. Writing on every other line accomplishes two things. It increases the "skyline effect" and handwriting becomes easier to read, and also there is plenty of room for additions, corrections, and suggestions by proofreading parents or correcting teachers.

11. Underline Misspellings: Too often students who are not good spellers—for whatever reason—seriously "sandbag" their written expression in order to cover up their inability.

When this happens, three results can be observed. First, the student spells only words that are known. The word/syllable ratio usually drops quite quickly from a comfortable conversational level to a stilted writing level. The second thing is that in a test, the student creates strange sentences to avoid important words. The third result is the student lulls himself into thinking he has everyone "off his back," when the truth is that the writing is costing him both grades and "points" by his instructors. Instructors are confused by good verbal behavior vs. the lazy appearing, if not intellectual embarrassing, written responses.

"The underlining option" is simple, In class, when students

write essay tests, papers, etc., tell them to use the appropriate vocabulary, but underline all words misspelled and no points will be deducted. Two benefits occur. First, if the student does trust the instructor, answers on tests will resemble closely the student's intellectual capability, or at least the knowledge acquired. Secondly, a whole area of unknown writing skills surface which can then be remediated. It is important to remember that an instructor should not use a student's handicap against him. In most states, the inability to spell is considered a handicap. By using the underlining notion, students produce better quality, which then allows their instructor to better assess the mastered knowledge of the student. In-class papers can be used as a basis for referral to the skill center resource staff.

One last note: Always require some-in-class writing to assess the student's true writing capabilities. Otherwise, the poor writer or speller remains undetected thanks to the efforts of a dedicated corps of proofreaders and few unsuspecting instructors.

12. Erase Erasures: A significant number of students have discovered that erasing words, lines and paragraphs is viewed by teachers as honest academic labor. These students use erasing as avoidance behavior usually to compensate for their inability—real or imagined—to spell, write legibly or compose intelligent thoughts in sentence form.

Those teachers who have in their possession stacks of papers not only full of erasure holes, but which also appear to have been slept on can take heart. There is an alternative: the draw-the-line-through-the-mistake approach. It is a simple approach which does not cost taxpayer's money; in fact, it saves money. Instruct all students they are not to erase any more. Instead, they are to draw a neat, single line through any error and continue with their work.

This approach produces several results. The first is that the line allows the teacher to see the mistake. This provides valuable insight as to the struggles a student experiences in writing. Secondly, the student's time can be spent on getting as much information down with a minimum of interruptions. The third result is helping the student understand it is OK to make mistakes in class; that's what rough drafts are for. The last result is that when all these errors surface, they can be noted and managed by both the teacher and the student.

Stopping the constant erasing is similar to breaking a bad habit. It is best done school-wide and in "cold-turkey" style. The student's initial resentment is soon lost in more productive work. Papers become neater, the writing becomes more legible and the level of production increases.

13. If a child asks how a word is spelled, spell it out for him. If the parent doesn't know, then use the dictionary. Adults have a better chance at looking up a word they can't spell than children. If a child can't spell it, how can he look it up? He does not know his spelling options.

14. If there is an assignment to be read, consider two options. First, is this assignment available on tape from either The Books for the Blind or tapes done by volunteers in the community? If it is, then make certain that the student follows the reading in the book as it is read to him. Never let the student just listen to the tape. He needs to use two sensed in order to learn and remember. The second option is for the parent to read one paragraph, then the student reads the next and so forth.

15. Ask the teacher for a duplicate set of books to be kept at home. This eliminates all sorts of "forgetting" problems.

16. Purchase a separate notebook for each class. It is the student's responsibility to write down the assignments in each class. The student has the teacher initial the written down assignment. If there is no assignment, the teacher initials the words, "No Assignment." If the student "forgets" to write the assignment, some penalty must be assessed such as doing an extra chore, or loss of a half hour of television.

17. On the last day of each school week, the student should carry

his own progress report which is to be brought home to the parents. Keeping current is to be greatly rewarded.

"Missing assignments" mean consequences until work is caught up.

18. The development of good self-esteem is always at risk—especially for the LD youngster. Increase verbal rewards and physical rewards for competing jobs and for a job well done. It usually takes five positives to undo one negative.

19. It doesn't take too many negatives to erase all the positives in a child's day. Choose one important area of behavior at a time that needs to be improved upon. Work on that behavior and ignore other areas until improvement is shown. Then target new behavior and work on that.

20. If the teacher provides a study guide for a text, it is an enormous help. A good study guide helps the child organize the information and helps the child distinguish between important and unimportant information. A good study guide will preview all of the vocabulary words that the student should know. If there is no study guide, then one must be created at home. Use a clean page in the notebook and put the chapter number and the text page number at the top of the page. Divide the page into four columns going down the page. Label them VOCABULARY, PEOPLE, PLACES AND DATES, IDEAS AND DISCOVERIES. Write the text BOLD PRINT chapter and subchapter headings as they appear. As the text is read, fill in the columns and the headings. Do this for each notebook page.

21. There are two ways of taking notes. The first is to ask a good note-taker to use either carbons or NCR paper. The second is to create note sheets just like the study sheets mentioned in idea number 20. The differences is that when the teacher lectures or the class discusses, the student fills out the paper just as he did when studying.

22. Start studying for spelling tests early. If the student learns

five a day, it is easier. Test cumulatively. Most LD students will remember only for the test. If words aren't used, they will slip away.

23. If a child asks a question and you don't know the answer, say, "I don't know. Let's find the answer." Too many adults are embarrassed to admit that they don't know and will try to bluff it. Kids should be able to see and appreciate that there are "gaps" in everyone's knowledge. Kids are also more perceptive about when adults stretch the truth, if not abuse it. Honesty is the best policy.

24. Let your child count change in your purse or pocket. One parent kept a glass jar of change and varied the amount each week. Her son was asked to tally the number of pennies, nickels, dimes, quarters, and half-dollars coming up with a weekly grand total. He then subtracted this total from that of the previous week. (He also did multiplication to figure out the value of the nickels, dimes, etc.) Math started to "make sense."

25. Plastic letters can be purchased inexpensively at your local variety store. Put them up on the refrigerator door. They'll stick because of the magnets. Get your child to answer a question you arrange, or to put a riddle there for you to solve. Arranging the letters is easy. It is manipulative, requires recall, involves sequencing and is fun.

26. Bathroom Newspaper. One family installed a table and pencil on a string in the bathroom. Each person going in and out has to answer the note on the previous page (writing and reading) and also write a note for the next person. IT WORKS!

27. Riddle and joke books, if short, can provide a stimulus for your child to read. Have him practice reading a few to one member of the family in advance so that he can share a few each night with the whole family.

28. Comic Books. Yes, they are of limited value in many ways,

but if they provide motivation to read, get them anyway.

29. "Beat the Clock." One parent found that her children dawdled excessively when carrying out assigned tasks around the home (cleaning their rooms, dumping the garbage, etc.). She used her kitchen timer, always giving a bit more time than was actually required, and timed her children. This is particularly good for children with a poor sense of time. The timer can also be used to show children that they'll only have to do "it" (whatever "it" is) for "this much time."

30. Sign Writing. Getting the pencil to the paper is one of the toughest of all academics tasks, particularly when it is laborious. Try getting your child to write signs, "KEEP OUT - My room," "Danger - Enter at your own risk," "These are Billy's books, handle with care," etc. Signs are limited in usefulness. Perhaps some signs can be changed on a regular basis.

31. Letter Writing. Long letters are a no-no. Try a postcard approach, but first, "stack the deck" by getting a relative far off to be sure to answer in such a way that your child must respond. Let your child pick the postcards he'll want to send. Keep the messages short.

32. Family Newspaper. This works if you have a typewriter or computer. One member can be the "editor" and collect interesting items from the other members. It can be "published" whenever there are enough items and then posted in the kitchen for all to see and . . . READ.

33. Recipes. All kids like to cook. But try this approach. Double recipes or "halve" them. For example, if a recipe calls for ½ cup of milk, by doubling it, "How much milk would that require?" math reasoning is involved in a practical way. The BEST way to learn math is to use it.

34. Watch your daily newspaper. Many have feature pictures

that really stimulate reading the short story underneath. A recent photograph in the newspapers, for example, showed a dog in a large city park that liked to climb trees and sit in them. A comment like "Oh look, here's a dog that climbs trees and plays with the squirrels," will motivate your child to pick up the paper and try to read the story about it.

35. Photograph Album. Let your child select photographs of himself and make an "All About Me" book. He can paste one photograph per page and then write a story about it. "This is me last summer when I caught three fish" or whatever the action is in the picture.

36. Dream Book. Encourage your child to write his or her dreams each morning in a special "Dream Book." The dreams can be illustrated either before or after they have been written abut. Purchase a special notebook your child can use just for this purpose. Try to have your youngster write them first thing in the morning so they won't be forgotten.

37. Tallying of any kind is a practical way to apply arithmetic to routines of daily living. Take time to play board games such as "Monopoly" or checkers and have your child be the scorekeeper.

38. Tape recorders are available inexpensively and have many, many uses in the learning process. Have your child, for example, tape his spelling list and then listen to it several times during the week. The way other parents have found helpful is this: The child says the word, pauses, then spells it, pauses, than says it again. By listening to the tape, he gets extensive auditory reinforcement. You can also make auxiliary tapes for basic math facts, which can be regularly listened to as your child is involved in some other task.

39. Use video and computer games or programs that are educational and teach academic skills.

40. The one common denominator that all of the school subjects

have is language. The vocabulary of each subject matter is critical to the comprehension of the subject. There is a saying in teaching, "Just because something has been said doesn't mean it has been taught." People have to use words many times before those words are learned. Don't overlook vocabulary development. Urge your children to tell you about what they have read or heard in their classes. Try to develop and increase your child's vocabulary.

CHAPTER 49

Cable TV, Video Games, the Computer and the Internet. A Friend Or Enemy To School Performance And Behavior.

Years ago a typical complaint from parents was "all my child wants to do is watch TV or listen to music. He does not do much with children his age and stays inside too much." "I have a hard time getting him to do his homework." Today the complaints are similar, but the radio, TV, and stereo have been replaced with video games, cable TV, the computer and the Internet. There is nothing inherently wrong or bad with the above electronic instruments and they can be used to positively influence to improve school performance if used correctly. However, problems arise when they are used excessively or without proper supervision.

Types Of Problems

A lack of supervision of these activities not only results in excessive involvement in these activities, but may also result in the child coming in contact with information and activities that are not age-appropriate, than can be sexually explicit and/or involve violence. Concerns related to this area discussed below and in the chapter on Violence in the School.

Excessive Involvement

Some children spend most of their waking hours outside of school watching TV, playing video games or on the computer. Excessive involvement with these activities generally results in problems in two areas.

First, required activities are neglected or get partially

completed. Homework may not be done and grades decline. Chores around the house and other responsibilities may not be completed. As a result of this, parents may not allow their child to become involved with watching TV or playing video games. However, if you prohibit a child from watching TV, playing video games or getting on the computer for not doing homework, the only thing we are sure of is that he will not be involved in this activity. There is no assurance that he will do homework. A better way to accomplish your goal is to restrict the activity and use it as an incentive to get the work done. For example, playing video games would be contingent on a behavior (completing homework, having a clean room).

The second problem that occurs is a reduction of socialization experiences and peer interaction. Eventually this means a minimal number or even no friends or peer involvement. To teenagers, being with friends and social activities is a major part of their lives. A child with minimal social involvement has a big void in his life, and many teenagers are unhappy with this. A teenager with no social life who is not motivated about school or is unhappy because all he does is go to school and watch TV is difficult to motivate and it is difficult helping him to modify his behavior. A child with an active social life who shows similar problems is much easier to motivate. Therefore, we would want to increase the isolated child's opportunity for socialization experiences and reduce the amount of time he is involved with video games, TV, and the computer. Use of these devices would be contingent of his involvement with other children. For example, the amount of time spent video games would be based on the amount of time spent outside the house or with peers. He would be allowed access to the computer if he joined an activity involving age-mates (youth groups, school clubs, and sports).

The use of video games, TV, and computers must be monitored and should be only one aspect of a child's life. Not a major part.

Problems With The Internet
Involvement with the Internet could result in problems related to excessive use, exposure to information that is not age-

appropriate and giving away personal information that may put the teenager or their family at risk. Unacceptable relationships with members of a marginal subculture, individuals with emotional problems or older people is also common. Problems pertaining to excessive use were discussed above.

Lack Of Supervision

The second group of problems is primarily related to a lack of supervision. Although the Internet contains a wealth of information than can be very helpful to the child in school, it can also provide them with information that can be detrimental. For example, the teenagers who committed the recent killings in a high school learned how to make bombs on the Internet. Guns can be purchased on line. Pornography and very explicit sexual pictures are available on the Internet. Children could be exposed to hate messages that promote violence. The Internet does not discriminate between fact and fantasy or truth and lies. It provides all types of information. The children could easily be given inaccurate information to be used in school assignments or to share with their peers.

Since numerous things can be purchased on-line, shopping sprees and gambling are possible using the parent's credit cards. Teenagers could also provide legitimate business or crooks with personal information (address, phone number, credit card numbers, Social Security number) about themselves or their parents that may prove detrimental.

Leaving a child alone with the TV on may expose him to sex and violence. On the Internet the major danger is not the sex and violence, it is the people the child could meet on-line which is the danger. If unsupervised, they can be easy pray for sexual predators. Children have been known to develop "relationships" and "fall in love" with individuals who were 10 to 15 years older than they, who they met and communicated with on Internet. Children can be exposed to people and information that are not consistent with the values and attitudes of some parents and what some people would feel to be appropriate.

Solving Internet Problems

The solution to this problem seems fairly simple—parental supervision. Some children require more supervision and structure than others. For example, you could tell your daughter "come home at a reasonable time" and she will come home at a reasonable time. You tell your other child the same thing and he will come home in two weeks and argue with you that this is reasonable time. With the self-discipline, responsible child you could say "Don't turn on the computer when I'm not home" and he will listen. For another child you could tell them the same thing and he will turn the computer on as soon as you leave the house. You probably have a pretty good idea about your children - who can be trusted or is more responsible and who is not. The self-disciplined, responsible child is easy to supervise - they listen, cooperate and comply with authority. The stubborn, strong-willed, manipulative and/or irresponsible child is more difficult to supervise and most of the following pertains to him.

The more difficult child is usually irresponsible in many aspects of his life (e.g. homework, keeping his room clean) and does not listen to authority in a number of areas (e.g. getting off of the phone at a certain time, doing chores, coming home on time). The parent's first job with this child is not to make him responsible with the computer and Internet, but to make him more responsible across the board in as many areas of his life as possible. See the chapters pertaining to this.

Placing the computer in the area of the house that usually contains adults or is a high traffic area would help monitor what is being done on the Internet. Limit or restrict solo surfing. If the Internet would be required foe school assignments and reports, the child could wait for the parent to assist them when access is needed. The parent could be with them when they surf the Internet and download the sites they need.

Screening software can be helpful. It is not foolproof, but it will filter some of the unacceptable material. Some Internet service providers offer their own screening systems. Screening software can black out undesirable information and web sites. Someone who knows about computers could give you information or programs that would allow you to block access to certain or provide techniques to help determine what was done on the computer that day.

Setting specific guidelines (e.g. don't talk to strangers, don't give personal information, don't use your real name, don't order anything without permission, don't post photos of yourself) are needed. Clear limits and rules need to be set along with specific consequences for compliance and non compliance.

Children also have access to the Internet outside of the home. Hopefully, the school, library, etc. has methods to prevent the child from being exposed to inappropriate material. In general, you would not let your child sleep by a friend's house or spend a weekend with a family until you got to know the parents. The same thinking should be used when allowing a child to visit a friend with access to the Internet.

For all the dangers that exist on the Internet, keeping children away form it can, in some cases, cause more harm than good. You need to communicate with your child and get involved in their life to know their interest, attitudes, friends, etc. Clear rules and consequences need to be set pertaining to use and misuse of the Internet. Attempts need to be made to develop responsibility and trust in all areas of your child's life. Supervision is absolutely necessary. As mentioned above the amount of supervision is dependent on the child's personality. For some children explaining the "do's" and "don'ts" is all that will be necessary. For others taking the keyboard to work with you may be needed to provide adequate supervision.

Using Cable TV, Video Games, The Computer And The Internet To Improve School Performance And Behavior

With appropriate parental supervision and control the above electronic devices can be used as an incentive or consequence that can be used to motivate your child, modify his school behavior and/or improve his school performance. However, the parents must be in control. Many children are allowed access to the cable TV, computer, etc. if they are alive. If they are still living after school they come home and play video games. They could have had a good day at school or a bad day. They could have cooperated with their parent in the morning getting ready for school or produced tremendous problems. They could have done their homework the night before or refused to do it. The only criteria for watching the Cartoon Network on your cable TV is that they remain alive and don't die! The only way they will not watch TV, play the video game or get on line is if they die before the end of school!

Parents Must Take Control

Many children think they are entitled to play video games, have access to the computer and watch TV. They think it comes with being a kid. I was working with a 7th grader who was doing poorly in school primarily because he wasn't doing his homework. We set up a communication system between the parent and teacher. Every Friday the parents would send a chart to school and the teacher would check whether or not the homework was completed. This child had cable hooked up to a TV in his room. He was told "If all your homework is completed on Friday you will be able to have the cable in your room the next week. If not you will not have cable in your room to the next Friday when we get the report from your teacher."

The first week of the system, he did not do all of his homework and lost the cable, I happen to see him that week and he told me "you've got to talk to my parents. They're going crazy. They took my cable away and all I have is a few local channels on my TV. They think cable is a luxury. They are use to the old days when they only had three channels on the TV. This is today not then and I need the cable." Obviously, this child felt that he deserved the cable and it was something that he should have if he was alive.

Another parent of a child who was a behavior problem at school and at home told me "I can't get him off the Internet each night. He won't get off and go to bed. He stays up late and it's a big fight every night." After listening to the parent tell me how his child would not cooperate regarding use of the computer, I asked "who is paying for the hookup to the Internet?" Naturally, the father said he was. The solution to this is simple. The child needs to be told "you need to get off the computer at 9:00pm. If you do, you can use the computer tomorrow. If you do not get off the computer by 9:00pm, I will not pay for the service for a week" and the parent needs to disconnect the service for a week. Parents need to take control and not allow a child unlimited access to these electronic devices regardless of his behavior, level of cooperation, responsibility, etc.

Use Natural Consequences

As mentioned in this book several times, most children do not have a job, money, checking account or credit card. They cannot watch cable TV, play video games or access the Internet unless the child uses the electricity and services you are paying for. He cannot play his hand held video game unless you buy the batteries. If I want you to cooperate with me, I have to be nice to you and cooperate with you. If I'm ugly or don't cooperate with you, you will not cooperate with me. If you're the person with the power and money, I'm in trouble.

A child could be told, "If you can cooperate with me and do not give trouble with homework, I'll cooperate with you and let you use my electricity and cable to watch your cartoons."

For the child who is a behavior problem in school, we could establish a home/school communication system and break the school day into six periods. The child brings it to school and the teacher checks off whether his behavior was acceptable or unacceptable during each of the six periods. The child is told "Each period that the teacher indicates that your behavior was acceptable you will earn 15 minutes to play with video games."

See the chapters on responsibility and home/school communication system for more information.

CHAPTER 50

Violence in Schools

In recent years, guns and shootings in schools, as well as children committing serious violence against other children have become more of a national concern. Some people blame video games, violence on TV, guns, and so on; however, a primary cause of this violence is a lack of parental supervision or involvement in their child's life. The teenagers who did the shooting and killings in high school learned to make bombs over the Internet and the parents were not aware of this. The 6-year-old who brought a gun to school and killed another 6-year-old appeared to be from a very unstructured home situation with minimum supervision. This lack of supervision does not always result from parental neglect. It is also related to the time factor. In many families, both parents work and the children are shuffled to and from before and after school care. Overall, the amount of time the parents are around their children and involved in providing supervision seems significantly different than it was as little as 15 years ago.

As mentioned in the chapter on cable TV and the Internet, parental supervision and involvement must be present in order to minimize a child's exposure to inappropriate media. You have to talk to your children, find out what they are doing and where they are going, meet their friends, and so forth. You must supervise what they watch on TV, the video games they play, and their use of the Internet. Access to guns must be restricted, and parental/adult supervision is required on occasions where a gun is used for sport. There is research that indicates that children who view aggressive behavior and violence are more likely to be aggressive than those who do not. While this is true, it does not mean that video games, movies, or TV programs are the main reasons for the aggressive behavior. A few other factors need to be considered when trying to predict the probability of aggressive behavior.

A history of violent or aggressive behavior would certainly increase the probability that this behavior would be seen in the future. The child's preoccupation or involvement with aggressive concerns or activities is another factor. The child who draws guns all the time or watches primarily violent movies, for example, would be more of a concern than a child who watches a variety of movies. How frequently this behavior is seen and how much this activity or interest consumes a part of the child's life are some pertinent questions. Another indication might be whether or not the child is part of a subculture or group that supports potentially violent or aggressive behavior or has ideas and values that are not consistent with mainstream thinking.

Although positive responses to some of the above questions will increase the probability of aggressive behavior, some children who become aggressive toward other children in school do not have a history of violence or preoccupation with aggressive concerns. Instead they have had a tendency to be passive with poor self-esteem. Therefore, personality factors must also be considered. Out of a caseload of about seventy children and teenagers referred by schools for psychological help because they said or did something with an aggressive intent ("I'm going to bring a gun to school and shoot Mrs. Jones." "I'm going to burn the school down." They drew a picture or wrote a poem or note that suggested they wanted to harm their classmates. Only two or three showed any real reason to be concerned. Predicting behavior from personality factors is not a simple thing to do. It involves many components. Here are a few of the most important factors. Very generally, the child to be most concerned about are the loners who do not have many friends and tend to "stay to themselves." I am not talking about the introverted; shy child who likes to read or write and generally is conforming and seems well adjusted. The children of more concern lack assertiveness and ability to openly compete or have poor confidence and are socially insecure, but, as compared to the shy, well-adjusted child, there seems to be a significant amount of underlying anger. When these characteristics appear with other factors, such as nonconformity, association with a marginal subculture, unconventional thinking, a red flag goes up and in some cases, the need for intervention is necessary.

CHAPTER 51

Support Groups and Organization

American Speech-Language-Hearing Association
10801 Rockville Pike
Rockville, MD 20852
(800) 638-8255
Provides information on speech and language disorders, as well as referrals to certified speech-language therapists.

Attention Deficit Information Network
475 Hillside Avenue
Needham, MA 02194
(617) 455-9895
Provides up-to-date information on current research, regional meetings. Offers aid in finding solutions to practical problems faced by adults and children with an attention disorder.

Association on Higher Education and Disability (AHEAD)
P.O. Box 21192
Columbus, OH 43221-0192
(614) 488-4972
An excellent organization to contact for individuals with disabilities who are planning to attend college and who will need special accommodations. Numerous training programs, workshops, publications, and conferences.

Candlelighters Childhood Cancer Foundation
7910 Woodmont Avenue, Suite 460

Bethesda, MD 20814
(800) 366-2223
Provides information and support for children treated for cancer who later experience learning disabilities.

Center for Mental Health Services
Office of Consumer, Family, and Public Information
5600 Fishers Lane, Room 15-81
Rockville, MD 20857
(301) 443-2792
This new national center, a component of the U.S. Public Health Service, provides a range of information on mental health, treatment, and support services.

Children and Adults with Attention Deficit Disorders (CH.A.D.D.)
499 Northwest 70th Avenue, Suite 101
Plantation, FL 33317
(954) 587-3700
(800) 233-4050
CH.A.D.D. (Children and Adults with Attention Deficit Disorders) is a national organization with over 32,000 members and more than 500 chapters nationwide that provides support and information for parents who have children wit ADD and adults with ADD.

Council for Exceptional Children (CEC)
1920 Association Drive
Reston, VA 22091-1589
(703) 620-3660
(703) 264-9446
The largest international professional organization committed to improving educational outcomes for individuals with disabilities.

Federation of Families for Children's Mental Health
1021 Prince Street

Alexandria, VA 22314
(703) 684-7710
Provides information support and referrals through federation chapters throughout the country. This national parent-run organization focuses on the needs of children with broad mental health problems.

HEATH Resource Center
One Dupont Circle, N.W., Suite 800
Washington, DC 20036-1193
(202) 939-9320
(800) 54-HEATH
A clearinghouse of information on topics related to postsecondary education and disabilities. Publishes an annual resource directory.

International Dyslexia Association (IDA)
8600 LaSalle Road, Suite 382
Baltimore, MD 21204-6020
(410) 296-0232
(800) ABCD-123
The IDA is an international, non-profit organization dedicated to the study and treatment of learning disabilities and dyslexia. For nearly 50 years, the IDA has been helping individuals with dyslexia, their families, teachers, physicians, and researchers to better understand dyslexia.

Learning Disabilities Association of America (LDA)
4156 Library Road
Pittsburgh, PA 15234-1349
(412) 341-1515
LDA is the largest non-profit volunteer organization advocating for individuals with learning disabilities. LDA has more than 600 local chapters and affiliates in 50 states, Washington, DC and Puerto Rico. LDA seeks to educate individuals with learning disabilities and their parents about the nature of the disability and inform them of their rights.

Library of Congress
National Library for the Blind and Physically Handicapped
1291 Taylor St. NW
Washington, DC 20542
Publishes Talking Books and Reading Disabilities, a fact sheet outlining eligibility requirements for borrowing talking books.

National Alliance for the Mentally Ill
Children and Adolescents Network (NAMI CAN)
2102 Wilson Boulevard, Suite 302
Arlington, VA 22201
(800) 950-NAMI
Provides support to families through personal contact and support meetings. Provides education regarding coping strategies; reading material; and information about what works—and what doesn't.

National Association of Private Schools for Exceptional Children
1522 K Street, N.W., Suite 1032
Washington, DC 20005
Provides referrals to private special education programs.

National Center for Learning Disabilities
381 Park Avenue South, Suite 1420
New York, NY 10016
(212) 687-7211
Provides referrals and resources. Publishes "Their World" magazine describing true stories on ways children and adults cope with LD.

National Information Center for Children and Youth with Disabilities
P.O. Box 1492

Washington, DC 20013
(800) 999-5599
Publishes newsletters, arranges workshops. Advises parents on the laws entitling children with disabilities to special education and other services.

Recording for the Blind & Dyslexic (RFB&D)
20 Roszel Road
Princeton, NJ 08540
(609) 452-0606
RFB&D is recognized as the nation's leading educational lending library of academic and professional textbooks on audiotape from elementary through post-graduate and professional levels. Students with print disabilities can request cassette or diskette versions of books and order 4-track tape players.

Printed in the United States
221713BV00002B/6/P

9 781935 235026